Political Parties and Democratic Linkage

Volumes of a Collaborative Research Program among
Election Study Teams from Around the World

Series editors: Hans-Dieter Klingemann and Ian McAllister

The Comparative Study of Electoral Systems (CSES) is a collaborative program of research among election study teams from around the world. Participating countries include a common module of survey questions in their post-election studies. The resulting data are deposited along with voting, demographic, district, and macro variables. The studies are then merged into a single, free, public dataset for use in comparative study and cross-level analysis.

The set of volumes in this series is based on these CSES modules, and the volumes address the key theoretical issues and empirical debates in the study of elections and representative democracy. Some of the volumes will be organized around the theoretical issues raised by a particular module, while others will be thematic in their focus. Taken together, these volumes will provide a rigorous and ongoing contribution to understanding the expansion and consolidation of democracy in the twenty-first century.

COMPARATIVE STUDY *of* ELECTORAL SYSTEMS

Further information on CSES activities can be obtained from:

CSES Secretariat
Center for Political Studies
Institute for Social Research
The University of Michigan
426 Thompson Street
Ann Arbor, Michigan 481042321
USA

CSES web site: http://www.cses.org

Political Parties and Democratic Linkage

How Parties Organize Democracy

Russell J. Dalton, David M. Farrell, and Ian McAllister

OXFORD

UNIVERSITY PRESS

OXFORD
UNIVERSITY PRESS

Great Clarendon Street, Oxford ox2 6DP

Oxford University Press is a department of the University of Oxford.
It furthers the University's objective of excellence in research, scholarship,
and education by publishing worldwide in

Oxford New York

Auckland Cape Town Dar es Salaam Hong Kong Karachi
Kuala Lumpur Madrid Melbourne Mexico City Nairobi
New Delhi Shanghai Taipei Toronto

With offices in

Argentina Austria Brazil Chile Czech Republic France Greece
Guatemala Hungary Italy Japan Poland Portugal Singapore
South Korea Switzerland Thailand Turkey Ukraine Vietnam

Oxford is a registered trade mark of Oxford University Press
in the UK and in certain other countries

Published in the United States
by Oxford University Press Inc., New York

British Library Cataloguing in Publication Data

Data available

Library of Congress Cataloging in Publication Data

Data available

Typeset by SPI Publisher Services, Pondicherry, India
Printed in Great Britain
on acid-free paper by
MPG Books Group, Bodmin and King's Lynn

ISBN 978–0–19–959935–6

1 3 5 7 9 10 8 6 4 2

For Richard Rose,
Pioneer of the Study of Political Parties

Series Editors' Preface

Few topics generate as much interest among observers and practitioners of politics as the quality of the democratic process. The expansion of democracy during the twentieth century, which accelerated rapidly after the collapse of communism in 1990, has meant that a majority of the world's countries are now electoral democracies. But not all democracies can be considered equal; they differ widely in terms of institutional arrangements and practices and in the levels of public support that they attract. It is the public support for democracy that the Comparative Study of Electoral Systems (CSES) project is designed to investigate. This volume series presents the key findings from this major research project that commenced in 1994.

The first CSES volume, edited by Hans-Dieter Klingemann, has documented much of its historical background, the basic principles of data collection, and provided sample chapters showing many of the analytical possibilities of this unique data collection. This volume is based on the first module of survey questions in the CSES, completed in 2001, which examines the interaction of political institutions and political behavior regarding attitudes towards the democratic regime, the political authorities and the quality of the political process generally.

As with the first volume, the second one, edited by Russell J. Dalton and Christopher J. Anderson, addresses the fundamental question of whether the institutional structure of elections affects the nature of the public's choices. The first question looks at explanations of turnout, and how institutions structure the likelihood of voting. The second question discusses determinants of individual electoral behavior and examines the role of institutions in shaping what kinds of political loyalties voters acquire.

Political Parties and Democratic Linkage, the third volume in the series, describes and explains the role of political parties in election campaigns, in forming the electoral choice of voters and their role in government and opposition. The theoretical arguments relate to the logic of the responsible parties model. It is the first study that tests these ideas using a comprehensive and comparative design. It demonstrates the importance of the left-right schema to enable political positioning, political communication, and political representation. There is no doubt that this volume makes an important contribution to understanding how representative democracy works.

These are key questions for extending our understanding of individual citizen behavior. Most studies of voting behavior have been based on single country studies, often covering just a single election. By comparing a wide range of countries, for the first time the CSES project enables the institutional environment to be brought into the equation, enhancing our understanding of the complex relationship between individual choice and institutional context. Indeed, such analyses were impossible until the CSES was established.

A fourth volume, edited by Jacques Thomassen, to follow soon, is set to inquire into the nature of political representation and accountability. Future planned volumes in the series, using all modules available, will examine among other topics electoral choices and institutions, globalization, and gender and political behavior.

All of the CSES data are freely available and can be downloaded from our website (http://www.cses.org).

Hans-Dieter Klingemann
Ian McAllister
Series Editors

Preface

In 1897 the *New York Journal* reported the death of American humorist Mark Twain, and the newspaper in Twain's hometown sent a reporter to verify the obituary. Meeting the reporter, Twain observed, "the reports of my death are greatly exaggerated." Political parties must feel like Mark Twain. For decades, scholars and political pundits have prognosticated about the declining health of political parties, and titles about the end of political parties are commonplace. Yet the number of political parties has actually increased in recent decades in most established democracies. Political parties are still the central actors in democratic politics, still structure electoral competition, and still manage the activities of government in most democracies. Reports of their death seem greatly exaggerated.

This book examines the role of political parties in contemporary democracies. Our theoretical approach is based on the party government model of democracy, in which political parties provide a linkage between citizens, government, and policy outputs. Such a reliance on parties is widely seen as the key in ensuring representative democracy really represents and is really democratic.

Using the unique resources of the Comparative Study of Electoral Systems as a core, and drawing upon other cross-national data projects, we examine the party linkage model across a wide range of established and developing democracies. While portions of this model have been tested in previous studies, our project assembles evidence of this linkage process across a large number of party systems. We also consciously wrote this book to be accessible to the wide range of scholars who research political parties, party leaders and activists, and students who want to understand the role of parties in the democratic process. This study is empirically based, but the presentations and logic reach beyond the statistics.

We find:

- Political parties inevitably dominate the electoral process and are still potent forces in mobilizing electoral turnout.
- Drawing upon Downsian spatial modeling, we demonstrate that citizens can think about themselves and political parties in Left–Right terms.

- Left–Right orientations strongly affect voting choices, which produces a basic political agreement between elected representatives and the represented.
- Finally, party control of the government leads to predictable shifts in the policy outputs of government to reflect the priorities of their voters.

In short, despite the decline of party literature, we find that political parties as agents of representative democracy are alive and well.

These empirical findings lead us to ask why analysts so often point to the decline of parties. In part, we agree that some features of partisan politics suggest a pattern of decline—such as decreasing party membership, declining turnout, and fewer citizens identifying with a political party. But these changes in citizens' connection with parties have not been paralleled by a similar decline in parties' performance of their institutional roles in democracy. Rather, political parties generally adapt to changing social and political circumstances to retain their preeminent role in the democratic process. In most nations, the decline in membership has been accompanied by new styles of campaigning, funding from public sources, and a more efficient campaign style. The decline in traditional political cleavages has been counterbalanced by parties responding to new issue agendas, or new parties forming to represent these agendas. This ensures that voters' opinions are ultimately represented. And when parties fail, voters hold them accountable. In the long run, contemporary representative democracy necessarily works through the party government linkages

This book is only possible because of recent advances in comparative politics research that produces large cross-national data on political parties and the democratic process. The key resource for our book is the Comparative Study of Electoral Systems (CSES) project and the more than three dozen diverse democracies surveyed in module 2 of the CSES. We are indebted to all these election study investigators (see www.cses.org for the full list) and we want to thank all those scholars who have contributed to the CSES project over the years. We also draw heavily upon the national statistics collected by the CSES, the party expert study conducted by Kenneth Benoit and Michael Laver, data from the Comparative Manifesto Project, and aggregate policy data collected by the Organization of Economic Co-operation and Development. This wealth of cross-national data makes it possible to systematically compare the workings of the party linkage model across a broad range of democracies in a manner that was previously not possible. We are indebted to all the researchers who contributed to these cross-national projects.

We especially want to thank a large group of colleagues who helped at various stages of our research: Christopher Anderson, Nir Atmor, Susan Banducci, Mihail Chiru, Natalie Cook, Bernard Grofman, Reuven Hazan, Ken

Janda, Byong-Kuen Jhee, Willy Jou, Tatiana Kostadinova, Shane Martin, Michael McDonald, G. Bingham Powell, Gideon Rahat, Robert Rohrschneider, Giulia Sandri, Susan Scarrow, Rein Taagepera, Benjamin Thomas, and Martin Wattenberg. Shaun Bowler, and Hans-Dieter Klingemann were exceptionally helpful in critiquing the full manuscript. The Center for the Study of Democracy at the University of California, Irvine provided research support at various stages of this project, particularly in hosting visits by Farrell and McAllister. Dominic Byatt and the wonderful team at Oxford University Press were highly supportive throughout, for which we are very grateful.

We are aware that parties are imperfect institutions, and contemporary publics are increasingly aware of these imperfections as well. Indeed, this growing distance between citizens and political parties presents a mounting challenge for representative democracies. However, the strength of political parties and democracy is that they adapt to changing conditions. By showing how the process of party linkage does function today, this may provide a basis for determining how it can work better in the future.

As the book was going to press we learned of the untimely death of our colleague and friend, Peter Mair. Despite disagreeing with some of our conclusions Peter very graciously wrote a lovely endorsement for this book. It is most regretful that he was denied the opportunity he would have relished to lock horns with us.

Finally, we dedicate this book to Richard Rose, who helped to pioneer the academic study of political parties five decades ago. In books such as *The Problem of Party Government* and *Do Parties Make a Difference?* Rose has sought to understand the role of political parties in modern society—and to suggest how it might be changed. A constant theme throughout his work, from elections to public policy to postcommunist politics, has been the contribution of political parties to the effective functioning of democracy. Those of us who study political parties owe Richard a lifelong debt for the insights he has brought to this field of study.

Russell Dalton
David Farrell
Ian McAllister

Table of Contents

List of Figures

List of Tables

List of Abbreviations

C	Centre Party (Sweden)
CD	Christian Democrats
CDA	Christian Democratic Appeal (Netherlands)
CDR	Romanian Democratic Convention
CDU	Christian Democratic Union (Germany)
CEP	Candidates for the European Parliament election
CMP	Comparative Manifestos Project
CSES	Comparative Study of Electoral Systems
CSU	Christian Social Union (Germany)
CU	Christian Union (the Netherlands)
DF	Union for French Democracy
ECOLO	Ecologists Confederated for the Organisation of Original Struggles (Belgium)
GDP	Gross domestic product
FDP	Free Democratic Party (Germany)
FP	Liberal People's Party (Sweden)
IDEA	Institute for Democracy and Electoral Assistance
LDP	Liberal Democratic Party (Japan)
MMP	Mixed member proportionality
MNP	Member of the national parliament
NLP	National Liberal Party (Romania)
OECD	Organisation for Economic Co-operation and Development
PCF	French Communist Party
PDS	Party of Democratic Socialism (Germany)
PDSR	Party of Democratic Socialism (Romania)
PP	Partido Popular (People's Party) (Spain)
PR	Proportional representation
PRM	Greater Romania Party
PSOE	Spanish Socialist Workers' Party

PUR	Humanist Party of Romania
PvdA	Dutch Labour Party
SD	Social Democrats
SMP	single-member plurality
SPD	Sozialdemokratische Partei Deutschlands (Social Democratic Party of Germany)
UDF	Union for French Democracy
UDMR	Democratic Union of Hungarians in Romania
UMP	Union for a Popular Movement
VVD	People's Party for Freedom and Democracy (Netherlands)
WVS	World Values Survey

Author Biographies

Russell J. Dalton is Professor of Political Science at the University of California, Irvine and was the founding director of the Center for the Study of Democracy at UC Irvine. He has received a Fulbright Professorship at the University of Mannheim, a Barbra Streisand Center fellowship, German Marshall Research Fellowship, and a POSCO Fellowship at the East/West Center in Hawaii. His recent publications include *The Good Citizen* (2009) and *Democratic Challenges, Democratic Choices* (2004); he is co-editor of *Citizens, Context and Choice* (2011), *Party Politics in East Asia* (2008), *The Oxford Handbook of Political Behavior* (2007), *Citizens, Democracy and Markets around the Pacific Rim* (2006), *Democracy Transformed?* (2003), and *Parties without Partisans* (2001). His scholarly interests include comparative public opinion, political parties, social movements, and political participation.

David M. Farrell holds the Chair of Politics at University College Dublin, where he is Head of the School of Politics and International Relations. Prior to that, he was Professor of Politics and Head of the School of Social Sciences at the University of Manchester. He is the co-author (with Roger Scully) of *Representing Europe's Citizens* (Oxford University Press, 2007) and (with Ian McAllister) of *The Australian Electoral System* (University of New South Wales Press, 2006). The second edition of his textbook *Electoral Systems* (Palgrave Macmillan) was published in 2010. He is co-editor of *Party Politics*, and of the "Comparative Politics" book series published by Oxford University Press and the European Consortium for Political Research. His scholarly interests include electoral systems, party systems, and representative politics in the European Union. He is currently engaged in collaborative research on political reform in Ireland.

Ian McAllister is Distinguished Professor of Political Science at the Australian National University. He is the co-author (with David M. Farrell) of *The Australian Electoral System* (University of New South Wales Press, 2006) and *Dimensions of Australian Society* (Palgrave Macmillan, 2010), and co-editor of the *Cambridge Handbook of the Social Sciences in Australia* (Cambridge University Press, 2003). He has been director of the Australian Election Study since 1987, and was Chair of the Comparative Study of Electoral Systems project from 2004 to 2009 and editor of the *Australian Journal of Political Science* from 2004 to 2010. He is a member of the Academy of Social Sciences in Australia and a corresponding member of the Royal Society of Edinburgh. His scholarly research covers comparative political behavior, postcommunist politics, and Northern Ireland and Australian politics.

Introduction

1

Parties and Representative Government

In September 2010 the voters of Tuvalu went to the polls. Onlookers specu-
lated that Prime Minister Apisai Ielemia's government would be elected for a
second term. In the event, a new coalition government emerged with Maatia
Toafa as prime minister. The unusual feature in this process is that neither
Ielemia nor Toafa are party leaders, for the simple reason that this nation state,
a long-established democracy, does not have any political parties.

Tuvalu is one of a tiny number of exceptions—indeed, many of them tiny
(Pacific Rim) island states—to the general rule that democracies need political
parties to operate their representative institutions. These exceptional cases
aside, the general picture is of democracies centered on political parties, of
democracies operating representative institutions that are operated by and for
parties—a picture of party government as "a synonym for representative
democracy."[1] This is the central theme of our study, namely that political
parties are vital agencies in the proper functioning of democracies.

By no means is our position unique. It is a well-established position of party
theorists that these entities have played a crucial role in the establishment and
proper functioning of democracy. James Bryce, for instance, was unequivocal
in his view that "parties are inevitable: no free country has been without
them; and no one has shown how representative government could work
without them."[2] In Max Weber's terms, political parties are "the children of
democracy, of mass franchise, of the necessity to woo and organize the
masses."[3] According to LaPalombara and Weiner they are "the creature[s] of
modern and modernizing political systems."[4] In Schattschneider's most mem-
orable refrain, "modern democracy is unthinkable save in terms of the
parties."[5] Schattschneider's perspective is unapologetically normative: he
calls for the development of what he refers to as a model of "party government," a term that became quite prominent in political science debates in the
1970s and 1980s. This culminated in a multi-volume project on "the future of
party government" directed by the late Rudolf Wildenmann.[6]

3

Flash forward a few decades and the centrality of political parties is still much discussed. Leading scholars continue to describe political parties as being "at the heart" of the political system, as "endemic to democracy, an unavoidable part of democracy."[7] The centrality of political parties is reflected in the vibrancy of this branch of the political science discipline. For example, by one estimate researchers have published more than 11,500 books and articles on European parties in the postwar era.[8] And since the mid-1990s the journal *Party Politics* has been dedicated solely to the study of political parties. In the words of one of the leading scholars of party politics, this is "a field which is brimming with health and promise."[9]

It is hard to find fault with the perspective that political parties are ubiquitous. On a daily basis, senior party figures dominate the news agendas. The leaderships of those parties in office set the policy agenda and drive the policy process through the parliamentary system. These same leaderships appoint our judges and other important office holders. At local level we have representatives (MPs, Congressmen, Senators) elected to look after our interests, who in virtually all cases are party representatives. Every several years, we vote in general elections to elect candidates for office, the vast bulk of whom have been nominated by a political party. These snapshots indicate how, in so many respects, there remain important areas of linkage between political parties and citizens.

But while parties are—practically and normatively—essential to the operation of representative democracy, there are also frequent claims that they are in decline in the established democracies, or at the very least experiencing significant change.[10] Voters are less inclined to identify with parties than at any time since public opinion polling was developed, and party membership is in precipitous decline in these same nations. Perhaps most tellingly, even in parliamentary systems governments are now routinely named after the party leader, rather than the party. Thus between 1997 and 2007 in Britain the government was usually labeled "the Blair government" rather than the "Labour government." The nature of this evidence of decline and what it means for the future of parties and representative democracy is the subject of this book.

Our research is motivated by two factors. The first is the availability of new research resources that allow us to systematically study the party government model in a way that was not possible in the past. We mainly rely on the Comparative Study of Electoral Systems (CSES) project data, but we also employ a range of other sources, mainly at the institutional level. These new sources complement one another in valuable ways, permitting us to make new insights into the role of parties and party government in the twenty-first century. Our second motivation in writing this book is to contribute to the vigorous debate about party decline or change. While there is much evidence of party change, whether this amounts to decline and what it may presage for parties is as yet unclear. A major part of the puzzle is the unresolved question of how parties are adapting to these new circumstances. These are the questions that we address in this book.

Why Parties?

Susan Scarrow writes of the rise of party-based politics as "one of the transforming inventions" of the nineteenth century.[11] As the first wave of countries in Europe and North America took their cautious steps to democratization—involving in particular the transfer of power to legislatures and the expansion of the electorate—political parties emerged as the primary linkage mechanism for facilitating the representative process. It took some time for scholars to catch up with this development, in part reflecting disquiet over whether parties were necessarily a force for good. For instance, many of the earliest scholarly writings tended to refer to these new entities as "factions," which were the organizational precursors of parties.[12] In part, the lack of scholarly attention was also because political theory lagged behind political practice. Scholars inevitably took time to recognize the emergence of parties as key linkage mechanisms in the day-to-day operation of representative democracies.[13]

From the 1840s onwards, scholarly writings on political parties gathered pace with prominent (if not always entirely favorable) commentaries. Alexis de Tocqueville provided less than rosy coverage of the American party politics of the Jacksonian era. Henry George, in observing the development of British parliamentary democracy, was possibly one of the first to coin the phrase "party government." Walter Bagehot stressed the importance of cohesive parliamentary parties as the unifying element of representative democracy.[14]

It was not until the midpoint of the following century that the scholarly community started to flesh out the roles and functions of political parties in modern representative democracies. A first big step came in the 1950s with the publication of the influential "responsible parties" report issued by the American Political Science Association's (APSA) Committee on Political Parties. The report placed greatest stress on the need for political parties to produce policy programs giving voters clear choices in elections, and for the parties to be sufficiently disciplined and cohesive in the parliamentary assembly to implement these programs. This emphasis on party functions—notably the aggregative and policy-implementation functions—was to presage an important epistemological development in political science, which became known as "structural functionalism."

Gabriel Almond was the first to assign a set of key roles or functions that parties (he also refers to other actors in his classic essay) fulfill in a democracy.[15] There have been countless other studies that have addressed this theme since, perhaps none more prominent than the 1980s' Wildenmann project on "the future of party government."[16] By any standards, the range of functions that parties seek to fulfill—within the mass population, as organizations, and in government—are impressive.[17] Within the mass population, parties simplify the choices that are open to voters, thereby reducing the policy complexity of modern government into a small number of options that voters can easily understand. Parties educate citizens into the advantages and disadvantages of the policy choices that are on offer. Not least among their roles within the mass population is the expectation that political parties will mobilize citizens to actively participate in the political process, thereby creating long-term stability for the political system as a whole.

At the organizational level, parties recruit and train potential political leaders and candidates for political office, socializing them into the norms and values of democratic governance and thereby contributing to long-term political stability. Organizationally, parties also articulate the political interests of their supporters, giving them expression and substance within the political sphere. And in parallel with their role of articulation, parties aggregate political interests, placing them in a comprehensive and coherent form that will guide government policy if and when they are elected to office.

At the government level, parties organize the work of government by seeking to create majorities and thereby win office. Once in government, most parties possess a comprehensive set of policy objectives for which they can claim an electoral mandate. The party in government—or coalition of parties—will then move to implement those policies, and organize the administration of government to that end. The electoral mandate also provides the legitimacy for its policies while in government, and crucially ensures accountability for its decisions to the electorate, who will judge the party's performance against what it had promised. If the party is in opposition, it too can contribute to accountability by evaluating and criticizing government decisions.

One of the more recent descriptions of this model of party government comes from Kay Lawson.[18] Instead of talking about functions, Lawson uses the term "linkage" to distinguish political parties from other organizations, marking them as the primary representative agents between citizens and the state. As she puts it, this is why linkage is often used as a synonym for representation. In practical terms, however, Lawson's linkages are very similar to the functional roles in other party government theories.

In this study we identify five main forms of linkage between parties and voters (Figure 1.1):

Figure 1.1. The Chain of Democratic Linkage

- **Campaign linkage**: parties recruit candidates and set the parameters of the electoral process;
- **Participatory linkage**: parties activate citizens during elections and mobilize them to vote;
- **Ideological linkage**: parties inform voters about policy choices in elections and voters strongly base their voting preference on these policy alternatives;
- **Representative linkage**: elections achieve a good congruence between citizen policy preferences and the policies of the parties represented in parliament and the government; and
- **Policy linkage**: parties deliver on the policies they advocated in the election.

When there is a strong connection between each of these linkages in the chain of party government, then representative government can function well as a means to connect citizen preferences to the outcomes of government. But when one or more of these linkages deteriorates, the model of party government suffers.

Giovanni Sartori encapsulates the first of these linkages in his famous "minimal definition" of a party as "any political group identified by an official label that presents at elections, and is capable of placing through elections (free or non-free), candidates for public office."[19] Classically this was seen as the main factor separating political parties from interest groups, the latter not fielding candidates, but rather seeking to influence the actions and policies of the former. Thus candidate recruitment (and training) is an initial linkage in the party government model.

Another aspect of the campaign linkage is the parties' dominance of the campaign process. Although political parties must react to changes in social and political conditions, they play a dominant role in defining the agenda of campaigns. Parties are the prime actors in political discourse during elections, through their programs, advertising, and education of the citizenry. In most nations, parties now receive state funding and other subsidies to allow them to spread their message. And in the end, in most parliamentary systems voters face a choice of parties on the ballot—not individual candidates—and even individual candidates stand as party representatives. Thus parties' control of the various aspects of the campaign process is essential to the party linkage model.

Parties need votes to survive, which brings us to their participation linkage. The factors that drive each of us to the polling station are many and varied. According to Sidney Verba and his colleagues there are three broad reasons: we can; we want to; and we were encouraged to do so by an individual or organization—primarily by the political parties. In their efforts to organize "the chaotic public will,"[20] parties chase votes, trying to mobilize as many of their supporters as possible to turn out and trying to convert others to their cause.

The next step in the process of party government can be described as the ideological linkage or the aggregation of voter interests into party choices. The APSA Committee on Political Parties viewed this as one of the core functions of parties. Almond similarly maintained that political parties have a core role to play in aggregating voter interests.[21] The aggregation function can come in several ways. From the perspective of the APSA Committee—which privileged the two-party majoritarian form of democracy found in the USA—the aggregation occurs in advance of polling day by the parties setting out their programs for government, guiding the voters in how they might want to direct their votes. In the alternative "proportional representation vision" of democracy that predominates in Europe, the aggregation process more normally occurs in the post-election bartering and negotiations between party leaders seeking to form coalition governments.[22]

Ideological linkage is an essential part of the party linkage model. The model makes three basic presumptions about citizens and their voting choices that are the basis of linkage in representative democracy:[23]

- People possess informed political preferences and policy choices;
- They make judgments about which party best represents these preferences;
- These perceptions guide voting behavior.

Without such content and a programmatic structure, the connection between citizen preferences and electoral outcomes weakens. Elections could become meaningless expressions of opinions or habitual expressions of group loyalties, rather than instrumental acts of governance. The ability of contemporary electorates to fulfill these three criteria is highly debated in the scholarly literature.

The fourth step in the linkage process involves the formation of government. Elections can allocate seats to political parties, but they do this in a representative or a non-representative way. Moreover, in most parliamentary systems the actual composition of the government does not directly depend on election outcomes, but on the coalition negotiations among parties that occur after the election.[24] Consequently, the congruence between seats and votes, and between majority opinions and the policy positions of post-election governments, is a crucial step in democratic governance.[25]

The fifth linkage is policy implementation. This is the corollary of voter aggregation: the party or parties that form the government should then implement the policies that they promulgated during the election campaign and/or in the post-election negotiations over government formation. This perspective lies at the heart of the "does politics matter?" argument, where the nature of the party/parties in office is found to have a significant effect on policy output. Cross-national analyses from the Comparative Manifesto Project find striking evidence that parties make a real difference in government policy outputs.[26] Various studies of political representation similarly find strong connections between voter preferences and those of their parties in parliament and government overall.[27] Party government does appear to function quite well.

These steps in the process of party government may seem familiar enough. But they still leave questions to be asked over whether they provide sufficient coverage of parties' role in representative democracy and, indeed, whether they still apply in the contemporary world.

The Challenges to Parties

Not everything is rosy in the garden of political parties. Even though parties appear central to the proper functioning of democracies, there seems little doubt that they are now in some difficulty. Like struggling ducks in an ever faster downstream current, they are working harder just to keep still. As Philippe Schmitter (not one of the most sympathetic of observers of parties at the best of times) opines, "parties are not what they once were."[28] The challenges to parties are even more intense in the newer democracies where parties have sought to consolidate in less than propitious circumstances.[29]

The thesis that political parties are in decline is not new, but there is no doubt that in recent decades it has become a veritable "growth industry."[30] Critics cite several indicators to support this view—many of which were summarized in an earlier volume that the current authors were associated with[31]—that are worth briefly summarizing here. The critics cite several trends that are apparent in contemporary democracies: growing public detachment with political parties; the rise of alternative actors in the electoral process; and the parties' growing reliance on the state apparatus for support instead of their own voters/members. Other observers claim that the increasing fragmentation of political interests has made it more difficult for parties to govern, and thus policy performance has deteriorated.

The first example amounts to what Peter Mair refers to as a failure by parties "in their capacity to engage ordinary citizens."[32] He provides four familiar enough sets of evidence to support his case: declining electoral turnout; the rise of voter volatility; falling levels of party identification; and the monotonic decline in party membership numbers. He draws a stark conclusion: "all over Western Europe, and in all likelihood all over the advanced democracies, citizens are heading for the exits of the national political arena."[33]

These trends are problematic if they signal the erosion of parties' ability to perform several of the linkages described in Figure 1.1. Declining turnout, for example, suggests that parties are less effective in mobilizing citizens into the electoral process, and declining party membership implies that participation by activists is also weakening. Indeed, when turnout drops to barely half the electorate, as it did in recent elections in the USA, Switzerland, the UK, and several other nations, this raises questions about the basic legitimacy of election outcomes.

In addition, the weakening of popular identification with a political party—and the concomitant increase in interelection volatility and voter fluidity—may imply that the voting bonds between citizens and parties are eroding. Some analysts argue that parties are losing their programmatic focus in their effort to respond to the policy preferences of the moment, which then change at the next moment. In addition, there is also much debate over whether the rise of candidate-centered voting would strengthen or weaken the system of party-based government.

Another set of trends suggesting that parties are under threat involves the growing competition they face from other actors, particularly at elections. It is not too much of an exaggeration to state that elections are central to the *raison d'être* of political parties. Indeed, as we have seen, this is central to Sartori's "minimal definition" of a party. The signs are that the parties now face stiff competition in this regard. This is shown, for instance, in the rise of "third-party actors" and better-resourced interest groups competing against parties in elections,[34] in the growing prominence of microparties and independents,[35] and in the more assertive role of the mass media during elections.[36]

Certainly there are a growing number of "non-party actors" entering the electoral fray.[37] There are prominent examples of joke parties (such as the Monster Raving Loony Party in Britain, or the Polish Beer Lovers Party). Independent candidates are enjoying greater electoral success in some countries (such as Australia and Ireland). And in parts of Latin America, presidential candidates have benefited from promoting an "antiparty" ticket (Alberto Fujimori in Peru, Fernando Collor and subsequently Fernando Henrique Cardoso in Brazil, and Rafael Caldera in Venezuela).[38] Another challenge to parties' control of candidate recruitment is the decentralization of candidate selection from party elites to the members at large, or even voters in general.[39] In addition, there appears to be an increasing tendency for successful individuals in social or economic domains to use these credentials to gain party nomination or positions in government. All of these examples suggest that parties no longer have an exclusive role in the recruitment of political leaders.

These developments show how parties are no longer the sole actors articulating and aggregating voter interests. Parties no longer provide the exclusive route into electoral politics for budding political candidates who seek election. In addition, parties may have lost their dominant role as gatekeepers in setting and determining the policy agenda in elections. Information flowing from the media and interest groups now impinges on a party's role as information provider. All in all, these changes may weaken the parties' roles in the campaign linkage.

Another factor is the growing connection between parties and the state. Peter Mair sees this as the corollary (or part cause) of the "popular withdrawal" of parties from society,[40] and as forming a core feature of the "cartel party" argument he developed with Richard Katz.[41] The gist of the argument is that the parties are making ever more use of state resources, both to bolster their positions in response to declining resources (*inter alia* from less membership dues), and to shore up their positions as the established cartel of dominant parties.

One of the concerns about the development of cartel party characteristics is that it will contribute to the decoupling of parties and the mass public.[42] When funding comes from the government, the economic contributions of a mass membership are less central. Similarly, when campaigns shift to media contests rather than grass-roots contacting, the value of mass memberships declines. This may decrease turnout in elections, and encourage parties to mobilize their core voters, especially in a parliamentary system, rather than convert new supporters to the party.

Another problem with cartel parties is that they may weaken the representative linkage of the parties. If parties can depend on the institutional support of the government, they may lessen their attention to voter preferences. In other words, cartel characteristics may partially insulate parties from the mass public. This leaves parties open to the charge that they are becoming little more than agents of the state, or public utilities, a point stressed in the writings of party scholars like Richard Katz[43] and Ingrid van Biezen.[44]

Other factors may also weaken the parties' ability, or interest, in representing the views of their voters in the electoral process. The fragmentation of policy interests and interest articulation may make it more difficult for parties to represent a theoretical median voter. The past era of clear programmatic differences between the parties, and clear party choices, has evolved into a more diverse policy agenda with more competing interests. For example, the

British Liberal Democratic voters supported the party and its liberal agenda in the 2010 election, only to see it partner with the Conservatives and enact major cuts in government programs. These post-election surprises seem to be a more common aspect of contemporary politics especially in developing democracies.[45] The growing alienation from parties in general and from the system of party government is one indicator of this phenomenon.[46] It appears that many members of the public do not feel that their views are being represented in the governing process.

In addition, policy research stresses the constraints that now face parties and governments in enacting desired policies. In particular, the growing interdependence among nation states, the more intrusive role of the courts in the policy process, and the growing complexity of government with the attendant outsourcing of policy to non-government organizations mean that the days of dominant party control over policy are over. These factors combine to raise fundamental challenges for the ability of political parties to perform in terms of representation and policy linkages.

A number of objections can be raised to the various arguments regarding the decline of parties. First, there may be a tendency to overexaggerate recent developments. Yes, voter turnout is dropping, party vote loyalty is decreasing, and fewer of us are inclined to become party members. But in many of these instances the trends are modest.[47] We do not dispute this evidence of a weakening of party loyalties within contemporary electorates. Indeed, in other research we have documented the decline in partisan ties and the increasing fluidity of voting choice in the established democracies.[48] But even an increasing non-partisan public face the choice of parties as they enter the ballot booth, and are heavily dependent on political parties to ensure the representativeness of party government. Thus, this book focuses on the actions of political parties as organizations, realizing that the patterns of partisanship in the electorate may also be changing.

These trends also need to be considered in the wider context of societal change which has affected institutions beyond political parties. Societal change has contributed to a breakdown of collective identities as citizens become increasingly individualized. Rudy Andeweg uses poetic license to illustrate this point succinctly: "religion is increasingly expressed outside churches, interest promotion is taken care of outside interest associations, such as trade unions, physical exercise outside sports clubs ... work outside permanent employment, love outside marriage, and even gender differences are becoming divorced from sex differences."[49] Little wonder, then, why parties should have fewer members, few loyal followers, and face growing competition from other non-party actors.

We believe that these changes in citizens' attachments to political parties are a real and continuing feature of established democracies, and are even apparent in some new democracies. It may be impossible to return to the halcyon days of the past when parties had larger memberships, more people voted, and more people identified with a political party. But changes in the public can be separate from the actions of parties as political institutions. Moreover, we argue that some of the observed changes in modern parties reflect an attempt to adapt to social and political changes in democratic publics. Indeed, to succeed and persist, political parties have to adapt to changing political conditions in order to contribute to the process of representative democracy.

Second, some analysts display a tendency to look back fondly to bygone days, to a Golden Age personified by the "mass party" model whose features were first elaborated in Maurice Duverger's classic study.[50] More specifically, many observers highlight the decline in the mass membership upon which this type of party relies for its organizational strength and from that conclude that parties are in terminal decline.[51] Yet, the mass party was already undergoing change from its earliest years, first to the "catch-all" party first outlined by Otto Kirchheimer, and more recently to the cartel party proposed by Katz and Mair.[52] In this context, focusing mainly on the organizational aspects of parties does not provide any evidence about how well or how badly parties are fulfilling their basic functions.

The mass party model emphasizes a loyal supporter base, the representation of particular social groups, and large mass memberships. That is, the very features that are singled out as evidence in support of the party decline thesis. Furthermore, this party model was arguably more an ideal typical than a widespread political reality.[53] Writing in an American context, John Aldrich makes much the same point, observing that rather than decline, we have witnessed a shift from the "party in control" form of the Van Buren era to a "party in service."[54] In other words, the party has changed, but it is not necessarily any weaker as a consequence. As Michael Saward puts it, "It may be, in the words of Schmitter, that these shifts lead to the conclusion that 'parties are not what they once were', but that does not necessarily mean that they are *less* than they once were."[55]

The corollary of fixating on a particular model of party is a tendency to pay undue homage to a style of democracy that may be well past its sell-by date. Once again, Mair provides a good example. He places Schattschneider's argument about "unthinkable democracies" on its head by suggesting that not only can parties fail but if they do, "so too fails popular democracy."[56] His point is that representative democracy as we know it is under threat, as democracies become "hollowed out," "shorn of their popular component," transforming into "stripped down versions" of Madisonian democracy.[57] However, this sort of perspective fails to recognize the potential for adaptability, in this instance of democratic forms. Michael Saward makes this point when he tracks a shift from one ideal typical form of democracy, which he refers to as the "popular mode"—the form of democracy lauded by Mair—to alternative ideal typical modes, such as "statal" or "reflexive" modes. Saward's point is that such a shift "do[es] not necessarily add up to a picture that is less democratic. It can, rather, be differently democratic."[58]

What is missing from many of the accounts of party decline is what is happening in place of the older patterns. The answer to that is obvious: parties are not being replaced; they appear to be adapting to the changed conditions within which they find themselves. This is a process that has been occurring, almost seamlessly, for more than a century. Parties are an essential component of the state, and as such they are in the driving position in altering political institutions if they are inimical to their long-term interests. Parties are, if nothing else, survivors. An important goal of this book is therefore to balance the party decline argument with the equally compelling evidence concerning how parties are adapting to change.

To sum up, our principal objection to the "decline of parties" thesis—and the principal rationale for this study—is that the evidence of decline is too selective, emphasizes changes in the mass public rather than in party performance, and is arguably too focused on the mass party ideal. As we show in this book, the prospect for parties is far less worrisome. In a large number of areas, political parties continue to have important linkages with citizens and with government. And where those linkages are under stress, parties seek to address the problem.

Our Empirical Base

Our project relies on a set of cross-national datasets to assemble the necessary empirical evidence on the various links of the party government model. We base the core of our analyses on the nations included in the second module of the CSES.[59] The CSES is a collaborative research program among national election studies in over fifty countries around the world. Participating countries include a common module of survey questions in their post-election surveys. All surveys must meet certain quality and comparability standards, and all are conducted as nationally representative surveys. The resulting survey data are combined with district- and macro-level voting, demographic, and institutional variables, providing a unique opportunity to examine how institutional arrangements shape political behavior.

The CSES fielded its second module in national surveys conducted between 2001 and 2006. Table 1.1 lists the 36 module 2 nations and the year of the elections that are the core of our analyses (including two elections in Portugal and Taiwan).[60] The CSES project also compiled ancillary data on the political

Table 1.1. Comparative Study of Electoral Systems Nations in Module 2

Nation	Election Year	Sample Size
Albania	2005	1116
Australia	2004	1769
Belgium	2003	2225
Brazil	2002	2514
Bulgaria	2001	1482
Canada	2004	1674
Chile	2005	1200
Czech Republic	2002	948
Denmark	2001	2026
Finland	2003	1196
France	2002	1000
Germany	2002	2000
Hungary	2002	1200
Iceland	2003	1446
Ireland	2002	2367
Israel	2003	1212
Italy	2006	1439
Japan	2004	1977
Korea, South	2004	1500
Mexico	2003	1991
Netherlands	2002	1574
New Zealand	2002	1741
Norway	2001	2052
Peru	2006	2032
Philippines	2004	1200
Poland	2001	1794
Portugal	2002	1303
Portugal	2005	2801
Romania	2004	1913
Russia	2004	1496
Slovenia	2004	1002
Spain	2004	1212
Sweden	2002	1060
Switzerland	2003	1418
Taiwan	2001	2022
Taiwan	2004	1823
UK	2005	860
USA	2004	1066

Note: We do not include Hong Kong or Kyrgyzstan from module 2 because the elections were not free, fair, and authoritative.

systems, electoral systems, and parties in each election that we use in some of our analyses, complemented by institutional data added by the authors.

The CSES project is especially valuable for comparing the workings of party linkage across democratic settings. The survey contains measures of electoral participation to study how parties mobilize citizens to participate. It asks respondents to position themselves and the major political parties in their nation on the Left–Right scale, which is a central variable in our analyses of voting choice and representation. Because all the surveys are conducted following a national election, we measure public opinion with a focus on representation through elections, using comparable measures and methodologies.

Most previous comparative research on party linkage has focused on the experience of established democracies in Western Europe and North America. The CSES offers a valuable mix of electoral systems, constitutional structures, and democratic experience that were generally underrepresented in past European-based studies. The CSES is especially valuable for examining political opinions and behaviors in the newly democratized countries of Central and Eastern Europe. The project also includes information on the parties and national characteristics that are available as ancillary datasets. Furthermore, the CSES nations represent a wider range of cultural zones, including West and East Europe, North America, East Asia, and Latin America.

We supplement the CSES data with information from other cross-national research projects in various chapters. Chapter 2, on parties' structuring of electoral campaigns, assembles information from a wide array of projects dealing with party organizational characteristics, party funding, and electoral system design. Chapter 5, on citizens' perceptions of party positions, compares the results from the CSES survey with three other sources: the Benoit and Laver survey of party experts, the Comparative Manifesto Project coding of party Left–Right positions, and surveys of European parliamentary elites conducted in the mid-1990s.[61] Chapter 8, on the policy impact of party governments, utilizes data on social spending provided by the Organisation for Economic Co-operation and Development (OECD).[62] Indeed, only the relatively recent development of large-scale collaborative cross-national research makes it possible to conduct the type of analyses presented in this volume.

Studying the Linkage between Parties and Citizens

In the chapters that follow we assess the five forms of party linkage in turn, to show how parties continue to play important roles in representative democracy. Figure 1.2 expands on the party linkage framework to highlight the theoretical bases of each step, the chapters that examine each linkage, and the primary empirical resources in each chapter.

Chapter 2 covers the theme of *campaign* linkage by examining the role of parties in the electoral process. This is one of the areas singled out in the party-decline thesis, where there are frequent references to the growing competition political parties face in the electoral arena from other "non-party" actors; declining party memberships, and potentially increasing competition from non-party actors (the media and interest groups). This implies that parties have a tougher battle with less indigenous resources to maintain their dominant position in the electoral process. Moreover, in partial reaction to these

Forms of linkage	Campaign	Participatory	Ideological			Representative	Policy
Theory	Interest articulation Interest aggregation Cartel party	Mobilization & civic volunteerism model	Downsian left/right spatial analysis of electoral choice			Congruence; coalition theory	Do parties matter?
Chapter	Chapter 2 Parties & electoral institutions	Chapter 3 Parties & political participation	Chapter 4 Citizens & policy preferences	Chapter 5 Party images & party linkage	Chapter 6 Voter choice & partisan representation	Chapter 7 Congruence between voters & government	Chapter 8 Parties & policies
Data	Institutional & aggregate data	Individual-level analysis (CSES)		Individual to party-level analysis (CSES & Benoit/Laver)			Party to state-level analysis (CSES & policy data)

Figure 1.2. A Flowchart of Democratic Linkage

17

developments, parties are relying increasingly on the state apparatus to buttress their positions in a manner consistent with the Katz and Mair "cartel party" thesis.[63]

We review a wide body of evidence to show how parties have responded to changes in the electoral environment in three main respects. First, by the introduction and steady expansion of a wide range of generous state supports (both financial and in-kind). Second, by the implementation of regulatory mechanisms (the quid pro quo of state support) that are, for the most part, light touch and often ineffectual. Third, by the steady evolution of controls over the electoral process which are designed to ensure the primacy of parties. The evidence points clearly and consistently to an electoral process still dominated by political parties. The battle for political office remains very much one between candidates selected and promoted by political parties—with the partial exception of the USA. One recent survey of trends across the advanced industrial democracies paraphrased Schattschneider in concluding that the "recruitment of candidates for representative and related governmental functions remains virtually inconceivable without political parties."[64] As we shall demonstrate in Chapter 2, the hold of parties over the recruitment of candidates is even stronger in the new and developing democracies.

Not only do parties still have a tight hold over the apparatus of elections, our analysis of the CSES survey evidence in Chapter 3 provides clear evidence that parties continue to play a key *participatory* role in turning out the vote on polling day. The party-decline argument makes much play of the point that electoral participation has been in decline in recent decades. However, the fact remains that far more people vote than abstain. As we (and others before us) show, political parties bear much of the responsibility for cajoling voters to the polling booths. The evidence in Chapter 3 shows that local campaign activity still features prominently in the activity of political parties and that this has a strong influence in turning out a vote at elections. It may be more difficult, but there is little doubt that the mobilization efforts of parties still "matters" in influencing voters both to turn out and also to decide on which parties to vote for.[65]

A third form of linkage—which we refer to as *ideological*—involves voter choice of parties. Oftentimes voters face a bewildering array of options, particularly in those cases of multi-party systems. Voters have a difficult job to determine their policy preferences, work out how these are best represented by the range of parties and party programs on offer, and then vote for the party that best represents those views. Chapters 4–6 examine this process of ideological linkage in three logical steps. Chapter 4 shows how citizens' political preferences and policy choices can be summarized by their positions on the Left–Right dimension. Many electoral analysts have demonstrated that the Left–Right dimension is a suitable summary means of mapping voter orientations cross-nationally.[66]

Having determined their own policy preferences, democratic accountability then requires that citizens have sufficient understanding of the choices available to them from among the range of parties competing for votes in the election. Chapter 5 determines whether most citizens can identify the parties' Left–Right positions, and then verifies these perceptions with evidence from elite surveys, expert analyses of parties, and party election manifestos.

The final stage in this linkage sequence has people voting for the parties that best represent their political preferences; this is the focus of Chapter 6. This produces clear evidence that Left–Right orientations—more specifically, the congruence between the orientations of the voter and the party—are a very strong predictor of the vote. This confirms the continuing strength of ideological linkage between parties and citizens.

Chapter 7 shifts our focus from elections to government, and to the *representative* linkage between parties and citizens that occurs after the votes are counted. We show that the accountability between citizens and the political decision-makers is a dynamic process. The positions of the parties and voters on polling day are taken at one point in time. Once the dust has settled, negotiations ensue and governments (more normally than not, coalition governments) are formed. This may attenuate the link between citizens and their government, especially if the resulting coalitions are not representative of electoral outcomes or are distorted by the outcome of elite negotiations in "smoke-filled" rooms after polling day.[67] This chapter studies this dynamic by comparing voter–government policy congruence before and after polling day. We show how party government functions as a steering mechanism to adjust the course of government based on past government performance and the options available in the election. Thus, elections improve the level of congruence between voters and their government, providing good evidence of healthy representative linkage between parties and citizens.

Chapter 8 draws on OECD data to examine how the constellation of parties in office can impact on the policy outputs of the government. These analyses address the theme of whether "parties matter" in setting policy priorities. If party control of the government does matter, then those who voted for the government have good reason to feel that their policy preferences are being met in a manner consistent with their expressed vote choice. *Policy* linkage is the most complex linkage of the party government model to test. Still, the evidence we unearth is generally supportive.

Finally, in Chapter 9 we draw the main threads of our argument together to examine how parties have survived the storms of time and social change through a strategy of adaptation that focuses on four main dimensions:

institutional design, policy development, organizational reform, and strategies to maintain a dominant role over the government process.

What Parties Do

The *Madmen* TV series takes us back to the 1960s, to a time when Madison Avenue first entered the fray in providing advertising and marketing campaigns for the presidential races of Richard Nixon and John F. Kennedy. This election is often seen as marking an important turning point in US party politics, and thereafter the party politics of other countries (as the process of "Americanization" of election campaigns unfolded).[68] If there ever had been a Golden Age of party politics, then this election supposedly marks its death knell. The 1960s also stand out as the heyday of the era of Network TV. The three TV networks of CBS, NBC, and ABC were at the height of their powers, between them encompassing over 90 percent of the national television market.[69] Indeed, the personification of just how dominant network TV had become was demonstrated in the first-ever TV presidential debates between Kennedy and Nixon in 1960, debates that are seen generally to have played a crucial role in securing Kennedy his narrow electoral victory.

How different things are for the "Big Three" networks today: they have long lost their market dominance; the nature of their operation has changed also, with increasing outsourcing of production to other entities; and there have also been questions raised over the future of television as we know it.

All of this is a very familiar tale to those of us studying party politics, where we can track much the same sorts of trends: growing fragmentation of party systems; dramatic internal organizational changes; questions raised over the future of parties as we know them—issues (among others) that we have been teasing out in this introductory chapter, trends that are seen by some as raising important questions over the future of parties.

As we explain in the following chapters, much of the hand wringing over the state of political parties is predicated on a certain type of party and a certain style of representative politics from bygone days. The detractors also focus their attention on what parties *are*—mass membership, branch-based organizations; their internal structures; their ability to hold on to a loyal following of voters—perhaps more so than what they *do*.

The critics also often ignore how parties are adapting their roles to ensure that they continue to fulfill these functions. It is these latter perspectives that are featured in this book. Party government requires a set of roles (or functions) that parties must perform, a series of "linkages" that they provide between citizens and government. This study seeks to show how, in a large number of respects, the political parties of today continue to provide these important linkages through a process of adaption and evolution.

Parties remain central to modern democracy and undertake a wide range of functions. Any consideration of the health of parties must therefore evaluate systematically the panoply of activities that parties engage in, both cross-nationally and longitudinally. Our evidence—necessarily limited in time and coverage—shows that parties remain a crucial link between the citizen and the government. And while there has been a decline in some aspects of partisan politics, there is at least as much evidence of adaptation, as parties transform themselves in order to meet the challenges of ongoing political change.

Notes

1. Richard Katz, Party government and its alternatives. In Richard Katz, ed., *Party Governments: European and American Experiences*. Berlin: de Gruyter, 1987, p. 2. Dag Anckar and Carsten Anckar, Democracies without parties, *Comparative Political Studies* (2000) 33: 225–47. Another tiny set of partial exceptions are presented by the parliamentary assemblies in the Philippines, Indonesia, and Thailand which imposed blocks to prevent established parties from winning some or all of the seats. On this, see Roland Rich, Designing Parties out of Parliaments: Non-Partisan Chambers in Indonesia, the Philippines and Thailand. PhD dissertation, Australian National University, July 2010.
2. James Bryce, *Modern Democracies*. New York: Macmillan, 1921, p.119.
3. Max Weber, The advent of plebiscitarian democracy. In Peter Mair, ed., *The West European Party System*. Oxford: Oxford University Press, 1990, p. 35.
4. Joseph LaPalombara and Myron Weiner, The origin and development of political parties. In Joseph LaPalombara and Weiner, eds, *Political Parties and Development*. Princeton, NJ: Princeton University Press, 1966, p. 3.
5. E. E. Schattschneider, *Party Government*. Westport, CT: Greenwood Press, [1942] 1977, p. 1. More generally, see Russell Dalton and Martin Wattenberg, eds, *Parties without Partisans: Political Change in Advanced Industrial Democracies*. Oxford: Oxford University Press, 2000; Seymour Martin Lipset, The indispensability of political parties, *Journal of Democracy* (2000) 11: 48–55; Susan Scarrow, ed., *Perspectives on Political Parties: Classic Readings*. Basingstoke: Macmillan, 2002.
6. Francis Castles and Rudolf Wildenmann, eds, *Visions and Realities of Party Government*. Berlin: de Gruyter, 1986. See also Richard Rose, *The Problem of Party Government*. London: Macmillan, 1974.
7. John Aldrich, *Why Parties? The Origin and Transformation of Political Parties in America*. Chicago: University of Chicago Press, 1995, p. 3; Susan Stokes, Political parties and democracy, *Annual Review of Political Science* (1999) 2: 245.

8. Stefano Bartolini, Daniele Caramani, and Simon Hug, *Parties and Party Systems: A Bibliographical Guide to the Literature on Parties and Party Systems in Europe since 1945*. CD-ROM. London: Sage, 1998.

9. Peter Mair, *Party System Change: Approaches and Interpretations*. Oxford: Oxford University Press, 1997, p. vii.

10. Paul Webb, David Farrell, and Ian Holliday, eds, *Political Parties in Advanced Industrial Democracies*. Oxford: Oxford University Press, 2002; Dalton and Wattenberg, eds, *Parties without Partisans*; John Coleman, *Party Decline in America*. Princeton, NJ: Princeton University Press, 1996.

11. Susan Scarrow, The nineteenth-century origins of modern political parties: The unwanted emergence of party-based politics. In Richard Katz and William Crotty, eds, *Handbook of Party Politics*. London: Sage, 2006.

12. Giovanni Sartori, *Parties and Party Systems: A Framework for Analysis*. Cambridge: Cambridge University Press, 1976, ch. 1.

13. Scarrow, ed. *Perspectives on Political Parties*. Party scholars may have long since caught up with the practical reality of parties, but to this day it remains an issue that democratic theorists and party scholars tend to talk past each other: the former down-playing, even sidelining, the linkage role of parties, the latter giving insufficient attention to variations in models of democracy and the differing role that parties might play. For discussion, see Ingrid van Biezen and Michael Saward, Democratic theorists and party scholars: Why they don't talk to each other, and why they should, *Perspectives on Politics* (2008) 6; Richard Katz, Party in democratic theory. In Richard Katz and William Crotty, eds, *Handbook of Party Politics*. London: Sage, 2006.

14. For more detail, see Scarrow, The nineteenth-century origins of modern political parties, pp. 21–22.

15. Gabriel Almond, Introduction: A functional approach to comparative politics. In Gabriel Almond and James Coleman, eds, *The Politics of Developing Areas*. Princeton, NJ: Princeton University Press, 1960.

16. Richard Katz, Party government: A rationalistic conception. In Francis Castles and Rudolf Wildenmann, eds, *Visions and Realities of Party Government*. Berlin: de Gruyter, 1986, p. 32. For a sample of other studies, see: David Abbott and Edward Rogowsky, Introduction. In David Abbott and Edward Rogowsky, eds, *Political Parties: Leadership, Organization, Linkage*. Chicago: Rand McNally, 1971; Stefano Bartolini and Peter Mair, Challenges to contemporary political parties. In Larry Diamond and Richard Gunther, eds, *Political Parties and Democracy*. Baltimore, MD: Johns Hopkins University Press, 2001, p. 331; Samuel Eldersveld, *Political Parties: A Behavioral Analysis*. Chicago: Rand McNally, 1964; Richard Gunther and Larry Diamond, Types and functions of parties. In Larry Diamond and Richard Gunther, eds, *Political Parties and Democracy*. Baltimore, MD: Johns Hopkins University Press, 2001, pp. 7–8; Anthony King, Political parties in Western democracies: Some skeptical reflections, *Polity* (1969) 2: 111–41; Charles Merriam and Harold Gosnell, *The American Party System: An Introduction to the Study of Political Parties in the United States* (4th edn). New York: Macmillan, 1949, p. 470; Sigmund Neumann, Towards a comparative study of political parties. In Sigmund Neumann, ed., *Modern Political*

Parties: Approaches to Comparative Politics. Chicago: University of Chicago Press, 1956, pp. 396–97.

17. See Leon Epstein, *Political Parties in Western Democracies*. New Brunswick, NY: Transaction, 1980; Dalton and Wattenberg, eds, *Parties without Partisans*; Angelo Panebianco, *Political Parties: Organization and Power*. Cambridge: Cambridge University Press, 1988.

18. Kay Lawson, Political parties and linkage. In Kay Lawson, ed., *Political Parties and Linkage: A Comparative Perspective*. New Haven: Yale University Press, 1980. See also, Andrea Römmele, David Farrell, and Piero Ignazi, eds, *Political Parties and Political Systems: The Concept of Linkage Revisited*. Westport, CT: Praeger, 2005.

19. Sartori, *Parties and Party Systems*, p. 63.

20. Neumann, Towards a comparative study of political parties, p. 397.

21. Almond, Introduction, p. 40.

22. G. Bingham Powell, *Elections as Instruments of Democracy*. New Haven, CT: Yale University Press, 2000.

23. Jacques Thomassen, Empirical research into political representation. In M. Kent Jennings and Thomas Mann, eds, *Elections at Home and Abroad*. Ann Arbor: University of Michigan Press, 1994 ; Angus Campbell, Philip Converse, Warren Miller, and Donald Stokes, *The American Voter*. New York: Wiley, 1960, ch. 8.

24. Kaare Strom, Wolfgang Müller, and Torbjörn Bergman, eds, *Cabinets and Coalition Bargaining: The Democratic Life Cycle in Western Europe*. Oxford: Oxford University Press, 2008; Michael Laver and Ian Budge, eds, *Party Policy and Government Coalitions*. New York: St Martin's Press, 1992.

25. G. Bingham Powell, Institutions and the ideological congruence of governments. In Russell Dalton and Christopher Anderson, eds, *Citizens, Context and Choice*. Oxford: Oxford University Press, 2011.

26. Hans-Dieter Klingemann, Richard Hofferbert, and Ian Budge, *Parties, Policies and Democracy*. Boulder, CO: Westview Press, 1994; also see Francis Castles, *Comparative Public Policy: Patterns of Post-War Transformation*. Cheltenham: Edward Elgar, 1998.

27. Richard Katz and Bernhard Wessels, eds, *The European Parliament, National Parliaments, and European Integration*. Oxford: Oxford University Press, 1999; Hermann Schmitt and Jacques Thomassen, eds, *Political Representation and Legitimacy in the European Union*. Oxford: Oxford University Press, 1999; Stuart Soroka and Christopher Wlezien, *Degrees of Democracy: Politics, Public Opinion, and Policy*. New York: Cambridge University Press, 2009.

28. Phillipe Schmitter, Parties are not what they once were. In Larry Diamond and Richard Gunther, eds, *Political Parties and Democracy*. Baltimore, MD: Johns Hopkins University Press, 2001.

29. Paul Webb and Steven White, eds, *Party Politics in New Democracies*. Oxford: Oxford University Press, 2007; Zolt Enyedi, Party politics in post-communist transition. In Richard Katz and William Crotty, eds, *Handbook of Party Politics*. London: Sage, 2006.

30. Webb, Farrell, and Holliday, eds, *Political Parties in Advanced Industrial Democracies*; Dalton and Wattenberg, eds, *Parties without Partisans*.

31. Dalton and Wattenberg, eds. *Parties without Partisans*.

32. Peter Mair, *Democracy beyond Parties*. Irvine: University of California, Center for the Study of Democracy, 2005, p. 7.

33. Mair, *Democracy beyond Parties*, p. 16.

34. David Farrell and Rüdiger Schmitt-Beck, eds, *Non-Party Actors in Electoral Politics: The Role of Interest Groups and Independent Citizens in Contemporary Campaigns*. Baden-Baden: Nomos Verlagsgesellschaft, 2008.

35. Webb, Farrell and Holliday, eds, *Political Parties in Advanced Industrial Democracies*.

36. Holli Semetko, Parties in the media age. In Richard Katz and William Crotty, eds, *Handbook of Party Politics*. London: Sage, 2006.

37. Farrell and Schmitt-Beck, eds, *Non-Party Actors in Electoral Politics*.

38. Schmitter, Parties are not what they once were, p. 75.

39. Reuven Hazan and Gideon Rahat, *Democracy within Parties: Candidate Selection Methods and their Political Consequences*. Oxford: Oxford University Press, 2010.

40. Mair, *Democracy beyond Parties*, p. 16.

41. Richard Katz and Peter Mair, Changing models of party organization: The emergence of the cartel party, *Party Politics* (1995) 1: 5–28.

42. Richard Katz and Peter Mair, The cartel party thesis: A restatement, *Perspectives on Politics* (2009) 7: 753–66.

43. Richard Katz, Democracy and the legal regulation of political parties, paper presented at the USAID conference on "Change in Political Parties," Washington, DC, October 2004.

44. Ingrid van Biezen, State intervention in party politics: The public funding and regulation of political parties, *European Review* (2008) 16: 337–53.

45. Susan Stokes, What do policy switches tell us about democracy? In Adam Przeworski, Susan Stokes, and Bernard Manin, eds, *Democracy, Accountability, and Representation*. New York: Cambridge University Press, 1999.

46. Russell Dalton and Steve Weldon, Public images of political parties: A necessary evil? *West European Politics* (2005) 28: 931–51.

47. Mair, *Democracy beyond Parties*, p. 8. In this context, it is worth noting Mair's own Damascene conversion to the cause of party decline. Barely two–three years before penning this piece he was using much the same evidence to propose the argument that, rather than declining, parties were adapting to changing circumstances. See, for instance, Peter Mair, Political parties and democracy: What sort of future? *Central European Political Science Review* (2003) 4: 6–20.

48. Russell Dalton, The decline of party identifications. In Russell Dalton and Martin Wattenberg, eds, *Parties without Partisans*. Oxford: Oxford University Press, 2000.

49. Rudy Andeweg, Beyond representativeness? Trends in political representation, *European Review* (2003) 11: 151.

50. Maurice Duverger, *Political Parties*. London: Methuen & Co., 1964.

51. Piero Ignazi, The crisis of parties and the rise of new political parties, *Party Politics* (1996) 2: 549–66.

52. Otto Kirchheimer, The transformation of Western European party systems. In Joseph LaPalombara and Myron Weiner, eds, *Political Parties and Political Development*. Princeton: Princeton University Press, 1966; Katz and Mair, Changing models of party organization and party democracy.

53. Paul Whiteley, Is the party over? The decline of party activism and membership across the democratic world, *Party Politics* (2011) 17: 21–44.

54. Aldrich, *Why Parties?*, pp. 245, 282.

55. Michael Saward, Making representations: Modes and strategies of political parties, *European Review* (2008) 16: 279 (emphasis in the original).

56. Mair, *Democracy beyond Parties*, p. 6.

57. Ibid., p. 7.

58. Saward, Making representations, p. 283.

59. We want to thank the principal investigators of the CSES member research groups for their efforts to collect these data and share them with the international research community. The datasets used in this volume are available for free from the project website: www.cses.org.

60. We exclude Hong Kong and Kyrgyzstan because these were not free, fair and effective elections. In addition, there are two surveys for the 2002 German Bundestagswahl: we rely on the telephone survey, as it is more representative of the population. Our analyses are based on the 2006 release of the module II data. We should note that there are several corrections and updates of these data since this release, and these corrections are noted in the relevant analyses.

61. Kenneth Benoit and Michael Laver, *Party Policy in Modern Democracies*. New York: Routledge, 2006; Ian Budge et al., *Mapping Policy Preferences: Estimates for Parties, Electors and Governments 1945–1998*. Oxford: Oxford University Press, 2001; Katz and Wessels, eds, *The European Parliament, National Parliaments, and European Integration;* Schmitt and Thomassen, eds, *Political Representation and Legitimacy in the European Union.*

62. Organization of Economic Co-operation and Development, *Social Expenditure Database* (SOCX). Available at http://www.oecd.org/els/social/expenditure.

63. Katz and Mair, Changing models of party organization.

64. Paul Webb, Conclusion: Political parties and democratic control in advanced industrial societies. In Paul Webb, David Farrell, and Ian Holliday, eds, *Political Parties in Advanced Industrial Democracies*. Oxford: Oxford University Press, 2002, p. 444.

65. David Farrell and Rudiger Schmitt-Beck, eds, *Do Political Campaigns Matter? Campaign Effects in Elections and Referendums*. London and New York: Taylor and Francis, 2002; Alan Gerber and Donald Green, *Get Out the Vote: How to Increase Voter Turnout*. Washington, DC: Brookings Institution Press, 2004; Jeffrey Karp, Susan Banducci, and Shaun Bowler. Getting out the vote: Party mobilization in a comparative perspective, *British Journal of Political Science* (2008) 38: 91–112; Miki Caul Kittilson and Christopher Anderson, Electoral supply and voter engagement. In Russell Dalton and Christopher Anderson, eds, *Citizens, Context and Choice*. Oxford: Oxford University Press, 2011.

66. For a tiny, but prominent, sample of a very large body of work, see: Anthony Downs, *An Economic Theory of Voting*. New York: Wiley, 1957; Dieter Fuchs and Hans-Dieter Klingemann, The Left-Right schema. In M. Kent Jennings and Jan van Deth, eds, *Continuities in Political Action*. Berlin: de Gruyter, 1989; Michael

McDonald and Ian Budge, *Elections, Parties, Democracy: Conferring the Median Mandate*. Oxford: Oxford University Press, 2005.

67. See especially G. Bingham Powell, *Elections as Instruments of Democracy*.

68. Margaret Scammell, The wisdom of the war room: U.S. campaigning and Americanization, *Shorenstein Center Research Paper*. R-17 (1997).

69. J. Fred MacDonald, *One Nation under Television: The Rise and Decline of Network TV*. Available at http://jfredmacdonald.com/onutv/index.htm.

I. Parties and Election Campaigns

2

Parties and Electoral Institutions

In April 2010 Prime Minister Gordon Brown called the long awaited British general election. All the political parties had already selected their candidates and resources were in place to mount the usual short, brisk campaign that characterizes politics in the United Kingdom and across much of the rest of Europe as well. An army of formal party members was in place to staff the campaigns, free campaign ads were available on the television, and other sources of state support were in place. A little over one month later the result was known: Mr Brown was out of office and the removal vans were pulling up to No. 10 Downing Street. Contrast this with how presidential elections are fought in the USA: the creation of a personal campaign staff and campaign workers; long fund-raising drives by prospective candidates; the endless round of primaries; the months of campaigning that then follow. At the heart of the differences between the two examples is the nature of parliamentary politics that predominates across much of Europe as well as the anchoring role of strong parties, with the parties picking the candidates, financing the election, and organizing the campaign. This is the subject matter for this chapter.

In Chapter 1 (Figure 1.1) we set out a flowchart of democratic linkage, outlining the five main forms of linkage between political parties and voters that are dealt with in this book. This chapter looks at the first of these, which we refer to as "campaign linkage," the stage that structures campaigns and elections. We assess the extent to which parties control the electoral process. This process has become ever more competitive over time, manifested in a number of respects: a less supine media providing more critical and intrusive coverage of the spectacle of politics; well-resourced interest groups, big business, and lobbying organizations taking full advantage of new media technologies to influence the parties and voters; atomized voters, cut loose of party loyalties and therefore much harder to entice out to vote and, from the perspective of each of the parties, to vote "the right way." All this and more speaks to a supposed crisis of parties, a threat to the core of the party government model we outlined in Chapter 1.

This chapter examines the evidence relating to the institutional links between parties and citizens during the campaign period. This is one area where there is some common ground in much of the party politics literature. Party scholars have tracked how, over time, political parties have forged ever-closer links with the state. Richard Katz and Peter Mair go so far as to suggest that this coincides with a collapse in the links between the parties and society—something that we (and others) take issue with (a topic for later chapters).[1] But we disagree with Katz and Mair in their characterization of the party–state linkage as one forged on the ideal of nurturing the "cartel" of established political parties, of protecting the interests of certain (elite) parties over other (outsider) parties. This thesis presupposes an institutional environment that disproportionally favors some parties over others.

By contrast, our contention is that over the past few decades, reforms to the relationship between parties and the state, rather than discriminating between different party types, are protecting the genus of political parties as a species. The evidence we have amassed shows how the parties' responses to threats from greater competition in the electoral process have involved three main steps:

- Generous state support (financial and in-kind), which, at least in the case of the established democracies, has amounted to a degree of institutional design of quite impressive proportions;
- A light-touch regulatory regime to "police" party activities and particularly those of a financial nature;
- The steady evolution of controls on the electoral process designed to ensure the primacy of party.

This chapter reviews four sets of evidence—on ballot access rules, media access and campaign communication, party finance and regulation, and electoral system design—that show the parties' continuing dominance over the electoral process, demonstrating how campaign linkage is alive and well. The chapter concludes with an assessment of the "partyness" of elections in contemporary democracies.

Who Runs? Ballot Access and the Emergence of Candidates

One of the classic functions of parties is their gatekeeping role in recruiting leaders and regulating access to political office.[2] Parties provide a vehicle for recruiting potential elected officials, socializing them into politics and the party's programs, and then selecting them as candidates. The Germans, for instance, refer to the *Ochsentour* (or the slog), the long period of party work and experience required of individuals before they become party candidates for office—something that will be all too familiar to parliamentary candidates across many parliamentary democracies.

Recently, however, some scholars have viewed this recruitment pattern as under some threat as political parties face growing competition from other, non-party actors in the electoral process, among them single-issue microparties and independent candidates, who directly threaten the parties' recruitment function.[3] The Irish 2002 election is a case in point, with microparties and independents winning 11 percent of the vote and 8 percent of the parliamentary seats. Virtually all of these seats were won by independents, which is not that unusual in recent Irish politics.[4] While the Irish case may well be at the extreme in this regard, there are other cases where independents have made significant breakthroughs in recent years, for example France and the UK among the established democracies, and Brazil and Russia among the newer democracies—both prominent examples of "personalized and clientelist regimes."[5] For instance, in the case of the Russian Federation Henry Hale shows how powerful "party substitutes" at regional level or in big business have successfully circumvented party structures in promoting their own non-party candidates, thus ensuring that Russia has one of the highest proportions of independent candidates among the postcommunist states (15 percent in 2003).[6] More generally, there is some anecdotal evidence that it is becoming more common for individuals to use success or celebrity in a non-political field to catapult themselves to higher political office, whether it is businessman Ross Perot in US presidential elections in the 1990s, or Rosie the Clown who ran for office in the 2004 Canadian federal election, or the Swedish porno star, La Ciciolina, who was successfully elected to the Italian parliament in the early 1980s.

Given that life appears to be becoming more difficult for the contemporary party, it is no wonder that we should see parties making ever more use of their access to the levers of power to shore up their positions. Table 2.1 surveys the present situation by describing the extent to which parties are official gate-keepers to the ballot for the thirty-six nations in the Comparative Study of Electoral Systems (CSES) (module 2).[7] The message from the table is simple and straightforward: political parties continue to be the principal gatekeepers in determining ballot access. In most cases, the political parties have the main roles in determining the field of candidates standing for election.[8] This is actually more the case for the newer and developing democracies, where in 94 percent of nations the parties determine candidatures, than for the established democracies (61 percent).[9] In the majority of nations, the parties have to be registered in order to be allowed to field candidates—although the evidence suggests that for the most part the barriers to entry are set quite low (a minimum number of signatures; a small deposit; perhaps some minimal rules about organizational structures).[10] Finally, a number of countries have even gone so far as to introduce legal or practical blocks to prevent the emergence of independent, non-party candidates.[11]

Not only do parties in most cases have a powerful hold over who can run for office, the state also tends to give parties free rein over how those candidates are selected. Only in a handful of countries are there laws regulating the

Table 2.1. Ballot Access and the Emergence of Candidates

	Party nomination determines candidature[a]	Party registration requirements[b]	Blocks on independents[c]	Level of candidate selection[d]
Albania	✓	✓		
Australia	✓	✓		14.8
Belgium	✗	✓		(13.8)
Brazil	✓	✓	✓	9.0
Bulgaria	✓	✓		8.1
Canada	✓	✓		16.2
Chile	✗	✓		8.5
Czech Republic	✓	✓	✓	9.3
Denmark	✓	✓		15.0
Finland	✓	✓		16.0
France	✗	✗		9.9
Germany	✓	✓		13.5
Hungary	✓	✓		
Iceland		✓	✓	(17.5)
Ireland	✗	✓		13.1
Israel	✓	✓	✓	11.5
Italy	✗	✓	✓	5.2
Japan	✓	✓		
Korea, South	✓	✓		15.0
Mexico	✓	✓	✓	11.5
Netherlands	✗	✓		15.4
New Zealand	✗	✓		(8.1)
Norway	✓	✓	✓	9.0
Peru	✓	✓		
Philippines	✓	✓		—
Poland	✓	✓		
Portugal	✓	✓	✓	8.0
Romania	✓	✓		8.6
Russia	✓	✓		
Slovenia	✓	✓		6.4
Spain	✓	✓		8.5
Sweden	✓	✗	✓	(12.6)
Switzerland	✓	✓	✓	
Taiwan	✓	✓		16.5
UK	✗	✓		13.0
USA	✓	✓	✓	22.0

Sources: sources are listed in endnote 7.
a. A party nomination establishes how the field of candidates who stand for election is determined
b. Are there registration requirements for parties running for national elections?
c. Known blocks/effective blocks
d. The Hazan and Rahat selectorate scale runs from 0 (single party leader decides MP candidates) to 24 (all the citizens select the candidate). Figures in brackets indicate that some CSES parties with Left–Right scores lack selectorate scores.

process of candidate selection, such as Finland, Germany, New Zealand, and Norway (until 2002) where the parties are required to have relatively open and democratic procedures. The more normal pattern is that parties are allowed to determine candidate nomination themselves.

The final column in Table 2.1 attempts to summarize the patterns of candidate selection for the CSES nations, providing further evidence of just how centralized candidate selection processes remain in most countries (the USA is the outlier in this regard).[12] In only a few countries have parties moved fully toward US-style party primaries: counted among these are parties in Iceland, Israel, Mexico, Spain, and Taiwan. Most nations score toward the centralized party selection end of the selectorate variable. Gathering longitudinal information is even more difficult; the available evidence suggests a general move toward opening up the candidate selection process to the mass membership (i.e., making the process more "inclusive"), with the party leadership retaining and in some instances increasing their veto power over candidate choice.[13] Still, most political parties continue to control the candidate selection process, either through the national party or by delegating to local branches of the parties.

One recent survey of trends across advanced industrial democracies paraphrased Schattschneider in concluding: "recruitment of candidates for representative and related governmental functions remains virtually inconceivable without political parties."[14] The evidence in Table 2.1 supports this and shows that, if anything, the hold of parties over the recruitment function is even stronger in the new and developing democracies.

Who Speaks? Campaign Communications and Media Access

Parties also play a crucial role in mobilizing votes, at the heart of which are their efforts to communicate their policies and image to prospective voters. Given the importance of campaign communications, parties seek to design the ground rules to maximize their role as the key campaign communicators, and to do what they can to beat off non-party competitors.

At the same time, there are many rival sources of information at election time, and these have proliferated in recent decades. In most nations, the media have become active reporters and participants in election coverage. The shift from a complete lack of broadcasting coverage of campaigns in Britain prior to 1959 to the first ever party leaders' TV debates in 2010 illustrates this development. In many nations, the media have also assumed a more active role in evaluating candidates and parties in the election, and not just in reporting the news. Similarly, the very circumscribed tradition of political reporting in Japan has given way to a more dramatic and critical coverage of the parties and their candidates.[15] In addition, interest groups and non-governmental organizations often provide formal and informal political cues at election time. This has led some experts to claim that parties have lost their information dominance in election campaigns.[16]

Nevertheless, political parties play the dominant role in campaign discussions and media coverage of the campaign, which is the primary way that citizens gain information during an election. The Comparative National Election Project coded the main actors in newspaper or television coverage of national elections in the United States, Britain, Germany, Spain, and Japan. While citizens, interest groups, and political parties all play a role in campaigns, political parties—either elected party officials or representatives of the parties—were overwhelmingly the prime actors in media coverage of the campaign. For instance, analyses of media coverage of the 1990 German election found that political parties and their spokespersons accounted for 95 percent of prime actors cited by the media.[17] Similarly, analyses of the 1992 British parliamentary election, the 1992 US presidential election, and the 1993 Spanish elections showed that political party actors dominated media coverage across all three nations.[18] Even when an event or extraneous actor alters the campaign discourse—as with the "War of Jennifer's Ear" controversy in the 1992 British election or claims about Clinton's youthful indiscretions in the 1992 US presidential election—the parties and their representatives are the prime actors in responding to such events and shaping the public discourse.

Additional cross-national evidence comes from the media component of the 2009 European Election Study.[19] We coded the first three actors mentioned in stories about the 2009 European Parliament election. In every nation, the most common pattern was for national candidates, parties or government officials to be the most frequently mentioned actors, averaging nearly two-thirds of the actor mentions across all these nations. EU political officials and party actors in the European Parliament were cited in more than a tenth of the references. Non-partisan national actors accounted for only about a fifth of all actor references, with only a sprinkling of non-political actors at the EU level. This dominance of newspaper headlines and the airwaves by political parties and elected officials leaves limited space for interest groups or other organizations to shape the public discourse of the campaign.

There is also a strong tendency (in well over half of the CSES nations) for media coverage to be strongly oriented by a partisan bias—often referred to as "media-press parallelism."[20] The first column in Table 2.2 reports the patterns.[21] Furthermore, the parties have shored up their dominant position through a variety of means, such as setting down rules relating to media coverage of elections, passing legislation to allow parties free airtime, and participating in high-profile TV debates. Therefore, our second step is to describe the current situation with regard to political parties' media access and the ability to disseminate information.

Table 2.2 shows the current patterns with regard to free airtime provided to parties on the public broadcasting networks of virtually all the countries in our sample; the only exceptions are: Bulgaria, Finland, Iceland, Switzerland, Taiwan, and the USA. From the outset, the public-service broadcasting ethos that predominated almost everywhere other than in the USA ensured that the influence of the broadcasting media was "an occupational privilege of politicians." As television established itself as the principal communication medium in elections the parties gave themselves rights of free access.[22] This is one of the most prominent and most common forms of support in kind provided to political parties. The number of free slots and their length (20–25-

Table 2.2. Campaign Communications and Media Access

	Highly partisan press	Free media access	Media access rules	Paid political ads on TV	TV leaders' debates	Opinion poll ban
Albania	✓	✓	✓	✓		
Australia	✗	✓	✓a	✓	✓	✗
Belgium	✓	✓	✓	✗	✓	✗
Brazil	✓	✓	✓a	✗	✓	✓
Bulgaria	✓	✗	✓a	✓	✓	✗
Canada	✗	✓	✓a	✓	✓	
Chile	✓	✓	✓a	✓	✓	✗
Czech Republic	✗	✓	✓	✓	✓	✓
Denmark	✓	✓	✓	✗	✓	✗
Finland	✗	✗	✗	✓	✓	✗
France	✓	✓	✓a	✗	✓	✓
Germany	✗	✓	✓a	✓	✓	✗
Hungary	✓	✓	✓	✓	✓	✓
Iceland		✗				✗
Ireland	✗	✓	✓a	✗	✓	✗
Israel	✓	✓	✓a	✓	✓	✓
Italy	✓	✓	✓a	✓	✗	✓
Japan	✓	✗	✓	✓	✓	✗
Korea, South	✓	✓	✓a	✓	✓	✓
Mexico	✗	✓	✓a	✓	✓	✓
Netherlands	✓	✓	✓	✓	✓	✗
New Zealand	✓	✓	✓a	✓	✓	✗
Norway	✓	✓	✓	✗	✓	✗
Peru	✗	✓	✓	✓	✓	✗
Philippines	✓	✓	✓a	✓		
Poland	✓	✓	✓	✓	✓	✓
Portugal	✗	✓	✓	✗	✓	✓
Romania	✗	✓	✓a	✓	✓	✓
Russia	✗	✓	✓	✓	✗	✓
Slovenia	✓	✓		✓	✓	✓
Spain	✓	✓	✓a	✓	✓	✓
Sweden	✓	✓	✓	✓	✓	✗
Switzerland	✓	✗	✓	✗	✗	✗
Taiwan	✗	✗	✗	✓	✓	✓
UK	✓	✓	✓a	✗	✗b	✗
USA	✗	✗	✗	✓	✓	✗

Sources: sources are listed in chapter endnote 21.
a. Proportionate access rules.
b. At the time of the CSES survey. In the subsequent 2010 election there was a TV leaders' debate.

second ads in Finland; 60-second ads in Italy; up to 10-minute-long slots in Japan and the UK) can vary, with some significant impacts on the parties' balance sheets, at least during election times. Nassmacher makes the observation that, in some instances, free advertising is almost as significant as state funding, saving on a "considerable amount of money that parties do not have to spend for electioneering." Estimates suggest that this can amount to as much as a quarter of total national campaign expenditure by Austrian parties or half the British total.[23]

The public-sector broadcasting ethos also helps to explain why in so many of the established democracies there are media access rules regarding the nature of broadcasting coverage of parties and candidates. This practice exists in virtually all of the new and establishing democracies. These regulations come in one of two forms: equal access for all eligible parties (such as in Scandinavian countries, the Czech Republic, Hungary, and Poland) and, more commonly, proportionate access (applies in most of the newer democracies, and in established democracies like France, Germany, Italy, New Zealand, and the UK). Proportionate access allows greater access to the broadcast media for the larger, more established parties, although the smaller parties are far from being excluded.

The counter to free media access is, of course, paid political advertising on television, or TV spots. This can be seen as another feature of the resourcing of parties in the sense that the parties that receive substantial state funding can spend their money on communication with the public. Table 2.2 reports on how many countries permit parties (or candidates) to purchase TV spots, three-quarters of our sample of countries. This is a significant increase on barely two decades ago, when Anthony Smith reported on a survey of twenty-one countries, finding only four cases in which private TV spots were permitted: Australia, Canada, Japan, and the USA.[24] The two things that most of all have driven this have been the rising prominence of commercial broadcasting (which, in many cases is where the spots are only permitted) and the more liberal attitude toward TV spots among newer democracies (88 percent permit them).[25]

The 2010 British party leaders' debates on television were the first of their kind in British electoral history. The jury is still out on just how significant a contribution these debates made to the election outcome, but most analysts agree that they improved the electoral profile of the smaller Liberal Democrat party. TV debates were rare until quite recently—Anthony Smith's survey found just ten cases[26]—whereas now they are a common feature of electoral politics in nine out of ten of the nations we study. On the one hand, they demonstrate the growing competitiveness of the electoral process, indicative of the more detailed scrutiny of the parties, their policies, and leading personalities. On the other hand, they also demonstrate the continuing hold of parties and their leaders over the electoral process.

The final column in Table 2.2 reports on one other development in recent elections, namely the restrictions placed on the reporting of opinion polls. There are variations in how long prior to polling day the ban is instituted (anything from twenty-four hours up to a week before), but the evidence is clear that this form of campaign regulation is a more prominent feature among the newer democracies (80 percent) than the older ones (just 21 percent).

The regulation of opinion polls in newer democracies notwithstanding, the patterns summarized in Table 2.2 are consistent with other studies. Over time, campaign communications have become less regulated and more liberalized, with fewer restrictions on what the parties and candidates can do.[27] In short, the media environment has become friendlier to the parties (and by this we mean all parties) over time.

Who Pays? Financial Regulations and Campaign Finance

Campaign finance is probably the key aspect of the institutional linkage of parties to citizens. In his classic study *The Costs of Democracy*, Alexander Heard claims that "the processes of political finance constitute one set of mechanisms through which political representation is achieved."[28] Heard was writing in the late 1950s, a time when political parties and candidates relied on their own devices to raise funds; a time when all politics truly was local, when elections and party politics appear to have been more genteel activities[29] and certainly less expensive.

Half a century later and all has changed: party politics and election campaigns are more national affairs that are far more expensive to run,[30] and the state now actively intervenes in providing substantial support, financial and in-kind. (see Table 2.3).[31] State support for political parties is a postwar phenomenon, implemented in part as a means of reducing corruption, in part to counteract declining membership dues, and in part to level the political playing field. Today, even if the appropriateness of state funding might be open to question,[32] its ubiquity is undisputed.

But it is worth noting just how recent all of this is. Just over fifty years ago, (West) Germany was the first country in this group of CSES nations to introduce state funding of political parties. This was in 1959 and at that point only four other countries—Uruguay (1928), Costa Rica (1954), Argentina (1955), and Puerto Rico (1957)—had gone down this route. Other countries followed suit, though the initial take-up was gradual. In the 1960s, Finland, Israel, and Sweden were among the pioneers; the spread went further afield in the 1970s

(Brazil, Canada, Italy, Norway, Spain, the USA) and 1980s (Australia, Belgium, Denmark, France, Korea, Mexico, Taiwan).[33] The 1990s was the decade of democratic renewal in East and Central Europe and the former Soviet Union, and state funding spread to a host of new democracies.[34] Two of the countries to bring up the rear at the end of the 1990s were Ireland, which substantially increased its funding of parties in 1997–98,[35] and the UK, which somewhat surreptitiously opened up some funding lines to parties at the turn of the millennium.[36]

Inevitably the information is quite patchy, but it appears that the funding regime has become ever more generous and encompassing over time. In an early review of the trends, Nassmacher refers to three stages of implementation among the pioneering cases: a stage of "experimentation," in which state funding was introduced quite tentatively and on a small scale; a stage of "enlargement" (late 1960s–early 1980s), during which "all countries in a stepwise procedure enlarged the parties' claim to public money by introducing new objects of subsidization"; and finally a stage of "adjustment" in the 1980s when the funding regimes were consolidated and embedded with built-in inflation-beating controls.[37] As party funding diffused into other countries, it is pretty apparent that in many cases these skipped straight to Nassmacher's third phase, to the extent that it is quite appropriate to talk of the "increasing financial dependence of parties on the state,"[38] even if this dependency can vary significantly across countries and indeed across parties within one country.[39]

In addition to the free media support described above, Table 2.3 reports on various direct and indirect financial supports that the parties receive from government across nations. In each and every country in our set, the state provides some form of support, whether this is in the form of funding party organizations and/or their campaigns or allowing parties free broadcasting time. The available evidence suggests that some of the most generous party financing from public funds is in the Czech Republic, France, Germany, Hungary, Ireland, Israel, Mexico, Norway, Portugal, Slovenia, Spain, and Sweden. In some other cases—such as Bulgaria, Denmark, Russia, and the UK—the funding is far less significant for party budgets. Drawing together the disparate sources, Nassmacher estimates that for every citizen in Israel, political parties receive €10.50 ($13.74): the equivalent figure for Norwegian parties is €4.40 ($5.75), and for French parties €4.20 ($5.50). He concludes that, in continental Europe at least, "on average 40 percent of the annual budget of national party organizations may be a fair estimate for the revenue shares that originate from public subsidies."[40]

One reason often given for state support of political parties is that it helps to root out corruption, reducing the need parties might feel to look for resources from less than savory routes. But that really only works if it is combined with

Table 2.3. Party Finance and Regulatory Controls

	State funding of parties[a]	Systems for regulating party finance	Expenditure limits	Ceiling on donations	Independent enforcement body for party finance	Independent Election Management Bodies[c]
Albania	✓	✓	✗	✗	✗	✓
Australia	✓	✓	✗	✗	✓	✓
Belgium	✓	✓	✓	✓	✓	✗
Brazil	✓	✓	✗	✓	✓	✓
Bulgaria	✓	✓	✓	✓	✓	✓
Canada	✓	✓	✓	✓	✓	✗
Chile	✓	✓	✓	✗	✓	✓
Czech Republic	✓	✓	✗	✗	✗	✗
Denmark	✓	✗	✗	✗	✗	✗
Finland	✓	✓	✗	✗	✗	✗
France	✓	✓	✓	✓	✗	✗
Germany	✓	✓	✗	✗	✗	✗
Hungary	✓	✓	✗	✗	✗	✗
Iceland	✓	✗	✗	✗	✗	✗
Ireland	✓	✓	✓	✓	✓	✗
Israel	✓	✓	✓	✓	✗	✓
Italy	✓	✓	✓	✓	✓	✗
Japan	✓	✓	✗	✓	✗	✗
Korea, South	✓	✓	✓	✓		✓
Mexico	✓	✓	✓	✓	✓	✓
Netherlands	✓	✓	✗	✗	✗	✗
New Zealand	✗	✓	✓	✗	✓	✗
Norway	✓	✗	✗	✗	✗	✗
Peru	✓	✓	✗	✓	✓	✓
Philippines	✗	✓	✓			✓
Poland	✓	✓	✓	✓	✓	✓
Portugal	✓	✓	✓	✓	✓	✗
Romania	✓	✓	✗	✓	✓	✓
Russia	✓	✓	✓	✓	✓	✓
Slovenia	✓	✓	✓	✓		✓
Spain	✓	✓	✓	✓	✓	✗
Sweden	✓	✗	✗	✗	✗	✗
Switzerland	✗	✗	✗	✗	✗	✗
Taiwan	✓	✓	✗	✓		✓
UK	✓	✓	✓	✗	✓	✗
USA	✗[b]	✓	✗[b]	✓	✓	✗

Source: sources are listed in chapter endnote 31.

a. Funding of party organizations or campaigns.

b. Matching funds are not available for Congressional elections, only for presidential elections; if parties opt for this they must abide by expenditure limits.

c. ✓ = Independent; ✗ = Governmental or Mixed

the quid pro quo of regulatory controls. Here the picture, as presented in Table 2.3, is more mixed. At first blush the trends look pretty impressive: in almost 90 percent of the countries in our sample there is a system for regulating party finance, and that figure rises to 100 percent for all the new and developing democracies. But the mere existence of regulatory systems does not of itself mean that there is a rigorous regulatory regime. Two areas where we would expect regulatory controls on party finance to focus are setting expenditure limits on how much parties and candidates can spend on their election campaigns, and ceilings on private donations. Two in five of the established CSES democracies operate both—in large part the same countries in each instance. By comparison, the practice is more widespread in the newer democracies, particularly with regard to donation ceilings which apply in three-quarters of the cases. The nations that stand out in terms of the lack of any regulatory controls are: Denmark, Iceland, Norway, Sweden, and Switzerland—all cases of established European democracies. In his comprehensive survey of regulations relating to donations, Casas-Zamora makes the point that one reason why many West European countries have "shied away from comprehensive controls" is because they have opted "to curb the financial influence of donors through other means, such as extensive public subsidy systems, short election campaigns and severe restrictions on electoral publicity."[41]

There is some evidence of a move to establish independent regulatory agencies with enforcement roles. These are either focused specifically on the issue of campaign finance regulation, or they may be in the more general form of an independent election management body (such as an electoral commission) whose remit, on occasion, includes campaign finance. In large part a phenomenon of the newer democracies (over three-quarters of which operate one or other form of agency, and most of which operate both), there are a growing number of established democracies moving toward the creation of independent enforcement agencies, though the numbers remain quite small to date.[42] Even in the nations where rules apply, however—including nations with an independent regulatory agency in operation—there is little evidence that the agency has a great deal of force. The metaphors and adjectives used to describe what is going on, speak for themselves—descriptions such as "fiction," "honesty" (lack thereof), "tip of the iceberg," "a joke" are commonplace. In his broad sweep of cross-national trends, Pinto-Duschinsky concludes that these rules are commonly "honored in the breach,"[43] either by being ignored (and not actively enforced) or through evasion.

Ireland provides an interesting example of evading regulation. The maximum value of donations parties can receive from any one person in a calendar year is €6,348.69 ($8,304.45), and any donations that exceed an aggregate value of €5,078.95 ($6,643.56) must be declared. In 2009, Irish political parties faced a general election, a European Parliament election, and a series of high-profile by-elections—all the hallmarks of an expensive year. Despite this, the official figures of recorded donations disclosed by Irish parties were the lowest since the introduction of financial controls in the late 1980s. All three main political parties exploited loopholes in the legislation to ensure that none of them needed to disclose any donations in 2009.[44]

It is not always the case that parties deliberately set out to evade; sometimes the issue is simply one of poor bookkeeping. As Pierre and his colleagues note, part of the problem is that the subsidies can get mixed up with other party funds and it becomes difficult to disentangle later. They report on how one Danish party official commented: "it is like mixing hot and cold water and then try[ing] to separate them again."[45]

These patterns tells us that today's political parties in most CSES nations face a fair wind of financial support from the state and few if any inconvenient restrictions (apart from the obvious) on what they can spend, or indeed on what other funds they might raise. The picture is of a light-touch regulatory regime, buttressed by a supportive system of state funding.

Who Wins? Proportionality and Electoral System Design

Eventually we reach the end of the campaign—polling day—when the question that matters is who wins the seats. Here perhaps is the greatest scope for the established parties to seek to influence things in their favor, which could include a number of devices. There are two dimensions worth focusing on, one relating to efforts to keep out, or at least make life difficult for, new and minor parties, and the other relating to maintaining order and discipline within party ranks, dampening down candidate orientations that could jeopardize the primacy of parties. The first of these is an inter-party dimension, the second is intra-party.

In the first instance, the established parties can protect their interests by operating barriers to entry. The most obvious way of achieving this is by using non-proportional (the Australian alternative vote, the French two-round system, or the single member plurality systems of Canada, the UK, and the USA) or semi-proportional systems (such as in Ireland and Spain) which use small electoral districts to keep down proportionality, or the mixed-member majoritarian systems (in Albania, Hungary, South Korea, Mexico, and Taiwan).[46] As is well known, as proportionality increases, so does the number of parties in the parliament. We can see this in Table 2.4: higher levels of disproportionality are associated with smaller effective number of parliamentary parties (r=-.53).[47]

However, as Josep Colomer, among others, has shown convincingly, there is a trend toward greater proportionality over time, whether this is through a switch to more proportional electoral systems or by making existing electoral systems more proportional; an example of the latter is Germany's shift to a more proportional electoral formula in 2008.[48] Other examples of the adoption of more proportional electoral systems are Russia's and Italy's replacement of semi-proportional mixed-member majoritarian systems with list

Table 2.4. Proportionality and Electoral Systems

	Electoral system[a]	Dispro-portion-ality[b]	Effective number of parliamentary parties[b]	Legal threshold	Candidate vs. party vote[e]	Candidate-oriented electoral system[d]
Albania	MMM	15.31	2.98	2.5% for list tier	0.5	3.6
Australia	AV	9.41	2.39	n.a.	0.0	8.6
Belgium	List	4.27	7.47	5% within a district	1.0	2.9
Brazil	List	3.04	8.90	No	1.0	2.9
Bulgaria	List	7.00	3.34	4% national vote	1.0	1.4
Canada	SMP	10.52	2.99	n.a.	0.0	4.3
Chile	List	6.25	5.72	No	1.0	2.9
Czech Republic	List	5.73	3.39	5%; 10% coalition of 2, etc.	1.0	2.9
Denmark	List	1.35	4.90	For tier 2, need 1 lower tier seat, Hare quota, or 2%	1.0	7.1
Finland	List	3.18	5.03	No	1.0	7.1
France	Runoff	17.77	2.38	n.a.	0.0	5.7
Germany	MMP	3.39	3.40	5% national vote or 3 district seats	0.5	3.6
Hungary	MMM	6.67	2.31	5% of PR tier votes	0.5	4.7
Iceland	List	2.64	3.84	5% national vote for upper tier seats	1.0	1.4
Ireland	STV	6.24	3.21	No	0.0	10.0
Israel	List	2.21	6.93	2% national vote	1.0	1.4
Italy	List	5.73[c]	3.07[c]	2% if in coalition; 4% if not	1.0	1.4
Japan	MMM	12.69	2.53	No	0.5	3.6
Korea, South	MMM	10.51	2.38	3% national vote or 5 district seats for PR tier	0.5	3.6
Mexico	MMM	7.06	2.77	2% national vote for PR tier	0.5	3.6
Netherlands	List	0.99	5.36	0.67% national vote	1.0	2.9
New Zealand	MMP	2.45	3.17	5% national vote or 1 district seat	0.5	3.6
Norway	List	2.97	4.66	4% national vote for upper tier seats	1.0	1.4
Peru	List	8.10	3.98	4% or 5 elected candidates in 2 districts	1.0	2.9
Philippines	MMM			2% national vote	0.5	3.6
Poland	List	5.99	3.56	5% for parties; 8% for coalitions	1.0	2.9
Portugal	List	5.34	2.73	No	1.0	1.4
Romania	List	5.21	3.51	5% for party; 8% for coalition, etc.	1.0	1.4

Russia	List	4.33[c]	1.92[c]	7%; parties winning 5–6% get 1 seat; 6–7% get 2	1.0	1.4
Slovenia	List	3.40	4.67	4% national vote	1.0	2.9
Spain	List	4.95	2.46	3% within a district	1.0	1.4
Sweden	List	2.27	4.19	4% national vote or 12% in one district	1.0	2.9
Switzerland	List	2.52	4.99	No	1.0	7.1
Taiwan	MMM	16.89	1.75	5% for PR tier	0.5	3.6
UK	SMP	17.25	2.32	n.a.	0.0	4.3
USA	SMP	2.43	1.99	n.a.	0.5	5.7

Sources: sources are listed in chapter endnote 47.

a. Electoral system at the time of the survey.

b. Averages for the 2000s, or most recent election in the 2000s for which data available.

c. Not including elections before recent electoral reforms.

d. Modifed Shugart index. For details see Appendix Table A2.1.

e. 1 = vote for party (including all list systems because voting is, by the nature of such systems, party conditioned); 0 = vote for candidate; 0.5 = vote for both (mixed-member systems).

proportional representation (PR) systems (albeit in the latter case with an inbuilt advantage for the winning coalition).[49] As we discuss shortly, PR systems can benefit parties in other ways.

An alternative strategy of exclusion is to set up roadblocks to keep out minor parties, especially the sorts of microparties that promote single-issue politics. Many potential new parties seem more interested in pushing particular (and particularistic) policy agendas than in seeking office. The recent spread of pirate parties in Europe is a good example, as is New Zealand's Bill and Ben party. To the established parties, these ways of operating give party politics "a bad name." A common method to reduce the numbers of micro-parties is to set legal thresholds, generally in the form of minimum vote percentages that a party must achieve before they are awarded any seats. Table 2.4 shows that the bulk of the countries using PR electoral systems apply a legal threshold. While many of these are set pretty low (just 2–3 percent of the vote), the bulk are set at 4–5 percent, which can keep out the most minor parties quite effectively.[50] The interesting cases are those PR countries which, despite having low levels of disproportionality, do not use a legal threshold: Finland, the Netherlands, Switzerland, and, among the newer democracies, Brazil. These four cases represent the most liberal electoral regimes for outsider parties.

Another way of maintaining order, this time within the ranks of the political parties themselves, is to operate electoral systems under which the electoral fate of candidates is determined by the parties and their selectorates—the intra-party dimension.[51] The distinction to draw here is between "open" electoral systems (such as open list PR, or single transferable vote) in which the electoral fate of candidates is very much dependent on their own personal vote-chasing activities, and "closed" electoral systems (such as closed list PR) in which the electoral fate of candidates is dependent on where they have been ranked on their party lists. There is a range of electoral systems that lie between these two extremes. Clearly, more open electoral systems are characterized by a higher degree of candidate orientation and, by definition, a lower element of party control over those candidates.

The final columns in Table 2.4 provide measures of the degree to which voting is party- or candidate-oriented. First, we code electoral systems into those in which the vote is for candidates, or for party, or for a mix of both—showing a clear bias toward party-based voting in our CSES democracies.[52] Second, we provide a summary index of candidate orientation, which is a modification of a scale derived by Matthew Shugart, in which higher scores reflect electoral systems that place greater emphasis on personal vote-chasing by individual parliamentary candidates.[53] The countries that stand out most in this regard—all of them established democracies—are: Australia, Denmark, Finland, Ireland, and Switzerland. These are very much the exception to the rule. The trends reported in Table 2.4 speak to an agenda of strong party control overall, the subject of our final section.

Party Framing of the Electoral Process

The evidence reviewed in this chapter supports the general contention that parties' control of the campaign and electoral processes remains very strong. Parties are dominant in the recruitment and socialization of political elites. Even though there have been inroads by other political actors, parties still predominately shape the discourse of election campaigns. Political parties receive substantial amounts of state support, both financial and in-kind. Whatever regulations and regulatory authorities exist operate on the basis of a light-touch regime, allowing parties great sway to work around inconvenient restrictions. This amounts to the steady evolution of an electoral process designed by parties for parties, with the singular aim of ensuring the primacy of parties in the electoral process.

While parties are clearly the central actors in the electoral process, the previous sections have demonstrated significant cross-national variation in this role as reflected by the different legal and procedural aspects of elections. Some of these comparisons focus on the centrality of parties to the electoral choice, such as whether the structure of the electoral system privileges parties or candidates. Other measures seek to institutionalize parties along the lines of the cartel party model, such as providing financial subsidies or free media access to parties. Then there are the various legal provisions, such as guarantees for political parties in the constitution or guaranteeing them ballot access for their candidates. Susan Scarrow argues that such provisions provide a legal guarantee for party activity, especially in developing democracies where new constitutions often contain such guarantees.[54]

To an extent, the literature presumes that all these characteristics contribute to the centrality of parties in the electoral process. However, some traits might not reflect a common factor of party-centered systems. For instance, legal recognition of parties may reflect historical conditions and legal traditions when the nation was founded, with less impact on current electoral politics. Similarly, we might assume that cartelist arrangements develop when elections are structured around fixed party choices rather than individual candidates. However, there are notable cases where parties receive direct government support while elections involve candidate choices (e.g., Australia and Canada). And there are cases where the government does not subsidize parties while the ballot structure offers a choice between parties (e.g., Switzerland, albeit with an open party list).

Therefore, the last stage of this chapter's analysis examines the interrelationship of different system characteristics that might identify the centrality of parties to the electoral process. Our first step was to select traits from the previous sections that might define the importance of parties in a nation:

- Party nomination ensures position on ballot. (Table 2.1)
- The degree of central party control in selecting parliamentary candidates. (Table 2.1)
- Does the government provide free media access to parties? (Table 2.2)
- Does the government provide financial support to parties? (Table 2.3)
- Is there government regulation of party finances? (Table 2.3)
- Electoral system rules that emphasize party choice over candidate choice. (Table 2.4)
- Does the ballot choice select between parties or candidates? (Table 2.4)
- Is there legal/constitutional recognition of parties as distinct from other groups?[55]
- Is there a presidential or parliamentary system?[56]

The previous sections presented additional indicators, but the modest number of nations in the CSES study requires a modest number of variables to compare. We selected these nine items to represent the diversity of the factors that have been linked to strong party-centered systems.

These nine indicators were then factor analyzed to determine if there are commonalities among these various traits, or distinct subgroups of traits. Table 2.5 identifies the first two factors extracted from this analysis.[57] The

Table 2.5. Party System Characteristics in the CSES Nations

Variables	Party-centered election	Party regulation
Party selectorate	.80	.16
Candidate/party-orientated system	.77	.20
Vote for party on ballot	.68	−.55
Free media ads for parties	.44	.58
Legal recognition	.50	.07
Public subsidy for parties	.19	.06
Regulation of party finance	.17	.76
Party nominations	.13	−.57
Parliamentary vs. presidential	−.17	−.30
Eigenvalue	2.25	1.71
Variance explained	25.0%	19.1%

Source: The source of each variable is described in the accompanying text.
Note: The table presents an unrotated principal components analysis, with pair-wise deletion of missing data. See text for details on the variables.

first factor reflects what we call "party-centered" electoral systems that combine several traits. Countries in which national parties play a larger role in candidate selection also tend to have ballots based on party choices rather than candidate choices, as represented by the strong positive coefficients of these variables on the first factor. In addition, government subsidies for free media access tend to be more common in these same nations. Public subsidies are weakly related, but this is likely because there is very little variation across nations (91 percent offer some subsidies). In other words, these traits tend to cluster together to define nations in which parties play a strong role in structuring central aspects of the electoral process—from selecting candidates, to coordinating campaigns, to presenting a choice of parties on the ballot paper.

The second factor is more diffuse, but it seems to represent aspects of a regulatory state for political parties. The regulation of party finances is linked to this dimension (.76), as well as access to free media (.58), as we suggest above; perhaps the quid pro quo of government support is government regulation.[58] And regulation is more common in nations that also provide free media access for parties.

Combining five of the variables identified as the first dimension in the factor analysis, Table 2.6 displays a summary index of party-centered electoral processes across nations.[59] We would expect the party linkage process in election campaigns to work more effectively in those cases in which parties play a larger role in structuring campaigns and the electoral process. Not for the first time, the USA is the outlier—scoring near zero on this index. At the other extreme, the most party-centered cases include the Czech Republic, Israel, and Spain.

Table 2.6. An Index of Party-Centered Electoral Process

Nation	Party-Centered Index
Albania	4.0
Australia	2.0
Belgium	4.0
Brazil	5.0
Bulgaria	4.0
Canada	2.5
Chile	4.0
Czech Republic	5.0
Denmark	3.0
Finland	3.0
France	3.0
Germany	4.0
Hungary	3.5
Iceland	3.0
Ireland	2.0
Israel	5.0
Italy	5.0
Japan	3.0
Korea, South	4.0
Mexico	4.0
Netherlands	4.0
New Zealand	3.0
Norway	4.0
Peru	5.0
Philippines	3.0
Poland	5.0
Portugal	5.0
Romania	5.0
Russia	4.0
Slovenia	4.0
Spain	5.0
Sweden	4.0
Switzerland	2.0
Taiwan	2.0
UK	2.5
USA	0.5

Source: See Table 2.5.
Note: The table displays the party-centered index, adding candidate/party-centered electoral system, party vote on ballot, party subsidies, free media ads for parties, and legal recognition. The index ranges from 0 = no party-centered traits to 5 = all five.

The overarching pattern is the continuing centrality of parties in the electoral process of most contemporary democracies—nearly 60 percent score 4 or 5 items on the index. Still, there is some cross-national variation in this party-centered index. We find that newer democracies score higher overall (averaging 4.22) compared with the established democracies (3.16), symbolic perhaps of greater effort by newer democracies to protect their fledgling parties. But most other national characteristics that are not already represented in the index appear weakly related to this measure of party centrality. For instance, the difference between parliamentary and presidential systems is insignificant, as noted by the relationship in the factor analysis. Indeed, the generally high centrality of parties to electoral politics should be expected across institutional forms if parties are still essential to the working of the democratic process.

Conclusion: Parties and Election Campaigns

As the German Bundestag election approached, Gertrude followed the election closely. She watched the ads and news discussions on television; there were even campaign spots during the previews at the movies. She studiously watched the party leaders debate on television. Then she decided. On Sunday she went to the polls to vote for a member of parliament, but she didn't know who was actually running for parliament in her district. Whoever was on the ballot paper representing Gertrude's preferred party would get her vote. Most Germans do not know the names of the major party candidates running in their district. Gertrude's experience is typical for many voters in PR systems, because the campaign and the voting decision focus on the parties and their programs.

With the sole exception of the USA, all of our CSES countries manifest clear signs of party-centered electoral processes: but this is an electoral process centered on all parties, not the privileged few. We see this in a number of respects. Ballot access rules are designed to ensure the primacy of party against the potential threat from non-party actors and independent candidates (Table 2.1). In most countries parties are given free media access and/or the right to run their own political advertisements on television, and the television networks host high-profile party leaders' debates (Table 2.2). The state provides generous support—financial and in-kind—to parties (Table 2.3).

The evidence we have amassed provides little support for the contention of scholars like Katz and Mair that these developments are to the benefit of a cartel of parties; the evidence, rather, points to a strengthening of links between parties and the state which is to the benefit of *all* parties *tout court*.[60] In saying this, we recognize of course that there are some disproportionalities of scale; that the larger more established parties are benefiting to a greater degree than smaller parties from the state largesse.[61] And clearly, too, there are undoubtedly some cases of barriers to entry that keep out the microparties, notably the application of electoral thresholds which can be 5 percent or more (Table 2.4).

But our contention is that such inequalities do not take from the main point, which is that the steps that have been taken in recent decades to shore up the position of parties are supporting the genus of parties rather than a privileged few. A small party that breaks through the electoral barrier and wins seats in parliament in most cases is able to access free media coverage during the election, receives state funding, and, providing it has sufficient funds, can run TV spots.

The fact that parties are making ever more use of state resources to buttress their positions is not the same as saying that they have "become absorbed by the state and begun to act as semi-state agencies."[62] To suggest that the greater dependence on parties by the state is in some way an insidious development, a threatening of the position of parties, is rather missing the point. Indeed, the point that lies at the heart of the party government framework is that the parties are effectively synonymous with the state, and always have been (at least since the origins of representative democratic systems).[63] The fact that the level of support may be greater merely reflects decisions by the parties (qua state) to provide it.

Appendix

Table A2.1 describes the procedures used in constructing the Candidate-Orientations Index. The scores column lists scores for ballot, vote, and district respectively. The rankings are based on the nature of the electoral system, and range from most candidate-centered (score of 10) to most party-centered electoral systems (score of 1.4). There are also adjustments variations in mixed member systems. **MM fix A**: For MM systems with runoff rules in the SSDs. Mean of 5.7 (SSD-plurality score) and 1.4 (closed list score) = 3.6. Mean of 3.6 and 5.7 (SSD-plurality score) = 4.7. **MM fix B**: For MM systems with plurality rules in the SSDs. Mean of 4.3 (SSD two rounds score) and 1.4 (closed list score) = 2.9. Mean of 2.9 and 4.3 (SSD two rounds score) = 3.6.

Table A2.1 Deriving the Candidate-Orientation Index

Index	Scores	Description of system	Cases
10	4, 5, 3	STV	Ireland
8.6	4, 5, 2	AV	Australia
7.1	2, 4, 3	Open list, panachage	Denmark, Finland, Switzerland
5.7	3, 3, 2	SSD, two rounds	France, USA
4.7	[MM fix A]	MM with runoff	Hungary
4.3	1, 3, 2	SSD, plurality	Canada, UK
3.6	[MM fix B]	MM with plurality	Albania, Germany, Japan, Korea, Mexico, New Zealand, Philippines, Taiwan
2.9	2, 2, 1	Ordered list	Belgium, Brazil, Chile, Czech Republic, Netherlands, Peru, Poland, Slovenia, Sweden
1.4	1, 1, 1	Closed list	Bulgaria, Iceland, Israel, Italy, Norway, Portugal, Romania, Russia, Spain

Notes

1. Richard Katz and Peter Mair, Changing models of party organization: The emergence of the cartel party, *Party Politics* (1995) 1: 5–28; Richard Katz and Peter Mair, Cadre, catch-all, or cartel? A rejoinder, *Party Politics* (1996) 2: 525–34; Ruud Koole, Cadre, catch-all, or cartel? A comment on the notion of the cartel party, *Party Politics* (1996) 2: 507–34.

2. Michael Gallagher and Michael Marsh, *Candidate Selection in Comparative Perspective: The Secret Garden of Politics*. London: Sage, 1988; Heinrich Best and Maurizio Cotta, eds, *Parliamentary Representatives in Europe, 1848–2000: Legislative Recruitment and Careers in Eleven European Countries*. Oxford: Oxford University Press, 2000; Reuven Hazan and Gideon Rahat, *Democracy within Parties: Candidate Selection Methods and their Political Consequences*. Oxford: Oxford University Press, 2010.

3. David Farrell and Rüdiger Schmitt-Beck, eds, *Non-Party Actors in Electoral Politics: The Role of Interest Groups and Independent Citizens in Contemporary Election Campaigns*. Baden Baden: Nomos, 2008.

4. The Irish parliament "usually contains more independents than all other West European parliaments put together." From Michael Gallagher, Stability and turmoil: Analysis of the results. In Michael Gallagher, Michael Marsh, and Paul Mitchell, eds, *How Ireland Voted 2002*. Houndmills, Basingstoke: Palgrave Macmillan, 2003, p. 103; Nicole Bolleyer and Liam Weeks, The puzzle of non-party actors in party democracy: Independents in Ireland, *Comparative European Politics* (2009) 7: 299–324.

5. Paul Webb and Stephen White, Political parties in new democracies: Trajectories of development and implications for democracy. In Paul Webb and Stephen White, eds, *Party Politics in New Democracies*. Oxford: Oxford University Press, 2007, p. 364.

6. Henry Hale, *Why Not Parties in Russia? Democracy, Federalism and the State*. Cambridge: Cambridge University Press, 2006, p. 238.

7. The sources for Table 2.1 are: ACE Electoral Knowledge Network (aceproject.org/epic); Reginald Austin and Maja Tjernström, eds. *Funding of Political Parties and Election Campaigns*. Stockholm: International Institute for Democracy and Assistance, 2003; Bowler et al. Changing party Access to elections; Brancati, Winning alone; Institutions and elections project (http://www2.binghamton.edu/political-science/institutions-and-elections-project.html); Hazan and Rahat, *Democracy within Parties*; Miki Caul Kittilson and Susan Scarrow, Political parties and the rhetoric and realities of democratization. In Bruce Cain, Russell Dalton and Susan Scarrow, eds. *Democracy Transformed? Expanding Political Opportunities in Advanced Industrial Democracies*. Oxford: Oxford University Press, 2003; Nir, *The Relationship between Candidate Selection Methods and Electoral Systems;* Plasser and Plasser, *Global Political Campaigning;* Jan Teorell, Nicholas Charron, Marcus Samanni, Sören Holmberg & Bo Rothstein. The Quality of Government Dataset, version 27 May10, 2010. University of Gothenburg: The Quality of Government Institute (http://www.qog.pol.gu.se); David Samuels, Political ambition, candidate recruitment and legislative politics in Brazil. In Scott Morgenstern and Peter Siavelis, eds. *Pathways to Power*. Pennsylvania: Penn State University Press, 2009.

8. This variable is coded to reflect whether a party nomination establishes how the field of candidates who stand for election is determined. For more details, see http://www2.binghampton.edu/political-science/institutions-and-elections-project.html

9. Established democracies are the following: Australia, Belgium, Canada, Denmark, Finland, France, Germany, Iceland, Ireland, Israel, Italy, Japan, Netherlands, New Zealand, Norway, Sweden, Switzerland, the UK, and the USA.

10. It is difficult to find comprehensive data on the constitutional and legal regulations relating to political parties. What cross-national evidence there is (most of this European-focused) reveals a strong tendency toward explicit legal regulations of parties. See especially, Kenneth Janda, *Adopting Party Law*. Washington, DC: National Democratic Institute for International Affairs, 2005; Ingrid van Biezen, Constitutionalizing party democracy: The constitutive codification of political parties in post-war Europe, *Legal Regulation of Political Parties Working Paper 3*, University of Birmingham, 2009.

11. Dawn Brancati, Winning alone: The electoral fate of independent candidates worldwide, *Journal of Politics* (2008) 70: 648–62.

12. These are national averages (weighted by party size) of codes derived by Reuven Hazan and Gideon Rahat, *Democracy within Parties: Candidate Selection Methods and their Political Consequences*. Oxford: Oxford University Press, 2010, ch. 3. The scale runs from 0 (candidates selected by all the public), to 24 (candidates selected by a single party leader). Atmor Nir generously provided additional party scores: Atmor Nir, The Relationship between Candidate Selection Methods and Electoral Systems: A Comparative Perspective, PhD dissertation, Hebrew University of Jerusalem, in progress. The authors of this book separately coded several other cases.

13. The move toward more inclusive candidate selection procedures is designed to sideline the troublesome activist base. It also helps the party leadership's efforts to usurp greater control over policy design by "buying off" the members with what purports to be a greater say over candidate selection. For further discussion, see Peter Mair, Party organizations: from civil society to the state. In Richard Katz and Peter Mair, eds, *How Parties Organize: Change and Adaptation in Party Organizations in Western Democracies*. London: Sage, 1994; R. Kenneth Carty, Parties as franchise systems: Stratarchical organizational imperatives, *Party Politics* (2004) 10: 5–24.

14. Paul Webb, Conclusion: Political parties and democratic control in advanced industrial societies. In Paul Webb, David Farrell, and Ian Holliday, eds, *Political Parties in Advanced Industrial Democracies*. Oxford: Oxford University Press, 2002, p. 444.

15. Ellis Krauss and Benjamin Nyblade, "Presidentialization" in Japan? The prime minister, media and elections in Japan, *British Journal of Political Science* (2004) 34: 357–68.

16. Farrell and Schmitt-Beck, eds, *Non-Party Actors in Electoral Politics*.

17. Holli Semetko and Klaus Schoenbach, The campaign in the media. In Russell Dalton, ed., *The New Germany Votes*. Providence, RI: Berg Press, 1993, pp. 201–202; also see Holli Semetko and Klaus Schoenbach, *Germany's "Unity Election": Voters and the Media*. New York: Hampton Press, 1993.

18. About an eighth of British media reports referred to primary actors that were not party representatives, and about a sixth of Spanish newspaper coverage featured non-party actors. Even in less structured American campaigns only about a fifth of primary actors were not party representatives (often the media themselves, the public in general, or interest groups). Russell Dalton et al., Partisan cues in the media: Cross-national comparisons of election coverage. Paper presented at the CNEP Conference, Madrid, 1998, supplemental table 2. Also see Holli Semetko, et al., *The Formation of Campaign Agendas: A Comparative Analysis of Party and Media Roles in Recent American and British Elections*. London: Routledge, 1990.

19. We analyzed the initial data release for the eighteen EU nations that were also included in the CSES study. For information on the media study see Andreas Schuck, Georgios Xezonakis, Susan Banducci, and Claes de Vreese, EES (2009) Media Study Data Advance Release Documentation, 31 March 2010 version (www.piredeu.eu).

20. Baek shows how partisan the press is in a country based on their content and their organizational affiliation. Mijeong Baek, A comparative analysis of political communication systems and voter turnout, *American Journal of Political Science* (2009) 53: 376–93. Baek's analysis draws on earlier suggestions by Hallin and Mancini and van Kempen. Daniel Hallin and Paolo Mancini, *Comparing Media Systems: Three Models of Media and Politics*. Cambridge: Cambridge University Press, 2004; Hetty van Kempen, Media-party parallelism and its effects: A cross-national comparative study, *Political Communication* (2007) 24: 303–20.

21. The sources for Table 2.2 are: Austin and Tjernström, eds. *Funding of Political Parties and Election Campaigns*; Mijeong Baek, A comparative analysis of political communication systems and voter turnout, *American Journal of Political Science* (2009) 53: 376–93; Shaun Bowler and David Farrell, The internationalization of campaign consultancy. In James Thurber and Candice Nelson, eds, *Campaign Warriors: Political Consultants in Elections*. Washington, DC: Brookings Institution Press, 2000; Bowler et al., Changing party access to elections; Kevin Casas-Zamora, *Paying for Democracy: Political Finance and State Funding of Parties*. Colchester: ECPR, 2005, p. 46; Claes de Vreese, Campaign communication and media. In Lawrence LeDuc, Richard Niemi, and Pippa Norris, eds, *Comparing Democracies 3: Elections and Voting in the 21st Century*. London: Sage, 2010; Plasser and Plasser, *Global Political Campaigning;* Pippa Norris, *A Virtuous Circle? Political Communications in Post-Industrial Democracies*. Cambridge: Cambridge University Press, 2000; Ingrid van Biezen, Political parties as public utilities, *Party Politics* (2004) 10: 701–22; Ingrid van Biezen, State intervention in party politics: The public funding and regulation of political parties, *European Review* (2008) 16: 337–53; Ingrid van Biezen and Petr Kopecky, The state and the parties: Public funding, public regulation and rent-seeking in contemporary democracies, *Party Politics* (2007) 13: 235–54.

22. Anthony Smith, Mass communications. In David Butler, Howard Penniman, and Austin Ranney, eds, *Democracy at the Polls: A Comparative Study of Competitive National Elections*. Washington, DC: American Enterprise Institute, 1981, p. 177.

23. Karl-Heinz Nassmacher, *The Funding of Party Competition: Political Finance in 25 Democracies*. Baden-Baden: Nomos, 2009, p. 297; Fritz Plasser and Gunda Plasser,

Global Political Campaigning: A Worldwide Analysis of Campaign Professionals and their Practices. Westport, CT: Praeger, 2002, Table 8.4.

24. Smith, Mass communications, Table 8.1.
25. Lynda Lee Kaid and Christina Holtz-Bacha, eds, *Political Advertising in Western Democracies: Parties and Candidates on Television*. London: Sage, 1995; Hallin and Mancini, *Comparing Media Systems*.
26. Smith, Mass communications, Table 8.1.
27. Hallin and Mancini, *Comparing Media Systems*; Claes de Vreese, Campaign communication and media. In Lawrence LeDuc, Richard Niemi, and Pippa Norris, eds, *Comparing Democracies 3: Elections and Voting in the 21st Century*. London: Sage, 2010.
28. Alexander Heard, *The Costs of Democracy*. Chapel Hill: University of North Carolina Press, 1960, p. 12.
29. Though see Gil Troy, *See How they Ran: The Changing Role of the Presidential Candidate*. Cambridge, MA: Harvard University Press, 1996.
30. David Farrell, Political parties in a changing campaign environment. In Richard Katz and William Crotty, eds, *Handbook of Party Politics*. London: Sage, 2006.
31. Austin and Tjernström, eds. *Funding of Political Parties and Election Campaigns*; Baek, A comparative analysis of political communication systems; Casas-Zamora, *Paying for Democracy*; Pinto-Duschinsky, Financing parties; Plasser and Plasser, *Global Political Campaigning*; van Biezen, Political parties as public utilities; van Biezen, State intervention in party politics; van Biezen and Kopecky, The state and the parties; Wall, et al., *Electoral Management Design*.
32. Jonathan Hopkin, The problem with party finance: Theoretical perspectives on the funding of party politics, *Party Politics* (2004) 10: 627–51.
33. Nassmacher, *The Funding of Party Competition*.
34. Ingrid van Biezen, *Political Parties in New Democracies: Party Organization in Southern and East-Central Europe*. Houndmills, Basingstoke: Palgrave Macmillan, 2003; Steven Roper and Janis Ikstens, eds, *Public Finance and Post-Communist Party Development*. Aldershot: Gower, 2008.
35. R. J. Murphy and David Farrell, Party politics in Ireland: Regularizing a volatile system. In Paul Webb, David Farrell, and Ian Holliday, eds, *Political Parties in Advanced Industrial Democracies*. Oxford: Oxford University Press, 2002.
36. Ben Clift and Justin Fisher, Comparative political finance reform: The cases of France and Britain, *Party Politics* (2004) 10: 677–99.
37. Karl-Heinz Nassmacher, Structure and impact of public subsidies to political parties in Europe: The examples of Austria, Italy, Sweden and West Germany. In Herbert Alexander, ed., *Comparative Political Finance in the 1980s*. Cambridge: Cambridge University Press, 1989.
38. Ingrid van Biezen, State intervention in party politics: The public funding and regulation of political parties, *European Review* (2008) 16: 337–53; Nassmacher, *Funding of Party Competition*, p. 317.
39. Jon Pierre, Lars Svåsand, and Anders Widfeldt, State subsidies to political parties: Confronting rhetoric with reality, *West European Politics* (2000) 23: 14–16.

40. Nassmacher, *Funding of Party Competition*, pp. 318, 324. Also: Petr Kopecky, Political parties and the state in post-communist Europe: The nature of symbiosis, *Journal of Communist Studies and Transition Politics* (2006) 22: 251–74; Michael Pinto-Duschinsky, Financing parties: A global view, *Journal of Democracy* (2002) 13: 251–73; Kevin Casas-Zamora, *Paying for Democracy: Political Finance and State Funding of Parties*. Colchester: ECPR, 2005, p. 46.

41. Casas-Zamora, *Paying for Democracy*, p. 20.

42. Alan Wall, Andrew Ellis, Ayman Ayoub, Carl Dundas, Joram Rukambe, and Sara Staino, *Electoral Management Design: The International IDEA Handbook*. Stockholm, International IDEA, 2006; Louis Massicotte, André Blais, and Antoine Yoshinaka, *Establishing the Rules of the Game: Elections Laws in Democracies*. Toronto: University of Toronto Press, 2004.

43. Pinto-Duschinsky, Financing parties, p. 80.

44. For more details, see http://www.sipo.gov.ie/en/Reports/AnnualDisclosures/DisclosurebyPoliticalParties/180510-DonationStatementsfurnishedbyPoliticalParties for2009/

45. Pierre et al., State subsidies to political parties, p. 12.

46. For more details, see David Farrell, *Electoral Systems: A Comparative Introduction*, 2nd edn. Houndmills, Basingstoke: Palgrave Macmillan, 2010.

47. For derivations of the disproportionality and effective number of parties indices, see Michael Gallagher, Proportionality, disproportionality and electoral systems, *Electoral Studies* (1991) 10: 33–51; Markku Laakso and Rein Taagepera, The effective number of parliamentary parties: A measure with application to Western Europe, *Comparative Political Studies* (1979) 12: 3–27. The source of table 2.4 data are the CSES macro files; http://www.tcd.ie/Political_Science/staff/michael_gallagher/ElSystems/index.php; Farrell, *Electoral Systems*.

48. Josep Colomer, It's parties that choose electoral systems (or, Duverger's laws upside down), *Political Studies* (2005) 53: 1–21; Alan Renwick, *The Politics of Electoral Reform: Changing the Rules of Democracy*. Cambridge: Cambridge University Press, 2010.

49. Farrell, *Electoral Systems*.

50. See Farrell, *Electoral Systems* for more details. An unusual twist is provided by Russia, which offers a sop to the smaller parties in the form of a threshold rule that awards the booby prize of one seat for parties winning between 5 and 6 percent of the national vote, and two seats for parties winning between 6 and 7 percent. Only those parties that win at least 7 percent of the vote are eligible to be awarded the requisite proportion of seats.

51. Another dimension that would be worth exploring is how candidates are actually selected by political parties. All that is known on cross-national trends is that there is much variation across countries, electoral systems, and political parties. See Hazan and Rahat, *Democracy within Parties*

52. We categorize all list systems (including the open systems used in Denmark, Finland, and Switzerland) as party-based on the grounds that, by their nature, such systems condition voters to think of party lists when voting.

53. Matthew Shugart, Electoral "efficiency" and the move to mixed-member systems, *Electoral Studies* (2001) 20: 173–93; David Farrell and Ian McAllister, *The Australian Electoral System: Origins, Variations, and Consequences.* Sydney: University of New South Wales Press, 2006. See Appendix Table A2.1 for more details.

54. Susan Scarrow, Political parties and party systems. In Lawrence LeDuc, Richard Niemi, and Pippa Norris, eds, *Comparing Democracies 3.* London: Sage, 2010.

55. This three-item index of legal provisions for parties is from Scarrow, Political parties and party systems.

56. We presume that the candidate orientation of presidential systems would limit the political role of parties as institutions. These data are from the CSES macrofiles (www.cses.org).

57. The table presents an unrotated principal factor result. We constrained the result to two dimensions based partially on the interpretability of the results and the decline in the eigenvalues for additional dimensions.

58. About 90 percent of CSES nations have government regulation of party finances, but the exceptions all tend to be nations where party nomination guarantees ballot access. This produces a modest negative correlation ($r=-.20$) between both variables.

59. This is an additive index of five items: a party-oriented electoral system, vote for a party vs. candidate on the ballot, free access to the media, legal recognition, and state support for parties. Each variable was coded to have a 0–1 range. We did not include the selectorate variable because we lacked data for several nations, but this is another strong indicator of the parties' role in elections.

60. Katz and Mair, Changing models of party organization; see also Nassmacher, *Funding of Party Competition;* Casas-Zamora, *Paying for Democracy.*

61. Shaun Bowler, Elisabeth Carter, and David Farrell, Changing party access to elections. In Bruce Cain, Russell Dalton, and Susan Scarrow, eds, *Democracy Transformed? Expanding Political Opportunities in Advanced Industrial Democracies.* Oxford: Oxford University Press, 2003.

62. Van Biezen, State intervention in political parties, p. 339. Also Ingrid van Biezen, Political parties as public utilities, *Party Politics* (2004) 10: 701–22.

63. See also, Nassmacher, *Funding of Party Competition*, p. 293.

3

Party Mobilization and Campaign Participation

Stephen Pound has represented the constituency of Ealing North, a borough of Greater London, since 1997. He is an old school politician who believes in the importance of canvassing his constituents as the election approaches. "There is no point in being a politician unless you absolutely love talking to people," says Pound.[1] "Also you get useful information and tips. There is no better way to take the temperature of a place. It is part of the job and I absolutely love it." Pound engages voters as he visits their homes, even though some householders have reacted to the appearance of his grinning face by aiming a boot at his backside. Indeed, canvassing by candidates and party activists is a regular part of British election campaigns, and has even increased in recent elections at a time when election turnout and party memberships have been in decline.[2] The candidates and party workers meet with individual voters, and develop a list of people's voting preferences. Then on election day a party worker knocks on the doors of prospective supporters at their homes to make sure they cast their ballot and often offers a ride to the polls if needed.

Traditionally, the two core functions of parties at the local level have been to encourage voters first, to turn out to vote and, second, to support them at elections. While these two functions are conceptually distinct, in practice there is substantial overlap and they are often difficult to distinguish from one another. A candidate canvassing voters in a shopping center will try to persuade them to support her, but she must also persuade them to show up at the polls and cast a ballot in order to gain any benefit from the encounter. The recent focus on declining turnout has led some analysts to assume that this phenomenon may partially reflect the decline of the mass political party, with the parties possessing fewer members or resources with which to mobilize the vote.[3] However, parties have a variety of ways they may engage citizens in an election, with the door knocking that Stephen Pound engaged in being just one of them. This chapter examines the parties' continuing importance in mobilizing citizens to participate in elections.

We start with a brief discussion of the theoretical debates over the parties' role as agents of mobilization. We first describe some of the reasons why we might expect party contacting to be important in mobilizing voters, and then turn to outline the levels of voting and campaign activity across the nations in the CSES study. Then we describe the levels of party contacting across these nations and the factors that affect levels of contacting. Finally, we develop a multivariate model of voting and campaign activity to assess the direct and psychological effects of party contact on participation.

Parties and Political Mobilization

Sidney Verba, Kay Scholzman, and Henry Brady described three broad reasons why people participate in politics: (1) they can (they have the resources to do so); (2) they want to (their views motivate them to vote and to influence government); and (3) they are asked to vote by an individual or an organization.[4] As the primary actors in campaigns whose fate is dependent on securing a reasonable vote, political parties have a special reason to fulfill the last criteria and ask potential supporters to vote and participate in the campaign. Even with interest groups and media potentially becoming more active in political discourse and voter mobilization, the parties' livelihoods and very survival depends on who turns out to vote.

Because of this, parties have developed extensive mechanisms to identify potential voters and to mobilize them on election day. The case of Stephen Pound at the beginning of this chapter is an example of traditional grass-roots politics where candidates personally go from door to door. This tradition of canvassing and election day visits is woven into the fabric of British elections and that of many other established democracies. In Ireland, for example, local election campaigning remains alive and well, and even the prime minister has to take to the streets in order to secure re-election.[5] At the same time, election campaigning is experiencing significant change in many democracies. In the article by Wheeler, Pound also expresses his loathing for "the blogosphere and Twitter and all of that." But many parties are adapting to changes in communication methods and embracing these new technologies as a means of connecting to voters—often combining the old and new to produce an even more effective connection to voters.

The adoption of new technologies to influence voters was taken to a new level by the 2008 Obama campaign in the United States, which developed an extensive database of supporters, regularly informing them about campaign issues, soliciting contributions via the internet, and even offering social networking through the campaign website (MyBo networking).[6] These computer databases provided the organizational basis for extensive telephone contacting through well-organized and targeted call centers, and personal contacting in competitive states. Almost daily, Obama supporters received a message from the campaign organization, Michelle Obama, or Barack Obama when they opened their emails or via text messages on their cell phones. The Obama election campaign represented an unprecedented effort to contact voters using new technology.

Longitudinal data for Britain show a similar pattern of parties adapting to change. As the number of party workers and campaign helpers has decreased in recent decades, the parties are using new methods of citizen mobilization.[7] The percentage of local party organizations that had computerized electoral rosters increased from 43 percent in 1992 to 80 percent in 2005. Simultaneously, the use of computerized databases to organize canvassing during the campaign and election day visits more than doubled during this period. In Australia, computerized databases maintained by the major political parties have become an essential campaign tool; each of the two major party databases now contains the voting preferences of over half a million individual citizens, representing in total about one in every ten voters.[8] The use of these technologies allows parties to be more efficient in their mobilizing efforts. In other words, political parties may remain very active in campaign mobilization, even if the means of mobilization have changed over time.

Interest groups and other organizations also try to mobilize individuals to participate in elections—but their resources and efforts pale in comparison with the activities of political parties. For instance, the much heralded efforts by youth groups to raise funds to increase turnout among the young in the 2008 US election was a small fraction of the funds available to the Obama campaign. In addition, with direct financial support from the government in many nations (see Chapter 2), and this support contingent on the votes that a party receives, there are even stronger motivations for parties to increase turnout.

Thus, previous studies of campaign participation have stressed the importance of parties as agents of mobilization. Steven Rosenstone and Mark Hansen argued that mobilization by political parties and interest groups was a key factor in explaining levels of voting turnout in the United States.[9] More recent experimental studies in the United States by Donald Green and Alan Gerber demonstrate persuasively the effectiveness of contacting, especially interpersonal contacting, for stimulating voting turnout.[10] Election research across a wide range of nations finds a similar pattern of party contacting mobilizing voting participation.[11]

Party contacting may also encourage citizens to participate in campaign activities beyond voting: attending a rally, reading campaign literature, or even working for a campaign can all be stimulated by coming into direct or indirect contact with a political party.[12] Contacting provides citizens with information about a party and its issues, which can encourage further involvement in the campaign. Such partisan effects can have a multiplier effect on overall levels of political activity.

Mobilization effects can vary with the institutional context of elections. For example, Jeffrey Karp and Susan Banducci find that the ideological polarization of a party system increases campaign involvement, and it increases the magnitude of contacting effects because the political choices are starker.[13] The amount and importance of party contacting also appear to vary across the range of established and new democracies that are included in the Comparative Study of Electoral Systems.[14] Political parties in new democracies typically are less institutionalized and command fewer resources, which limits their ability to mobilize voters during the campaign. Party membership also tends to be lower in new democracies, which limits the resources for in-person contacting. These factors can contribute to lower levels of turnout and campaign activity in new democracies.

The decline in turnout has led some scholars to link this to decreased party mobilization and thus to a diminished political role for parties. For instance, Rosenstone and Hansen attribute most of the decrease in turnout in the USA during the 1970s and 1980s to the decline in mobilization as parties shifted to more candidate-centered campaigns, local party organizations atrophied, and greater emphasis was placed on campaign advertising in the media.[15] But a variety of factors contribute to the trends in turnout, such as changing political norms and other societal forces. Moreover, there is also evidence that the electoral mobilization of some traditional interests, such as labor unions, has waned in recent decades.[16] In any case, with cross-sectional data we focus on the impact of party mobilization on contemporary electorates to assess its persisting role.

Another way that parties can mobilize citizen participation is through psychological factors that make people *want* to participate—fulfilling Verba, Schlozman, and Brady's second criteria for political action mentioned above. The clearest party-based mobilization factor is a psychological identity with a party.[17] This encourages individuals to strongly support their party at election time by voting and being active in the campaign. Like sports fans showing up at the game to support their team, partisans express their loyalty by showing up to cast their vote; these effects typically are even stronger for campaign activity, which represents the peak of the political cycle.

These partisanship effects also might vary systematically across the nations in our study. Feelings of partisanship tend to be stronger in more established democracies, and are still forming in the new democracies where political parties and party labels are less stable. Thus the impact of partisanship may also vary with the democratic development of a nation. Partisanship is also a valuable heuristic for making political choices when other information is limited, so we expect partisanship may play a greater role in low information environments or among those with limited political knowledge. Although there are many factors that affect participation levels, this chapter focuses on the role of parties—through contacting and partisan attachments—in explaining voting and campaign activity. In the next section we examine the effect of party contacting on election turnout.

Election Turnout

Voting in elections is widely seen as one of the essential elements of democracy. Thus, the near universal decline in election turnout that has occurred across the established democracies over the past three decades has received considerable attention. Among twenty-nine established democracies, turnout in the 1970s averaged 83.1 percent; in the same countries in the early 2000s, the average turnout was nearly 10 percentage points lower, at 73.9 percent.[18] Turnout was initially very high in many Third Wave democracies, but voting has generally declined in these nations as well.[19] Scholars often interpret decreasing turnout as an indicator of the weakening of political parties that have lost party members and party identifiers over this same period (see Chapter 1). Even with the decline in turnout, however, this remains the most common form of political action, and the total number of votes cast has generally increased in advanced industrial democracies as populations have expanded.[20]

Stimulated by the general decline in turnout, recent research has generated considerable evidence concerning what motivates citizens to vote and the reasons for the decline in turnout. We know that the decline in turnout is largely a result of the young not voting, while voting among older citizens has remained stable. Researchers have attributed the decline to lower levels of newspaper readership among the young, a weaker sense of citizen duty, and lower levels of "voter initiation."[21] Changing images of government and feelings concerning political efficacy are often cited as additional factors in explaining levels of turnout.[22] In many nations the decline in turnout has been greater among the less educated and less affluent, those who are least likely to possess the resources to participate. Our concern here is whether in this changing context parties still play a major role in mobilizing those citizens who do vote.

Measuring election turnout in surveys is always problematic, since reported turnout in a survey is consistently higher than the actual turnout in the election, largely because non-voters are less likely to admit to abstaining. The bias resulting from the over-reporting of turnout is a perennial problem in survey research where checking the validity of self-reports of voting against actual voting records is not possible.[23] The problem has apparently increased in recent years, as turnout has generally declined in advanced industrial societies, and survey respondents have become more hesitant to admit to abstaining.[24]

The CSES survey suffers from the problem of the over-reporting of turnout since self-reports could not be checked against actual turnout. However, we can partially mitigate the effects of the problem by utilizing the two measures of turnout that are included in the module 2 dataset: for the election held just before the survey was conducted; and for the election preceding that election. This provides a valuable opportunity to ascertain the broader habits of voting by distinguishing between those who report having not voted in two elections, and those who report voting in both elections. In principle, since turnout is measured across two elections, this should provide a more robust measure of turnout than if just a single election is examined. Our dependent variable for turnout is therefore measured as zero if the respondents reported not voting in either election, 1 if they voted in one election only, and 2 if they voted in both the current and the preceding election.

The patterns of reported and actual turnout are shown in Table 3.1. Both reported and actual turnout (the latter measured by voting age population) is highest in the two countries with enforced systems of compulsory voting— Belgium and Australia. In Australia, for example, 86 percent of the survey respondents reported voting in both the 2001 and 2004 elections, and actual turnout as a proportion of the voting age population was 82.4 percent in the 2004 election. Both measures of turnout are also high in Peru and Chile, which have mandatory voting, although the level of enforcement is more limited. At the other end of the scale, both measures of turnout are low in Poland and Mexico. In Poland, just 58 percent of the survey respondents reported voting in the 2001 election, while actual turnout was 47.6 percent. Among the countries with the lower levels of turnout, we also find the largest disparities between actual and reported turnout. For example, in Ireland, 85 percent of the survey respondents said that they voted in the 2002 Dáil Éireann election, but the actual level of turnout was 67 percent.[25]

Among the countries included in the analysis, actual turnout in the elections covered by the CSES was 62.3 percent.[26] The reported turnout among the CSES survey respondents in the same elections was 79 percent. However, the relative ranking of countries is largely preserved in both turnout statistics. Since we are interested in the relativities, the bias caused by self-reported turnout should be minimal.[27] In summary, even though turnout levels have decreased significantly in most established democracies, it remains the most common form of political action and one that is inexorably linked to the activities of political parties.

Table 3.1. Reported and Actual Turnout by Country (Percent)

	Voted recent election	Voted previous election	Voted both elections	(Actual turnout)
Albania	89	75	69	(47.8)
Australia	92	92	86	(82.4)
Belgium	86	77	73	(85.9)
Brazil	83	75	69	(68.4)
Britain	72	72	64	(58.3)
Bulgaria	79	72	64	(72.1)
Canada	91	—	91	(55.3)
Chile	96	80	78	(66.5)
Czech Republic	73	57	52	(59.0)
Denmark	95	91	89	(84.3)
Finland	80	76	69	(70.0)
France	79	74	64	(47.3)
Germany	94	89	86	(73.5)
Hungary	83	80	72	(55.9)
Iceland	91	79	76	(89.1)
Ireland	85	76	70	(67.0)
Israel	89	81	75	(76.1)
Italy	77	—	77	(82.1)
Mexico	72	80	63	(43.4)
Netherlands	97	88	87	(76.8)
New Zealand	81	84	71	(72.5)
Norway	83	81	71	(76.5)
Peru	95	77	73	(84.1)
Philippines	86	78	72	(27.1)
Poland	58	68	48	(47.6)
Portugal (2002)	75	75	67	(69.2)
Romania	79	68	60	(62.3)
Russia	79	77	67	(54.3)
Slovenia	76	74	65	(61.1)
South Korea	78	82	70	(59.5)
Spain	89	77	74	(79.8)
Sweden	88	81	76	(78.0)
Switzerland	74	71	64	(37.3)
Taiwan (2004)	91	80	76	(54.0)
United States	79	69	64	(56.7)
(Means)	(83)	(74)	(67)	(65.2)

Source: CSES module 2, final release. Actual turnout figures are based on voting age population from International IDEA.

Campaign Activity

The types of activities that political parties undertake to mobilize citizens can vary widely. Traditional local party activities can include organizing community meetings on issues of local concern, door-to-door canvassing of voters, and encouraging members and supporters to put up posters to rally support for their favored candidate. These activities have been undertaken virtually since the introduction of mass political parties at the end of the nineteenth century. They constitute the "sound and fury" that sums up the image of the modern election campaign.

In practice, these activities seek to accomplish two goals. First, they are intended to mobilize citizens to turn out to vote by heightening activity and interest in the election. This is most often accomplished by articulating a clear choice for voters, who then find it easier to opt for one or other candidate based on their stated policies. Second, these local party activities are also designed to convert voters by persuading them that the election of one particular party will offer them a better and more prosperous future. The mobilization and conversion functions that parties undertake are conceptually distinct, but in their day-to-day application, and especially during the frenetic pace of a modern election campaign, they often overlap considerably.

The second module of the CSES survey included two questions designed to measure the level of local party activity among the survey respondents:[28]

Here is a list of things some people do during elections. Which if any did you do during the most recent election?

...talked to other people to persuade them to vote for a particular party or candidate?

...showed your support for a particular party or candidate by, for example, attending a meeting, putting up a poster, or in some other way?

Table 3.2 shows the level of party activity across the CSES nations for which data are available. Averaged across all of the countries in the table, just over one in every four citizens reports engaging in some form of local party activity. This is a relatively high proportion, particularly in view of the argument that political parties are in significant decline. Indeed, if we focus just on the most directly party-related of the two activities—attending a meeting or putting up a poster in support of a candidate or party—then around one in every nine citizens across the countries reported participating in such an activity.

In practice, persuading others how to vote and showing support for a party or candidate are closely related. At the individual level, the average correlation between the two items is $r=.37$, which is a very substantial overlap between the two activities. Across the nations in the table, the national levels of both activities are even more strongly correlated ($r=.70$). In short, both items tap a general aspect of campaign involvement.

Across these countries, Canada ranks highest, largely because of the remarkably high proportion—64 percent—who report persuading others how to vote, and 35 percent who report some form of local party activity.[29] In second and third place are Albania and the United States, respectively. Albania represents an interesting case; apart from being a new democracy, it is also one of only three countries (the other two being the Philippines and Mexico) where the proportion of citizens engaging in campaign activities is greater than the

Table 3.2. Campaign Activity by Country (Percent)

	Persuade others	Campaign activities	(At least one)
Albania	34	45	54
Australia	32	16	38
Belgium	12	7	16
Brazil	35	17	40
Britain	17	13	23
Bulgaria	7	7	10
Canada	64	35	69
Chile	23	12	26
Czech Republic	26	20	31
Denmark	22	8	26
Finland	13	11	19
France	29	7	31
Germany	28	7	31
Hungary	15	10	19
Iceland	22	16	30
Ireland	13	9	17
Israel	32	11	36
Italy	9	8	13
Mexico	9	13	17
Netherlands	12	7	17
New Zealand	24	7	27
Norway	18	7	21
Peru	29	16	36
Philippines	26	27	36
Poland	7	4	9
Portugal (2002)	10	7	13
Romania	17	7	21
Russia	25	4	26
Slovenia	7	5	10
South Korea	21	4	22
Spain	8	6	11
Sweden	13	3	14
Switzerland	16	7	19
Taiwan (2004)	24	17	32
United States	44	31	53
(Means)	(21)	(12)	(26)

Source: CSES module 2, final release.

proportion saying that they persuaded others how to vote. At the bottom of the scale, just around a tenth of the public in Poland, Bulgaria, Slovenia, and Spain report engaging in one or other of the activities. It is perhaps no surprise that three of these four countries are postcommunist democracies, where there are a large number of competing parties, often transitory in nature and weakly organized, vying for the popular vote.

To what extent are campaign activity and turnout related? In principle we might expect some relationship, since higher levels of activity should produce more local interest in the election and, ultimately, a higher turnout. In practice, of course, many other factors are associated with turnout, as we show below. Most obviously, system characteristics, such as compulsory or mandatory voting, will drive turnout more than campaign activity. And in voluntary systems, such factors as the competitiveness of the party system or the closeness of the contest in the constituency are likely to have a greater impact.[30] Nevertheless, the individual level correlation between local campaign activity and turnout (using the weighted measure) is r=.06; this is a significant relationship if not an overwhelmingly important one. At the national level, the correlation between campaign activity and turnout is r=.23, which suggests that a much stronger relationship exists at the country level. In summary, nations that engage citizens in one form of campaign activity generally engage them in others.

Contact with a Candidate or Party

The preceding sections have described cross-national levels of turnout and campaign activity, and this section presents the level of party mobilization across nations. More specifically, it measures the extent to which parties and candidates directly contact the voter.

Contact with the election campaign represents a precise measure of the extent to which the parties undertake activities, such as leafleting and canvassing, that directly connect to the ordinary citizen. In turn, we expect that people who have such direct contact with a candidate or party will be more likely to engage in campaign activity and to show up at the polls on election day. To measure contact with a candidate or the campaign, the CSES survey included the question: "During the last campaign did a candidate or anyone from a political party contact you to persuade you to vote for them?"[31] This directly assesses the parties' efforts to mobilize the public.

As with citizens' campaign activity, there is a large variation in the proportions of people who reported having been contacted by the candidate or party workers during the election campaign (Table 3.3). There are high levels of contact in Ireland and Canada, with 56 percent and 55 percent, respectively, reporting contact by a candidate or party representative; Ireland is, of course, the example par excellence of localism.[32] The Philippines and the United States also report high levels of contact, at 50 and 49 percent, respectively. At the other end of the scale, Poles, Spaniards, and Russians report negligible contacts with parties or candidates. However, perhaps surprisingly, several established democracies also come far down the list, notably France, Sweden, Germany, and the Netherlands. There is, then, considerable variation in party contacting across the CSES nations which does not appear to be strongly associated with the length of time that the country has been a democracy. In the next section we examine what some of these factors might be.

Table 3.3. Contact with the Candidate or Party by Country (Percent)

	Contact
Albania	35
Australia	29
Belgium	28
Brazil	47
Britain	32
Bulgaria	8
Canada	55
Chile	27
Czech Republic	30
Denmark	24
Finland	21
France	7
Germany	13
Hungary	8
Iceland	28
Ireland	56
Israel	18
Italy	22
Mexico	18
Netherlands	14
New Zealand	22
Norway	15
Peru	15
Philippines	50
Poland	5
Portugal (2002)	15
Romania	11
Russia	6
Slovenia	15
South Korea	18
Spain	6
Sweden	7
Switzerland	18
Taiwan (2004)	14
USA	49
(Means)	(22)

Source: CSES module 2, final release.

Predicting Contacting

In order to better understand the processes of party mobilization, we need to ask what institutional features might shape national levels of party contacting.[33] Several potential influences flow from the structure of the electoral system, and these form the first set of variables in the model. Less proportional electoral systems should result in more party activity, since small changes in votes can reap large rewards in seats; the PR/majoritarian form of the electoral system tests this idea. District magnitude is often used as a more precise measure of the proportionality of the electoral system, and should have similar effects to PR. A candidate-oriented electoral system places greater emphasis on personal vote-chasing by individual parliamentary candidates and thus may stimulate higher levels of contacting.

A second set of variables taps the characteristics of the party system. The polarization index measures the extent to which voters have ideological choices among the political parties and is based on the dispersion of parties on the Left–Right scale.[34] We expect higher levels of contacting when the partisan differences are greater, because this presumably mobilizes citizens to be concerned about election outcomes. The effective number of electoral parties should in theory stimulate the level of party activity because more parties are fielding campaign organizations.[35] Marginality is the percentage of the vote separating the first and second parties in a national election, and we would expect closer contests to encourage more party activity.[36] We also might expect more contacting in nations with *less* party control of elections (Chapter 1). This is because party-centered elections often focus on mobilizing a core set of habitual supporters rather than marked efforts to broaden a party's appeal, while candidate-oriented systems often follow this broader strategy of attempting to convert new supporters as well as mobilize existing supporters. And in some developing democracies, weak party systems coincide with personalistic appeals for voter support, such as in the Philippines and Brazil. We also include a measure for compulsory voting, and we might expect that countries with compulsory voting would exhibit higher levels of party contact.

A third set of variables measures the characteristics of the political system or constitutional design. For instance, party contacting may tend to be more common in established democracies because the parties are more institutionalized, better organized, and with greater resources. A similar pattern should emerge as a function of the socioeconomic development of a nation, with higher levels of party contacting in more affluent nations. Finally, a presidential election tends to stimulate higher levels of political activity, at least in comparison with legislative turnout in the same nation.

Table 3.4 displays the relationships between these national characteristics and aggregate levels of party contacting. The first panel in the table displays three characteristics of the electoral system. All three measures (PR electoral system, district magnitude, and party-based voting) have a negative effect on party contacting. This actually seems contradictory to the party linkage model, but it implies that candidate-oriented campaigns—with candidates who run as party representatives—tend to stimulate local party activity to mobilize prospective voters. Since gaining election in these systems depends more on the visibility and profile of the local candidate and less on their party affiliation, it is logical that local candidates would seek to gain as much visibility within the electorate as is possible. The image of a candidate shaking hands at a railway station or moving from door to door would be familiar in

Table 3.4. Which Country Characteristics Shape Party Contact?

	Correlation
Electoral System	
Proportional representation	−.33*
District magnitude	−.24*
Party-oriented vote	−.40*
Compulsory voting	.29*
Party System	
Party-centered index	−.44*
Left–Right polarization	−.38*
Effective number of electoral parties	−.04
Disproportionality	−.05
Political System	
Established democracy	.12
Presidential election	−.08
Socio-economic development (HDI)	.19

Note: Entries are Pearson r correlations. Correlations significant at $p < .05$ are denoted by an asterisk. Maximum N=36.

Source: CSES module 2, final release.

some, mainly candidate-centered systems, but much less familiar in other, mainly party-centered systems. Proportional and party-based voting systems may stimulate turnout, but there is less grass-roots contacting in such systems. Finally, countries with compulsory voting also have higher levels of party contact, possibly because parties in these countries can focus their resources on conversion since mobilization is assured by the electoral institutions.

The next panel of the table displays several potentially relevant features of the party system. The party-centered index developed in Chapter 2 shows a strong negative relationship with party contacting, again suggesting that strong party systems may concentrate on maximizing turnout by mobilizing committed supporters rather than engaging in diverse grass-roots mobilization. Similarly, we might expect that highly polarized systems would encourage greater political competition, but polarization tends to diminish broad efforts at party contacting. The two other party system traits, the effective number of electoral parties and disproportionality, are essentially unrelated to national levels of party contacting.

The final panel of the table considers whether the characteristics of the political system are related to the level of party contacting. Established democracies and those with higher levels of socioeconomic development have somewhat higher levels of contacting, but the relationships are not statistically significant. In addition, presidential elections lead to lower levels of contact, as we might expect, since they are generally less partisan than legislative elections, but again the relationship is not significant. Overall, the relationships between the characteristics of the political system and party contacting are generally weak, and certainly of much less importance when compared with the characteristics of the electoral and party systems.

These results largely accord with those of Jeffrey Karp and Susan Banducci,[37] who also used the CSES data to examine patterns of party contacting. In line with our results, they show the importance of candidate-centered rather than party-centered systems in shaping contacting, and the significant role of party system polarization. In particular, they show that party systems with strong polarization are reluctant to engage in contacting voters; they conclude that "parties in polarized systems may follow a more targeted strategy by contacting only their own supporters in order to mobilize them to participate."[38] There is, then, an important mediating factor in the political context, which shapes how parties go about the business of contacting voters.

Of all the party activities that are likely to impinge on an ordinary citizen during an election campaign, direct contact with a candidate or a party worker is potentially the most important. While advertising in the mass media or a public debate will have some resonance with voters, meeting the local candidate or party representative in person—for example, by having the candidate knock on the person's door, or shake their hand in a shopping center—is an event that is likely to be remembered, and to have potential electoral consequences. In the next section we test whether this hypothesis finds any support in campaign participation of contemporary publics.

Mobilizing Electoral Participation

As we argued in the first section of this chapter, during an election campaign the political parties mobilize voters to turn out to vote on election day and ideally to support the party's cause. For most of the first half of the twentieth century these functions were conducted at the local level, through door-to-door canvassing, community meetings, and the distribution of leaflets. However, with the advent of electronic media, coupled with the declining resources that parties have available at the local level, the conversion function has increasingly been carried out by the nationwide marketing activities of parties. These activities include paid and free advertising and policy launches, and the myriad activities that parties and leaders engage in with the goal of capturing the—hopefully favorable—attention of voters.

To what extent, then, is party mobilization of the mass electorate still important in predicting who decides to vote and who participates in the campaign? Party mobilization is based on the citizen being contacted by an election candidate or a party worker. Turnout is measured by reported participation in the current and preceding election. We measure campaign activity by reported participation in two activities—persuading others how to vote, and activities such as attending a meeting or putting up a poster. Our basic presumption is that party contacting stimulates both types of election participation. This is most directly tested by the correlation between contacting and these two forms of election activity. At the individual level, there is a modest correlation between contacting and voting in the most recent election (r=.08) and a robust correlation with campaign activity (r=.24).

However, these individual relationships do not uniformly carry over to national patterns. The positive correlation between party contacting and voting turnout ranges from .00 (in Norway) to .30 (in the United States), which implies that the institutional context shapes the mobilization process. In addition to the United States, Italy (r=.20) and Finland (r=.14) also show a strong relationship between party contacting and turnout. Moreover, we expect that nations with high levels of party contacting will also have high levels of voting turnout, since contacting is one way of mobilizing the vote. Yet, as we noted above, there is a surprisingly modest relationship between national turnout levels and contacting (r=.08). For instance, the Philippines, which ranks third in terms of the level of contacting, has one of the lowest levels of turnout in the set of CSES nations, while Sweden, which is fourth from the bottom in terms of contacting, returned a 78 percent turnout in their 2002 elections.

Part of the explanation for these patterns may be the distortions produced by survey respondents over-reporting their participation in the election. But there is a similar weak aggregate correlation between party contacting and actual turnout as reported by the International Institute for Democracy and Electoral Assistance (IDEA). Instead, we suspect the explanation lies in the institutionalized structure of elections. Methods of voter registration, compulsory voting, and the relative ease or difficulty of voting can significantly affect turnout levels independently of party activity.[39] The positive influence of contacting on turnout may be masked by these other institutional factors in simple two-variable comparisons.

However, national levels of party contacting are strongly related to both campaign activity and trying to persuade others during the campaign.[40] The combined index of campaign activity is strongly correlated with levels of contacting (Figure 3.1). For instance, the personalistic nature of election campaigns in the Philippines with high levels of contacting is now consistent with a high level of campaign activity by Filipinos; and the low levels of contacting evident in Swedish campaigns are consistent with low levels of campaign activity. Less fettered by institutional constraints, campaign activity more directly reflects the effects of party contacting in stimulating participation.

Certainly the causes of voting turnout and campaign activity are complex and occur at both the individual and system levels as the previous results suggest. To illustrate these forces, and to put the effect of party mobilization in this larger context, we developed a multilevel model to predict voting turnout

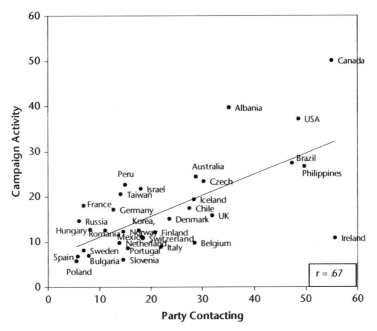

Figure 3.1. Party Contacting and Levels of Campaign Activity

Source: CSES, module 2; party contacting is the average of the two items in Table 3.3.

and campaign activity. Besides being contacted by a party, the individual-level predictors include partisanship to tap the psychological mobilization of party loyalties. In addition, we include a common set of demographic predictors that are generally related to political participation: age, gender, marital status, and tertiary education.

To this model we added several national-level factors. In large part, these are the aggregate predictors of turnout, and campaign activity should mirror the predictors of party contacting discussed above. An electoral system based on compulsory voting will obviously produce higher turnout, so that is an important control; but we would also expect that compulsory voting might influence the levels of campaign activity. Similarly, whether the election was a presidential election, or a legislative election held in conjunction with a presidential election, may influence turnout and the nature of the campaign. Also included in the model is the party-centered index; as we argued earlier, a party-centered system may see fewer attempts to campaign more widely beyond core supporters, while a more candidate-centered system might see a more wide-ranging campaign aimed at conversion. The polarization index measures the degree of ideological difference within the country. As Russell Dalton has argued, it may not be the choice in the number of parties that matters, but the diversity of choice, with citizens who are presented with

71

clearer choices being more motivated to vote and participate.[41] Finally, the model controls for the effective number of electoral parties, and whether or not the country is an established democracy.

The results presented in Table 3.5 show that contact with a party or candidate does indeed matter, in shaping both higher turnout and higher levels of campaign participation. Indeed, in predicting participation in the election campaign, party contact is second only to being a party identifier. The other notable result is the consistently greater importance of individual over country characteristics. At the individual level, a citizen's socioeconomic status shapes participation in line with other research on turnout and campaign activity. Older citizens are more likely to vote, while younger ones are more likely to participate in campaign activity; more education and being a party identifier increase the levels of both behaviors.

Our expectations about which country characteristics might influence who votes or participates are largely unsupported. With the exception of the polarization index and the occurrence of a presidential election, none of the factors are statistically significant, and in the case of a presidential election, there is only a modest effect for such an election enhancing campaign activity and no impact on turnout.[42] Party polarization is significant in both

Table 3.5 Predicting Turnout and Campaign Activity

	Turnout		Campaign activity	
	Est	(SE)	Est	(SE)
Party contact	.08**	(.01)	.26**	(.01)
Individual characteristics				
Gender (male)	.01	(.01)	.07**	(.01)
Age (decades)	.08**	(.00)	−.01**	(.00)
Tertiary education	.14**	(.01)	.08**	(.01)
Married	.18**	(.01)	.01	(.01)
Party identifier	.20**	(.01)	.26**	(.01)
Country characteristics				
Compulsory voting	.06	(.09)	.06	(.08)
Presidential election	−.06	(.06)	.09*	(.04)
Party-centered index	.06	(.05)	.00	(.03)
Polarization index	.14*	(.08)	−.30**	(.10)
Effective number electoral parties	.03	(.03)	.00	(.01)
Established democracy	.06	(.04)	−.03	(.03)
Constant	1.98		.83	
N of countries	35		35	
N of individuals	50,294		55,774	

Note: Parameter estimates and standard errors from multilevel models with fixed and random effects. ** significant at p < .01, * significant at p < .05. Turnout is coded zero if did not vote in two elections, 1 if voted in one election only, 2 if voted in both elections. Campaign activity is coded zero if did not participate in either persuasion or other campaign activity, 1 if participated in one only, 2 if participated in both.

Source: CSES module 2, final release.

models, but it operates in different directions. Higher levels of party polarization within a system increase turnout, but decrease campaign activity. The diversity of choice that results from a polarized party system does present citizens with clearer choices and motivates them to vote; but it has the opposite effect in terms of drawing them into the election campaign. These results are consistent with those of Karp and Banducci, who show that the degree of polarization in the party system is an important intervening factor between party contact and the involvement of citizens in campaign activity.[43]

The answer to our question—does contact with the local candidate matter?—is yes, and contact is especially important for local campaign activity. In local campaign activity, reporting having been contacted by the local candidate or a party representative is second in importance among the variables in the equation, and is only surpassed (and only marginally) by being a party identifier. In practice, then, for the ordinary voter the act of meeting the local candidate is almost as important as having a party attachment in stimulating the voter to engage in these local campaign activities. Mobilization in the form of voting is also significantly influenced by having met the local candidate, but to a lesser degree than by local campaign activity. In this model, while contact with the candidate is important in shaping mobilization, the magnitude of the effect is much less than the other factors that we know about the voter, including her socioeconomic situation.

Why is contact with the candidate more important in shaping campaign activity compared with voting? One explanation may be that a candidate shaking hands in a shopping center or door-stopping a voter will be more likely to talk about the party's policies and what that candidate might do for the local area, rather than simply persuading the person to vote (though they may do this as well). Another explanation may be self-selection, and voters who have already decided to vote may be more likely to seek out the local candidate to elicit their views on issues or simply to meet them. The differential effects of voting registration and rules may also attenuate the impact of contacting on voting. A non-registered citizen might still talk to others about the campaign, even if they cannot vote.

Despite the changes that have taken place in the 100 and more years since mass political parties were born in the established democracies, local campaign activity remains important. The results presented here do suggest that it is especially important in engaging citizens in the campaign, even after a wide range of other factors are taken into account. But it is also clear that contact varies considerably by political context, and especially by the diversity of choice within the party system, measured by the degree of ideological polarization. By implication, then, changes to institutional rules and procedures will affect the level of contact, and therefore the degree to which it can help to mold conversion and mobilization.

Conclusion

When the then Australian prime minister, Paul Keating, was campaigning in the 1996 general election he was faced with a constituent who complained about the high level of university fees. Keating's response was "go and get a job!" Keating lost the election, and presumably the vote of the constituent. The encounter highlighted, in slightly melodramatic form, the importance of personal contact between a party candidate and a voter, although this was not the sort of party contact that wins votes. As we have argued in this chapter, party contact remains an important function for political parties, and it has significant effects on local campaign activity and on the mobilization of the vote.

Despite the declining memberships of political parties and the fewer local resources that they can command, the findings in this chapter are broadly consistent with the notion that parties continue to play an important mobilizing role in elections. Moreover, there is clear evidence of extensive local campaign activities by political parties across a wide range of countries, and that activity is shaped, for the most part, by the institutional rules that govern party competition. Similarly, contact with a local party candidate is driven more by the design of the electoral and party system than by the individual characteristics of citizens. In short, parties remain important agencies of mobilization at the local level across most democracies.

Our evidence also suggests that parties are adapting to the declining human resources that they can command at the local level. With fewer members and activists available to conduct local canvassing and leafleting, the parties have been concentrating their resources on maintaining comprehensive, sophisticated databases of constituents, and using the information contained therein to target potential swinging voters. There has also been an exponential growth in the use of the internet and in mobile phone technology in order to mobilize voters. Local parties may have declining members at the local level, but they are compensating for this change by investing in technology.

We started the chapter with a pessimistic picture of growing threats to the primary election function of parties—namely, that of mobilizing voters. The (now) expansive literature on declining election turnout would appear to sound the death knell for the role of political parties as agents of voter mobilization.[44] Based on all of this existing research, the future for parties appears to be bleak. And yet, as the analysis in this chapter shows, things may not actually be so bleak after all. Voting may well be in decline, but for those who do vote, there is strong and compelling evidence that it is the efforts of the political parties that have been important in cajoling those voters to the polling booth. In short, parties still do have their place.

Notes

1. Brian Wheeler, What's the point of canvassing, *BBC News* (April 9, 2010). http://news.bbc.co.uk/2/hi/uk_news/politics/8605756.stm
2. Justin Fisher, David Denver, Ed Fieldhouse, David Cutts, and Andrew Russell. Constituency campaigning in the 2005 British General Election. Paper presented at the EPOP meetings, 2005.
3. See Chapter 1. For a review of the literature, see Susan E. Scarrow, Political activism and party members. In Russell J. Dalton and Hans-Dieter Klingemann, eds, *The Oxford Handbook of Political Behavior*. Oxford: Oxford University Press, 2007.
4. Sidney Verba, Kay Schlozman, and Henry Brady. *Voice and Equality: Civic Voluntarism in American Politics*. Cambridge, MA: Harvard University Press, 1995.
5. Michael Marsh, Candidates or parties? Objects of electoral choice in Ireland, *Party Politics* (2007) 13: 501–28.
6. David Plouffe, *The Audacity to Win*. New York: Viking, 2009.
7. Fisher et al. Constituency campaigning in the 2005 British General Election.
8. Peter Van Onselen and Wayne Errington, Electoral databases: Big brother or democracy unbound? *Australian Journal of Political Science* (2004) 39: 349–66.
9. Steven Rosenstone and John Hansen. *Mobilization, Participation and Democracy in America*. New York: Macmillan, 1993.
10. Donald Green and Alan Gerber. *Get Out the Vote: How to Increase Voter Turnout*, 2nd edn. Washington, DC: Brookings Institution, 2008.
11. Jeffrey Karp, Susan Banducci, and Shaun Bowler. Getting out the vote: Party mobilization in comparative perspective, *British Journal of Political Science* (2008) 38: 91–112; Jeffrey Karp, Shaun Bowler, and Susan Banducci, Electoral systems, party mobilization, and turnout: Evidence from the European Parliamentary Elections, *British Elections and Parties Review* 13. London: Frank Cass Publishers, 2003; Miki Caul Kittilson and Christopher Anderson, Electoral supply and voter turnout. In Russell Dalton and Christopher Anderson, eds, *Citizens, Context and Choice*. Oxford: Oxford University Press, 2011; Charles Pattie, Patrick Seyd, and Paul Whiteley, *Citizenship in Britain: Values, Participation and Democracy*. New York: Cambridge University Press, 2004; David Denver, Gordon Hands, and Iain MacAllister. The electoral impact of constituency campaigning in Britain, 1992–2001, *Political Studies* (2004) 52: 289–306; Michael Marsh, None of that post-modern stuff around here: Grassroots campaigning in the 2002 Irish General Election, *British Elections and Parties Review* 14. London: Frank Cass Publishers, 2004.
12. Rosenstone and Hansen. *Mobilization, Participation and Democracy in America*; Jeffrey Karp and Susan Banducci, The influence of party and electoral systems on campaign engagement. In Russell Dalton and Christopher Anderson, eds, *Citizens, Context and Choice*. Oxford: Oxford University Press, 2011; this study is based on the same CSES surveys used in this chapter, with a particular focus on the impact of contextual factors.
13. Karp and Banducci, The influence of party and electoral systems on campaign engagement.

14. Jeffrey Karp and Susan Banducci, Party mobilization and political participation in new and old democracies, *Party Politics* (2007) 13: 217–34; Bernhard Wessels and Mark Franklin, Turning out or turning off: Do mobilization and attitudes account for turnout differences between new and established member states at the 2004 European Parliament elections? *Journal of European Integration* (2009) 31: 609–26.
15. Rosenstone and Hansen. *Mobilization, Participation and Democracy in America.*
16. Mark Gray and Miki Caul, Declining voter turnout in advanced industrial democracies 1950–1997, *Comparative Political Studies* (2000) 33: 1091–122.
17. Russell Dalton, *Citizen Politics*. Washington, DC: CQ Press, 2008, ch. 4; Verba, Schlozman, and Brady, *Voice and Equality*, ch. 12.
18. André Blais, Turnout in elections. In Russell Dalton and Hans-Dieter Klingemann, eds, *The Oxford Handbook of Political Behavior*. Oxford: Oxford University Press, 2007. Blais's chapter is an up-to-date summary of the current literature on turnout.
19. Tatiana Kostadinova, Voter turnout dynamics in post-communist Europe, *European Journal of Political Research* (2003) 42: 741–59.
20. Russell Dalton and Mark Gray. Expanding the electoral marketplace. In Bruce Cain, Russell Dalton, and Susan Scarrow, eds, *Reforming Democracy: Institutional Change in Advanced Industrial Democracies*. Oxford: Oxford University Press, 2003.
21. Martin Wattenberg, The decline of party mobilization. In Russell Dalton and Martin Wattenberg, eds, *Parties without Partisans*. Oxford: Oxford University Press, 2000; Martin Wattenberg, *Is Voting for Young People?*, rev. edn. New York: Longman, 2008; Mark Franklin, *Voter Turnout and the Dynamics of Electoral Competition*. Cambridge: Cambridge University Press, 2004.
22. Kees Aarts and Bernhard Wessels, Electoral turnout. In Jacques Thomassen, ed., *The European Voter*. Oxford: Oxford University Press, 2005.
23. Jeffrey Karp and David Brockington, Social desirability and response validity: A comparative analysis of over-reporting voter turnout in five countries, *Journal of Politics* (2005) 67: 825–40; Brian Silver, Barbara Anderson, and Paul Abramson, Who overreports voting? *American Political Science Review* (1986) 80: 613–24.
24. Barry Burden, Voter turnout and the national election studies, *Political Analysis* (2000) 8: 389–98.
25. Canada shows one of the widest discrepancies between survey reported turnout and government turnout statistics. We attribute part of this difference to the methodology effects described in note 29 below.
26. These results are based on voting age population statistics from the International Institute for Democracy and Electoral Assistance (www.idea.int/vt).
27. Karp and Banducci, Party mobilization and political participation in new and old democracies.
28. In actuality, the stem question and the response options varied somewhat across nations as election teams adapted this question to their standard national format. We suspect this affects the level of campaign activity in some nations that had significantly "harder" or "softer" measures of participation. For full question wording see the CSES codebook (www.cses.org). We use the 2002 Portuguese timepoint because it had full data on all three participation items; and the 2004 Taiwanese survey because the 2001 survey had an anomalous result for one variable. The New

Zealand question on trying to persuade others was miscoded in the final CSES release, and this was corrected in our datafile.

29. Personal communications with the principal investigator of the Canadian surveys suggest that the high levels of campaign activity in the CSES may be partially due to the panel survey design of the Canadian study and the use of a mailback interview for the CSES module. Both factors can produce a more politically interested set of respondents. Some effects of sampling design are apparent for other nations that used panels or mailback questionnaires. These factors might affect individual nations, but we expect such method effects do not have the same impact on the correlation analyses within nations.

30. Blais, Turnout in elections; Kittilson and Anderson, Electoral supply and voter turnout.

31. The exact wording of the question and response options varied in some nations. See the CSES codebook.

32. Marsh, None of that post-modern stuff around here.

33. Karp and Banducci, The influence of party and electoral systems on campaign engagement.

34. Russell Dalton, Left–Right orientations, context, and voting choices. In Russell Dalton and Christopher Anderson, eds, *Citizens, Context and Choice*. Oxford: Oxford University Press, 2011.

35. M. Laakso and Rein Taagepera, The effective number of parliamentary parties: A measure with application to Western Europe, *Comparative Political Studies* (1979) 12: 3–27.

36. It could be argued that constituency marginality is a more reliable indicator of a voter's incentive to turn out, but that was not available for all of the countries in the analysis.

37. Karp and Banducci, The influence of party and electoral systems on campaign engagement.

38. Karp and Banducci, The influence of party and electoral systems on campaign engagement, p. 67.

39. Kittilson and Anderson, Electoral supply and voter turnout.

40. There is a positive individual-level correlation between these two-variables in every nation, but it ranges from a weak .04 in Australia to .35 in Finland and .38 in Bulgaria. This suggests that contextual factors influence the impact of contacting.

41. Russell Dalton, The quantity and quality of party systems, *Comparative Political Studies* (2008) 41: 899–920.

42. Only one country in the sample had a presidential election only (France); the others coded as having a presidential election are based on a presidential and a legislative election being held simultaneously or in close proximity. The measure may therefore be picking up the heightened activity surrounding the occurrence of two elections held together, rather than suggesting that a presidential election produces more campaign activity compared with a legislative election.

43. Karp and Banducci, The influence of party and electoral systems on campaign engagement.

44. See Wattenberg, *Is Voting for Young People?*

II. Electoral Choice

4

Citizens and their Policy Preferences

Once people decide to cast a vote in an election, as discussed in Chapter 3, they often confront a challenging task. In many parliamentary systems, voters face a wide choice of parties. Each party offers its own view of political reality, and its proposals for the future. In the French parliamentary election of 2007, for instance, thirteen parties won at least a quarter million votes in the first tour, and twelve won at least one seat in the National Assembly. Conservative voters could select between four parties that comprised the conservative presidential majority, plus the right-wing National Front. Leftist voters also faced a handful of parties that claimed to represent their views. Friends, family, the media, and other pundits weighed in on the merits of each party. Moreover, each party takes positions on a wide range of issues, and judging each party's policy intent is a challenging task—even for political experts. In short, the simple act of voting is not such a simple decision in many cases. However, the party linkage model presumes that voters can find expression for their policy preferences in the choice of available parties, and vote for a party that represents their views.

This chapter begins a section of three chapters that examine the linkage between voters' preferences and their party choices in elections. We argue that broad political orientations, such as Liberal–Conservative or Left–Right, and the issue positions they reflect, should be a major basis of citizens' voting choices and the origins of the electoral linkage if elections serve as an effective means of democratic influence. Elections should provide opportunities for citizens to address contemporary political problems.

The party linkage model makes three basic presumptions about citizens and their voting choices, which are described in the voting behavior literature:[1]

- People have informed political preferences and policy choices.
- They make judgments about which party best represents these preferences.
- These perceptions guide voting behavior.

Without such content and a programmatic structure, elections could become ephemeral expressions of opinions or habitual expressions of group loyalties, rather than instrumental acts of governance. The scholarly literature debates intensely the ability of contemporary electorates to fulfill these three criteria, and the three chapters in this section take up each of these points in turn.

This chapter describes the broad political orientations of contemporary publics as represented by the Left–Right scale. We treat the Left–Right dimension as summarizing citizens' and parties' positions on the issues of the day, accepting that the terms Left and Right can have different meanings for different political actors as well as change over time. The Left–Right dimension thus provides the framework for our model of electoral linkage as described in Chapter 1.

We first discuss the concept of policy voting and the use of the Left–Right framework to capture this process. Then we examine whether most voters can position themselves on the Left–Right scale, and how they are distributed along this continuum in the CSES nations. We next consider the bases of these orientations in terms of social structure, political issues, and partisanship. The results provide a foundation for using Left–Right congruence to measure the workings of the party linkage model through the electoral process.

Elections as Policy Choices

If elections are to be meaningful guides to democratic government, there must be substantial policy content to electoral choices. Elections should provide a means for citizens to express their policy preferences, and to seek representation for these views within the democratic process. For example, in the 1998 German Bundestag elections Gerhard Schröder encouraged voters to judge him on his government's policy performance if he won the election; and they should have followed this directive in 2002. Similarly, in the 2009 elections Germans should have evaluated the policy positions and performance of the Merkel-led government since 2005, and what Merkel and her rivals offered for the future.

In contrast, a considerable literature argues that a large proportion of the public lacks the ability or motivation to make informed electoral choices. Some researchers stress the limited political sophistication and knowledge of many citizens.[2] Another critique emphasizes the non-policy bases of electoral choice, noting that some voters cast their ballot based on the personal idiosyncrasies, habitual partisan loyalties, or even the attractiveness of candidates.[3] Other research suggests that elections have decreasing policy content as parties have become less programmatic and predictable in their policy positions. Thus, the degree of policy voting is an important step in our party linkage model. If citizens' voting choices lack a meaningful political content, then the party government linkage ends at this point.

A large and rich literature examines the impact of issue voting in specific nations or in specific elections.[4] Contemporary issue voting in the established democracies often involves long-standing economic or religious cleavages and the issues derived from these cleavages. Downward economic cycles inevitably generate concerns about the economic role of government and individual economic security. Similarly, events stimulate policy controversies, such as the recent debate over immigration in several Western democracies. Contemporary democracies are also grappling with new foreign policy issues: the post-Cold War international system, the global economy, the threat of Jihadist terrorism, and new international conflicts throughout the world. Concerns about nuclear energy, gender equality, and environmental protection have entered the political agenda in recent decades. Until fairly recently, politicians and voters did not even know that problems of global warming and ozone depletion existed.

Faced with a variety of issues across elections and nations, it is difficult to systematically and meaningfully compare the impact of specific issues on voting choices cross-nationally. Indeed, the salient issues should change across time and space since they represent a dynamic element of elections. One cannot simply draw up a set of common issues and include them in a cross-national survey because no list is sufficiently detailed to include all the possible themes of debate, and the themes even change in the midst of campaigns.[5] With partial or incomplete coverage of the issues of the campaign, estimates on the overall level and content of issue voting will be biased in unknown ways. Yet, our goal is to compare the level of policy-based voting across nations, and identify the factors that systematically affect these correlates of voting.

This project assesses the impact of political preferences on voting behavior by examining the relationship between Left–Right attitudes and vote. Left–Right terminology is common in elite discourse; it is frequently heard in press descriptions of parties and candidates. Experts (and candidates) claim that one party is too liberal on a certain political issue, or another party is becoming less conservative. Electoral scholars routinely interpret shifts in party vote shares as reflecting this dynamic; a party gained votes by moving closer to the public, or lost votes for moving away from its electoral base.[6] In media and academic analyses of elections, at the least, the Left–Right dimension is a shorthand for summarizing issues, party positions, and the dynamics of electoral choice.

Nevertheless, many public opinion researchers have questioned whether ordinary people understand and utilize abstract political concepts like "Left" and "Right." *The American Voter* argued that few individuals in the 1950s understood the meaning of the terms; only half received a passing score in their recognition of "Liberal" and "Conservative."[7] Moreover, only 11 percent of the American public actively used the Liberal–Conservative framework in describing the good and bad points of the parties and the candidates. When this latter measure was repeated in 2000, still only 20 percent of the public were rated as ideologues.[8] Similarly, when surveys first asked voters to place themselves on the Left–Right scale in British election studies in the 1960s, a full 60 percent of respondents did not recognize the terms as they apply to politics.[9] These researchers claimed that most people do not organize their political orientations according to broad, abstract standards derived from a political ideology.

Ideological liberal–conservative thinking as meant by political theorists is largely confined to a small sophisticated stratum of the public. Moreover, these arguments about the public's limited ideological thinking were based on established democracies with affluent, educated publics and an active free press. Given the range of nations included in the Comparative Study of Electoral Systems project, we might expect even shallower belief systems in new democracies where electoral competition and political parties are still developing.

A contrasting research literature offers a more positive perspective on the use of the Left–Right dimension among contemporary publics. This approach accepts that most citizens do not have a sophisticated philosophical understanding of ideological concepts such as socialism or liberalism that are traditionally embedded in the terms Left and Right. Instead, the Left–Right framework provides a *political heuristic* that helps orient the individual to politics. Part of its value is that it simplifies choice by framing the options in terms of a dichotomy between Left and Right poles. Another part of its heuristic value is that it provides a general reference framework so people can discuss the broad course of government without being knowledgeable on each specific issue. In fact, such broad guidance of government is probably the most that elections can achieve. Anthony Downs, for example, viewed Left–Right labels as a way to reduce information costs, rather than as fully informed ideological orientations. As he explained, "With this short cut a voter can save himself the cost of being informed upon a wide range of issues."[10] Such broad orientations presumably shape issue opinions, evaluations of political events and political actors, and ultimately political choices—at least this is the logic underlying our party linkage model.

Contemporary public opinion research finds that most citizens can position themselves on a Left–Right scale, even in relatively new democracies. For instance, in the first wave of the Comparative Study of Electoral Systems, nearly four-fifths of all the respondents expressed a Left–Right position.[11] Evidence from an even larger and more diverse set of nations in the World Values Survey similarly found that a large majority in most nations can position themselves on the Left–Right scale.[12]

Left–Right orientations are important to the extent that they have a political content, although the nature of this content is also a source of debate which we discuss later in this chapter. Historically, the terms Left and Right were most commonly identified with contrasting positions on economic and social welfare issues.[13] A citizen who identified with the Left generally supported more extensive social services, a larger role of government in managing the economy, and ensuring the well-being of the working class. The Right was synonymous with smaller government, modest social programs, and the advocacy of middle-class economic interests.

Today, however, the Left–Right framework does not appear limited to traditional socioeconomic issues or even religiously linked social issues. A host of other issues have entered the political agenda, and been integrated into the Left–Right framework. For instance, a recent survey asked Germans to identify those issues that are associated more with "the Left" and those that are associated more with "the Right."[14] The term "Left" was most closely linked to voting rights for foreigners, support for more asylum-seekers, and limitations on German military participation in UN missions (limitations on social programs was fourth on this list). Germans described opposition to foreigners, a desire for more law and order, opposition to the environmental tax, and opposition to a shorter working week as Right issues (the issue of social programs was fifth on this list). This illustrates how Left–Right orientations can represent a range of very different issues for different individuals that can expand beyond traditional class or religious issues. To a German blue-collar worker, Left may still mean social welfare policies; to a young German college student it may mean environmental protection and multiculturalism.

Indeed, the Left–Right scale is valuable because of its inclusiveness. Even if the specific definitions of Left and Right vary across individuals and even nations, the simple structure of a general Left–Right scale can summarize the political positions of voters and other political actors.[15] Ronald Inglehart describes the scale as a sort of super-issue that represents the "major conflicts that are present in the political system."[16]

Much of this book relies upon the Left–Right dimension to estimate citizen, party, and government political positions. This allows us to examine the nature and efficacy of party linkage between citizens and voters as well as later stages of the linkage process. We acknowledge that this one-dimensional framework is an oversimplification of contemporary party competition. In almost every election, parties compete along different policy dimensions that often may have different absolute and relative positions on these dimensions.[17] And some issues appear to remain separate from the Left–Right framework, at least temporarily. To compress political analysis into a single Left–Right dimension is an oversimplification.

Nevertheless, even if the Left–Right dimension oversimplifies political reality, we believe the dimension provides a good approximation of the nature of party competition in contemporary democracies.[18] And if we accept that the meaning of these terms can vary across individuals and nations, then the Left–Right positions for each citizen represent the policy dimensions most salient to them. This allows us to compare citizen orientations across nations, their perceptions of the political parties on this same dimension, and thus the linkage between citizens and parties across democracies.

At the same time, if expressions of Left–Right orientations lack meaning for many individuals, this should limit the ability of these orientations to predict party choice. If citizens and parties have different conceptions of Left and Right, this should also limit the potential of elections to connect like-minded citizens and voters. If elections involve complex multidimensional spaces not fully captured by a single Left–Right dimension, this should decrease our ability to demonstrate party linkage. In short, if our analyses overestimate the validity of the Left–Right framework to citizens and parties, then this should limit our ability to find meaningful relationships at each stage of party linkage. Our reliance on the Left–Right scale therefore may yield a conservative estimate of the actual workings of the party linkage in electoral politics.

Measuring Citizens' Left–Right Positions

We begin our empirical analyses by determining whether people have a Left–Right orientation. The Comparative Study of Electoral Systems surveys asked respondents to position themselves along a Left–Right scale using the following commonly asked question:[19]

In politics people sometimes talk of left and right. Where would you place yourself on a scale from 0 to 10, where 0 means the left and 10 means the right?

0   1   2   3   4   5   6   7   8   9   10

A prime criterion for a meaningful party linkage model is that individuals have political orientations that enable them to position themselves on the Left–Right scale. Figure 4.1 shows the percentage of the public in each CSES module 2 nation who locate themselves on the scale. On average, almost 90 percent of the public in this diverse set of nations have a Left–Right position. This high level transcends old and new democracies, and nations of quite different heritages. For instance, more than 90 percent of Albanians, Czechs, Bulgarians, and Hungarians have a Left–Right self-location, even though these are relatively new party systems. The nations with low levels of Left–Right self-placements are also relatively mixed. The percentage of people placing themselves on the scale only drops below two-thirds in Slovenia and Taiwan.[20] Furthermore, the generally high levels of Left–Right self-placements in the CSES are consistent with evidence from the World Values Survey which asked the same question in many of these same nations.[21]

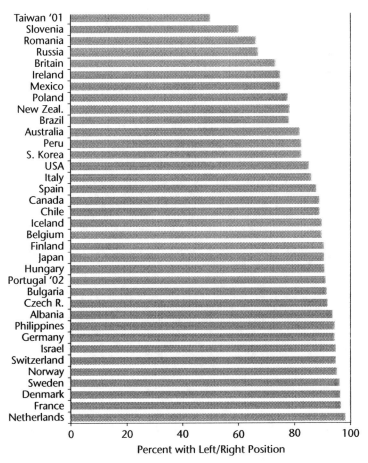

Figure 4.1. The Percentage of the Public Positioning Themselves on the Left–Right Scale

Source: CSES module 2.

Note: The figure displays the percentage of the public in each nation who position themselves on the Left–Right scale.

Relatively few people do not have a Left–Right position, but the possession of these orientations varies as one might expect. People with higher levels of education are more likely to position themselves on the scale, as are those who score highly on an index of political information.[22] Strong partisans are more likely to have a Left–Right position, because these orientations are often party-linked. Left–Right identities are predictably more common among those who actually voted in the previous elections. These patterns suggest that these orientations are linked to cognitive skills and political engagement. Nevertheless, even the majority of less sophisticated and less involved citizens can identify themselves in Left–Right terms.

The Distribution of Left–Right Positions

Most surveys find that people locate themselves along the Left–Right dimension in something like a bell curve, with most people in the center of the scale and the numbers trailing off to the Left and Right. Early theoretical writers, such as Downs and Sartori, argued that this was the common pattern, and it was confirmed in most empirical studies of the Left–Right dimension.

As a rough illustration of this pattern, Figure 4.2 summarizes the Left–Right positions of all those interviewed in the CSES module 2 nations in a pooled analysis. The figure has the rough shape of a bell curve, with the largest proportion of individuals located near the center of the scale. The median position is the center of the scale (5.0), although the average is slightly right of center (5.2). Some analysts claim that the center point is another way to

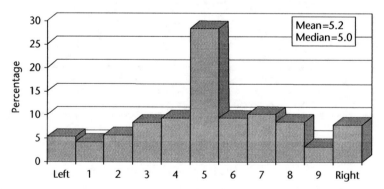

Figure 4.2. The Pooled Left–Right Position of Contemporary Publics

Source: CSES module 2.

Note: The figure displays the percentage of the public at each position of the Left–Right scale. All the CSES nations are weighted to have equal size, and the figure presents the pooled results.

express the lack of a Left–Right identity by selecting a position that is neither Left nor Right. This might be the case for some individuals, such as those who do not vote or follow politics. However, we expect that most of these individuals are as they say: centrists who hold a moderate position between Left and Right.

The combined Left–Right distribution in Figure 4.2 averages together different national patterns. In some nations, people display more consensus so the center of the distribution is more heavily populated. In other nations, orientations are more polarized, spreading out along the dimension. Or, Left–Right positions are not perfectly symmetrical; some publics lean Left and others lean Right.

Figure 4.3 shows the distribution of Left–Right orientations for each nation. The horizontal bars in the figure estimate the range of opinions that encompasses approximately two-thirds of the public. This shows whether citizens gravitate toward the center of the distribution or are spread out across the scale. The vertical hash mark on each bar shows the average score for all those who place themselves on the scale. The figure lists nations from those with the most leftist public to those with the most rightist.

Most people locate themselves near the center of the scale, and thus most national mean scores are close to the midpoint of the Left–Right scale. A diverse handful of nations fall outside of this range to the left: Spain, Germany, South Korea, Poland, the Czech Republic, and Hungary. And a few nations are distinctly more conservative: Romania, the United States, Russia, the Philippines, and Mexico.

We suspect these cross-national patterns reflect a mix of long-term political traditions, and the short-term effects of specific elections. One apparent generalization is almost tautological—nations with strong leftist traditions (France, Italy, and Spain) have electorates that lean toward the Left, and nations with strong rightist traditions lean to the Right. For instance, the CSES replicates the findings of other cross-national studies by locating the American public toward the Right end of the dimension. This presumably reflects the religious and individualist traditions of American politics, as well as the absence of a traditional socialist or social democratic party to mobilize the Left.

The heritage of post-communist nations is surprisingly diverse. Several of these nations—Poland, the Czech Republic, and Hungary—are skewed to the left, while another set tend toward the right end (Albania, Bulgaria, Romania, and Russia).[23] These latter nations have struggled to democratize, partially because of their more conservative, autocratic political cultures.

Short-term patterns are apparent in a case such as Korea, where comparisons over time suggest that President Moo-hyun Roh's policies and the parliament's attempted impeachment of him in 2003 dramatically polarized the party

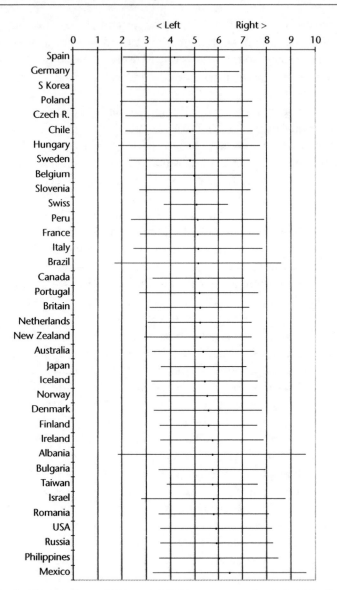

Figure 4.3. The Distribution of Citizens' Self-Placement on the Left–Right Scale

Source: CSES module 2.

Note: The length of the bars represents the range covered by approximately two-thirds of the respondents; the cross-hatch in the center of the bar displays the mean for the total public.

system, and shifted Korea's center of gravity to the Left. Similarly, the Czech and Peruvian publics moved significantly to the Left between the first and second CSES modules. In overall terms, however, the public's average Left–Right position is relatively stable over time, producing an enduring framework for political competition between elections. Frequent claims of dramatic shifts in public positions from election to election are not typically seen in overall Left–Right positions, because of the breadth of these orientations.

The other apparent difference across nations is the spread of the public along the Left–Right scale (that is, the length of the horizontal bar). In Switzerland, for instance, the spread is very small. Two-thirds of the Swiss are within 1.34 points of the mean—a bell-shaped curve with a tall bell. In contrast, the Albanian, Brazilian, and Mexican publics are much more widely dispersed so that the range of public opinions more resembles a block rather than a bell-shaped curve. Beyond these extremes, however, the range of Left–Right opinions tends to be fairly similar across nations. In most political systems, two-thirds of the public are within 2 scale points of the overall public mean score.

The ability of most citizens to locate themselves along a Left–Right dimension is a first indication of the validity of this scale as a framework for political competition. This provides a single metric that citizens, parties, and other political actors can use to locate themselves relative to each other. However, we also recognize that the content of these self-identities varies across nations, which we examine in the next section of this chapter.

What Shapes Left–Right Positions?

The Left–Right schema is normally considered as a short cut that people use to make decisions about the political parties and leaders they will support in an election. This occurs in much the same way as party identification acts as a means by which voters can reduce the amount of information they require in order to understand and interpret the political world.

What shapes a person's position on the Left–Right scale? And how closely is it related to party identification? This section examines the content of a voter's particular position on the scale from three perspectives. The first perspective is the degree to which Left–Right positions are systemically associated with social groups within a society. The second perspective connects citizens' Left–Right orientations to their positions on the issues of the day. The third perspective assesses the degree to which people align their Left–Right orientations with their party identity.

Our goal is to show that Left–Right attitudes are rooted in a society's existing political cleavages. We acknowledge that our analyses will be incomplete, because we lack evidence on all of the specific issues that might structure

Left–Right attitudes in each nation. In Taiwan, for instance, these orientations are presumably linked to positions on Taiwanese independence and relations with China, in Europe the European Union provides an additional dimension of cleavage, while in Mexico the issue of corruption and now the drug cartel are important. As we noted earlier, a fully specified definition of Left–Right would require such country-specific measures. However, we can illustrate broad cross-national patterns as evidence of the political content of these orientations.

Because the CSES does not include issue questions, we turn to the World Values Survey to compare the social structural and issue correlates of Left–Right cross-nationally. To increase the comparability with the CSES analyses, we examine the electoral democracies from the fifth wave of the World Values Survey that are also included in the CSES module 2.[24] These include both established and new democracies, from Europe, North America, Latin America, and Asia.

Social Structure

In principle, one's position in the social structure should influence where a person places themselves on the Left–Right scale. For instance, Seymour Martin Lipset's early cross-national study of electoral politics described the class cleavage as one of the most pervasive bases of party support: "Even though many parties renounce the principle of class conflict or loyalty, an analysis of their appeals and their support suggests that they do represent the interests of different classes. On a world scale, the principal generalization that can be made is that parties are primarily based on either the lower classes or the middle and upper classes."[25] Thus, a person's socioeconomic status reflects their social conditions and, as such, should determine their political preferences. While socioeconomic status was once measured simply by whether a person was employed in a manual or a non-manual occupation, the concept has become much more complex, reflecting not just occupation (itself now often measured across several dimensions encapsulating autonomy and skills, and authority in the workplace) but also human capital, such as education.

In practice, class interests have become much less important for political competition across a range of established democracies, encouraged by party convergence on class-based policies.[26] There is also evidence that class-based political conflict is much less structured in developing democracies which lack the long tradition of institutionalized class competition that formed West European party systems.[27] At the same time, the economic tensions in many developing nations are more intense and severe than in established Western democracies.

Another historically important part of social structure, particularly for many European societies, is religion. Religion defined a cleavage between different denominations or between religious and secular values. The religious cleavage generated issues such as state support for Church schools, adherence to traditional lifestyles, and endorsement of family values. Again, the impact of religious divisions in developing democracies is less predictable, often because these cleavages were not linked to political competition and because of the varied nature of religious traditions.[28] To broaden the potential relevance of this social cleavage, we use religious practice and religiosity to represent a religious/secular divide.

Additional aspects of social structure are defined characteristics such as age and gender. Age may tap different meanings of Left and Right across generations, and thus a different self-location on the Left–Right scale. In addition, age can also reflect the impact of historical events that changed public values, especially in post-communist nations and other developing democracies. Gender can represent differences in life chances and socialization experiences, which influence Left–Right orientations. However, the direction of these effects in Left–Right terms can be ambiguous as the meaning of Left and Right varies. In Western democracies, for example, women historically favored conservative parties, and only in recent years have they voted disproportionately for leftist parties.[29]

We correlated these five social structure variables with Left–Right attitudes for all twenty-two nations from the 2005 World Values Survey (the variables are described in the chapter appendix). These social structure traits have a limited ability to predict a person's position on the Left–Right scale, as the first part of Table 4.1 shows. Left–Right position is most strongly related to the frequency of church attendance and feelings of religiosity. The two social status measures—occupation of the head of the household and family income—have a limited relationship with Left–Right positions in this pooled set of nations. Neither age nor gender has a substantial relationship with Left–Right position. Even including all six predictors in a multivariate model of Left–Right attitudes yields a modest Multiple R correlation (.17).

We also conducted these analyses separately for each nation (data not shown). Among individual countries, religion has its strongest correlations with Left–Right position in Poland (0.25), where Catholicism played a pivotal role in the downfall of communism, and in Finland (0.10).[30] Income is most important in predicting Left–Right position in the Scandinavian countries (Sweden, with a correlation of 0.18, and Finland, 0.19) where the economic cleavage has dominated electoral politics since the end of the nineteenth century. There is also a strong economic correlation in Bulgaria (.24). Notwithstanding these variations, we would have to conclude that the overall impact of social structure on Left–Right position is modest, at least for the twenty-two nations included in the analysis.

Table 4.1. Social Structure and Issue Correlates of Left–Right Self-Placement

Social Structure		Economic Attitudes		Environmental Attitudes		Cultural Attitudes	
Family income	.05	Need large income differences to encourage effort	.19	Protect environment at expense economic growth	.07	Gender equality index	.18
Head occupation	.03						
Church attendance	.14	Increase government ownership of business and industry	.10	Increase taxes to prevent environmental pollution	.06	Democracy vs. autocracy	.11
Religious person	.12			Would give part of income for environment	.04	National pride	.10
Gender	.02	People should provide for themselves	.16			Social tolerance	.10
Age	.05						
Multiple R	.17	Multiple R	.22	Multiple R	.09	Multiple R	.23

Source: Twenty-two democracies from the World Values Survey, 2005 (see Figure 4.4). Variables are described in chapter appendix.

Note: Figures are Pearson's r between the item in question and Left–Right self-placement, based on the countries listed in Figure 4.4. Mean correlations ignore signs. See appendix for question wordings.

Political Issues

The political issues that dominate day-to-day debate are likely more important than social structure in shaping Left–Right orientations because they explicitly tap policy interests. We examine issues in three areas—economic policy, environmental policy, and cultural issues—as examples of the possible content of Left–Right positions.

Anthony Downs originally saw Left–Right positions as representing the preferred degree of the government's intervention in the economy; the extreme Right seeking a free market with few restrictions on economic activity, and the extreme Left favoring complete government control of the economy.[31] Previous analyses of Left–Right attitudes have often found that economic conflicts are strongly related to citizen positions on this dimension, at least for the established democracies.[32]

More recently, a new set of cultural or postmaterial issues have developed in advanced industrial societies that stand outside of traditional economic policy debates.[33] These are illustrated in the earlier examples in this chapter of the Left–Right meaning of various issues for the German public, including issues of immigration, multiculturalism, and the quality of life. One of the most prominent examples of these new issues is environmental policy. While some Green groups explicitly claim they are neither Left nor Right, Green groups have increasingly become viewed as being on the Left, both by the parties and by voters.

A different set of political cleavages may exist in new democracies. Often the transition to democracy involves differences in regime orientations, between democratizing forces and those with attachments to the previous regime.[34] Daniel Bell has emphasized the importance of nationalism, ethnicity, pan-Arabism, and other ideological conflicts in the developing world.[35] Territorial disputes and conflicts over national identity, or political divisions based on race or ethnicity, could provide political content to the meaning of Left–Right position. Gender roles also reflect a conflict over traditional and modern values in many of these same nations. Consequently, research shows that variables such as national identity, support for democracy, and issues more relevant to developing democracies are more strongly related to Left–Right orientations in these nations.[36]

The World Values Survey (WVS) included a battery of questions intended to measure economic issues, environmental issues, and cultural issues (see chapter appendix). The three rightmost panels in Table 4.1 display the relationship between each set of issues and Left–Right orientations for all the WVS nations combined. As we would expect, economic attitudes—views about income inequality, the role of the state in providing welfare, and the role of government in business and industry—are significantly related to Left–Right positions in our pooled set of WVS democracies.

The second set of issues in Table 4.1 taps the potential environmental concerns. The three issues show modest correlations with Left–Right attitudes, significantly less than for the economic cleavage. However, we expect that these issues are more relevant in advanced industrial democracies, and thus are attenuated in these pooled analyses.

The third set of issues in Table 4.1 tap cultural conflicts. Gender equality, for instance, is nearly as strongly related to Left–Right positions as are economic attitudes. For the pooled set of nations, Left–Right position is modestly correlated with support for democracy, national pride, and social tolerance of different nationalities and religions. These cultural variables explain as much variation in Left–Right attitudes (r=.23) as do economic issues (r=.22).

There is, of course, substantial cross-national variation in the importance of these issue dimensions for Left–Right attitudes. Since economic and cultural dimensions display the largest correlations for the pooled set of nations, we focus on these two dimensions.[37] Figure 4.4 shows the Multiple R correlation by nation between these two sets of issues and Left–Right position. As prior research would suggest, the economic cleavage is strongly related to Left–Right positions in the class-based party systems of Scandinavia and in several other established democracies. For example, in Sweden, the Multiple R correlation between economic attitudes and Left–Right position is 0.63, twice the correlation for cultural values (and three times that for environmental attitudes). At the other end of the scale, the economic cleavage is less salient in the

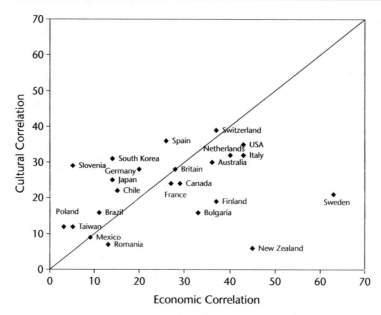

Figure 4.4. Correlation of Issue Dimensions with Left–Right Attitudes

Source: World Values Survey (2005).

Note: Figure entries are Multiple R correlations, omitting decimals, between issues from Table 4.1 and Left–Right self-placement, by country.

developing democracies. The five weakest economic correlations are in Poland, Slovenia, Taiwan, Mexico, and Brazil. To some extent this contrast is ironic because in the poorest nations where economic needs are greatest, economic issues are not strongly linked to Left–Right orientations. We attribute this to several factors. In contrast to many established democracies, public opinion is still fluid in many of these developing nations and the political parties lack the historic linkage to the class cleavage that underlies this orientation. In addition, lower education and income levels, as well as more limited access to political information, probably limit the political sophistication of publics in these new democracies, and thus the percentage who can articulate the basis of their Left–Right positions. Furthermore, many new democracies lack the history of social democratic activism that framed the class cleavage in Western Europe, and even the contemporary union movement in these nations often lacks the partisan linkages found in Western Europe.

We expected that cultural issues would be more relevant to Left–Right attitudes in developing democracies, and this expectation is partially confirmed. In relative terms, cultural variables tend to be more important in developing democracies, and thus generally lie above the 45-degree line representing equality of the two dimensions. Conversely, economic issues are more important in the established democracies which generally lie below the line. Yet many established democracies have relatively strong Left–Right polarization based on both economic and cultural dimensions: the United States, Switzerland, the Netherlands, Italy, and Australia. Indeed, debates over cultural values have often polarized contemporary politics in these nations, with subjects ranging from immigration to the changing role of women.

Figure 4.4 shows that Left–Right attitudes tend to be more grounded in issue positions in established advanced industrial democracies. In these countries, Left–Right has been used to describe political positions for an extended period, and voters have grown comfortable with using these terms. The developing nations with the weakest economic correlations also tend to have the weakest cultural correlations. As we noted earlier, it is difficult to have a full comparison of all the relevant issue dimensions in such broad cross-national comparisons, and it is possible that other country-specific issues display strong correlations with Left–Right attitudes when economic and cultural cleavages are weak. However, we expect that a visible, stable Left–Right cleavage is less common in developing democracies, and part of the development process is to institutionalize such political and partisan structures.

Still, the main point of these analyses is that Left–Right attitudes do display significant issue groundings even for the limited cross-national evidence available from the World Values Survey. As country-specific research demonstrates, adding items on current issue conflicts would predictably increase the relationships we have found.[38] This evidence points to the meaningfulness of citizen self-locations on the Left–Right scale.

Partisan Cues

A third perspective holds that Left–Right positions overlap with party attachments. Congruence can occur in multiple ways. A person might identify with a party through early life socialization or social group cues, and then position themselves to the Left or the Right accordingly as a summary of their political preferences. Or, their position on political issues and the Left–Right scale may lead them to support a party consistent with their position (see Chapters 5 and 6).

Previous research has found a strong congruence between Left–Right orientations and partisanship in the established democracies, and this logic should extend (perhaps in attenuated form) to developing democracies where party identities and Left–Right orientations are still evolving.[39] Left–Right orientation, like party identification, "is an efficient way to understand, order and store political information."[40] Partisanship can be a very useful short cut for citizens since voting involves party choice, although Left–Right attitudes may also exist separate from partisan ties. The personalization of politics may also make partisanship more easily associated with Left–Right position, since it is

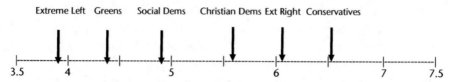

Figure 4.5. Left–Right Position of Public by Party Families

Note: Figure entries are the mean Left–Right scores of partisans grouped by party family. The scale runs from 1 (Left) to 10 (Right).

Source: World Values Survey, 2005.

often linked to the individual party leader, who is more easily understood and identifiable.[41]

Furthermore, most political parties describe themselves in Left–Right terms, thereby providing voters with important cues. The leftist tendencies of labor or socialist parties are easily apparent to voters, as are the rightist tendencies of conservative or Christian Democratic parties. However, Peter Mair noted that "a reasonably large group of parties seem happy to use the term 'left' in their titles, and although even more parties employ some version of the term 'center,' it is relatively difficult to find parties which are willing to use the term 'right.'"[42] Many of the parties that describe themselves as being on the right are actually found in Central and Eastern Europe, where the term implies a repudiation of the nation's communist past.

To illustrate the overlap between Left–Right positions and partisanship, we plotted the Left–Right means of citizens grouped by their partisan family among our subset of WVS nations (Figure 4.5). The figure shows a basic relationship between these two orientations. Supporters of communist, post-communist successor parties, or similar parties position themselves to the extreme left of the scale. At the other extreme, supporters of conservative parties, such as the British Conservative Party or the US Republican Party, position themselves a full point to the right of the scale's midpoint. Supporters of Green parties also locate themselves on the left, as do social democrats. Christian democrats are at about the midpoint of the scale, and right-wing parties, such as the French National Front and the Danish Progress Party, have supporters located between Christian Democrats and Conservatives.[43] Overall, there is a significant relationship between both orientations, but Left–Right attitudes are not identical with partisanship.

Multivariate Analysis

The social group and issue relationships in this section illustrate the varied content of Left–Right across nations, but the impact of these separate variables may overlap. This makes it difficult to identify the independent impact

Table 4.2. Predictors of Left–Right Position

	Demographics and Issues	Adding Party Families
Economic issues	.22*	.19*
Cultural issues	.17*	.15*
Demographic variables	.13*	.13*
Environmental issues	.00	.02
Social Democrat	—	−.09*
Conservative	—	.10*
Christian Democrat	—	.02
Green	—	−.04*
Extreme Left	—	−.06*
Extreme Right	—	.10*
Multiple R	.40	.45

Note: *significant at p < .01. Ordinary least squares regression analysis showing standardized (beta) regression coefficients predicting Left–Right position. See note 44 of this chapter on methodology.

Source: World Values Survey, 2005.

of each subset of variables, and their combined impact in structuring Left–Right attitudes. Therefore, to identify the broad bases of Left–Right positions cross-nationally, we conducted multivariate analyses. We first conducted a regression analysis separately for each nation using the six demographic variables in Table 4.1—and saved the predicted Left–Right attitudes based on these demographics. We repeated this procedure separately for economic issues, cultural issues, and environmental issues. This allowed the weight of the separate items to vary across nations, and yielded a summary index for each of the four sets of items.[44] For instance, the weight of the secular/religious variable may be greater in Poland with its sharp religious cleavage, while social class may have more weight in the Scandinavian nations. The weighted sum of demographic influences provides our cross-national measure of demography as a predictor. The same method was applied to the three issue indices.

The first column in Table 4.2 displays the results of predicting Left–Right positions with four measures: demographics, economic issues, environmental issues, and cultural issues. The results underscore the importance of the traditional economic cleavage as a basis of Left–Right self-locations (ß=.22), which is stronger than the other predictors. Cultural issues also have a large impact on Left–Right attitudes (ß=.17), and, surprisingly, demographics have an impact independent of issue positions (ß=.13). The only measure without a significant independent effect on Left–Right attitudes is the environmental issue index.

We have also shown that Left–Right attitudes are related to party preferences, although the causal direction of this relationship is ambiguous. On the one hand, party cues may shape Left–Right positions. If a voter supports the

German *Die Linke* (The Left) party, then we expect them to position themselves to the left on the Left–Right scale; similarly, a British Conservative should be located on the right. On the other hand, we expect that Left–Right orientations influence voting choice independently—we test the party linkage model in subsequent chapters. Consequently, we wanted to add partisanship to the multivariate model predicting Left–Right self-location, while admitting the uncertain causality of such a relationship.

To add party to the multivariate models, we recoded using the party family groupings from Figure 4.5. Party families give a label of "Social Democratic" or "Christian Democratic" to a party to illustrate its ideological position. We also use party families in Chapter 5 to compare the content of Left–Right for political parties.

The second model in Table 4.2 adds voters for six party families to our multivariate analysis.[45] All but one of these coefficients are statistically significant, but all are modest. In part, these modest coefficients reflect the diversity of party choices in each nation, with a wide variation in the partisan offerings and their alignment with party families. Because of this diversity, only a small minority are coded in any of these party families for the pooled set of WVS nations. Yet party preferences are independently related to Left–Right attitudes beyond the impact of issues, as the larger Multiple R and significant party coefficients in the second model demonstrate.

We can further illustrate the separation of Left–Right positions and party preferences using the CSES dataset which includes a question on party attachments (closeness to any party). About half the pooled sample say they are not close to any party. But even among this group of non-partisans, over 80 percent locate themselves on the Left–Right scale. In short, the possession of Left–Right attitudes and partisanship overlaps, but Left–Right attitudes are not merely partisanship with another label.

In answer to the question raised at the beginning of this section—what shapes Left–Right position?—partisanship is the strongest correlate, followed more distantly by economic attitudes, cultural attitudes (and presumably other issue positions), and demographic traits. Both in theory and in practice, this is much as we would expect. Party identification provides people with a means of interpreting the political world and helps them to choose a party in an election, in much the same way that Left–Right position provides a short cut to party choice. As we observed in the country differences, the established democracies display stronger relationships than their emerging democracy counterparts, emphasizing the importance of lifelong learning.

Citizens Left and Right

Gilbert and Sullivan once described the political orientations of the British public in the following terms:

> I often think it's comical how nature always does contrive,
> that every boy and every gal that's born into the world alive,
> is either a little Liberal or else a little Conservative.[46]

The refrain is from an opera criticizing British politics of the late 1800s. The reference to liberal and conservative orientations reflected Gilbert and Sullivan's view of the political divisions and orientations of the British public of the era—implying that liberal and conservative positions were commonplace among the public over a century ago.

This chapter has put Gilbert and Sullivan's presumption to an empirical test. We first determined what percentage of the public holds Left–Right attitudes in the nations included in the CSES survey. Contrary to the views of some skeptics, an overwhelming majority of the public locate themselves on the Left–Right dimension in most of the nations. The value of such identities is seen by the commonness of these orientations, even in the new democracies. For instance, in the relatively new democracies of Albania, the Czech Republic, Bulgaria, and Hungary, more than 90 percent of the public express a Left–Right self-location. These opinions are common both in systems with few parties and in those with many parties. We suspect the use of these terms in elite discourse affects the commonness of Left–Right self-locations in a nation: Britain, ironically, is one case among the established democracies where fewer individuals possess Left–Right attitudes. However, the cross-national breadth of these opinions suggests that Left–Right is a common metric in the political landscape of most democracies.

That people can express a Left–Right position still leaves open the question of whether these are meaningful responses or the ephemeral replies to a survey interviewer. Certainly many of these respondents lack the deep philosophical understanding of liberalism and conservativism that might be implicit in the Gilbert and Sullivan refrain—modern political scientists continue to debate this point. However, we have argued that these Left–Right positions represent a meaningful summary of where individuals stand on the issues of concern to them and the nation. The Left–Right dimension is a heuristic that citizens and elites use to summarize their overall political orientations.

The content of this heuristic varies over time and space and among individuals, but these are not ephemeral responses. It is difficult to fully describe the content of Left–Right attitudes cross-nationally with the available empirical evidence. However, we have demonstrated that economic and cultural attitudes are often strongly related to Left–Right self-locations, especially in established democracies with institutionalized party systems. Individual national surveys with a larger and more nation-specific set of issues typically find even stronger relationships between Left–Right attitudes and issue positions. We expect that most dimensional analyses of issue cleavages would find Left–Right attitudes as strongly correlated with the major dimensions of cleavage in a nation. Still, the Left–Right scale may underestimate the total policy concerns of the public. In addition, the single most important reference point appears to be party attachments, as party identities and Left–Right orientations naturally overlap. However, Left–Right attitudes are not simply partisanship by another name. These are overlapping political orientations, with some independence for each.

In summary, if we use Left–Right orientations as our metric, then we believe that most electoral systems fulfill the initial requirement of meaning electoral linkage: most people have meaningful political preferences. These opinions may vary in their clarity and content across individuals, but they exist for most citizens. However, stronger proof of the meaningfulness of opinions is whether they coexist with the other elements of the party linkage model, which require people to rely on these orientations in making electoral choices that continue the chain of party government.

Appendix

A4.1. World Values Survey Questions

Variable	Question wording	Coding
Left–Right Self-Placement	In politics people sometimes talk of left and right. Where would you place yourself on a scale from 0 to 10, where 0 means the left and 10 means the right?	0=Left to 10=Right
Family income	On this card is a scale of incomes on which 1 indicates the "lowest income decile" and 10 the "highest income decile" in your country. We would like to know in what group your household is. Please, specify the appropriate number, counting all wages, salaries, pensions and other incomes that come in.	1=lowest decile to 10= highest decile.
Head occupation	In which profession/occupation does he/she work (or did work)? If more than one job, the main job? What is/was his/her job there?	1 Employer/manager with 10 or more employees 2 Employer/manager with less than 10 employees 3 Professional worker lawyer, accountant, teacher, etc 4 Supervisory – office worker: supervises others 5 Non-manual – office worker: non-supervisory 6 Foreman and supervisor 7 Skilled manual worker 8 Semi-skilled manual worker

Church attendance	Apart from weddings and funerals, about how often do you attend religious services these days?	1 More than once a week 2 Once a week 3 Once a month 4 Only on special holy days 5 Once a year 6 Less often 7 Never, practically never
Age	Age	Coded in discrete years, 18+
Gender	Gender of respondent	1 = male, 2 = female
Party preference		Recoded into party family dummy variables

Economic Issues

Need large income differences	How would you place your views on this scale? 1 means you agree completely with the statement on the left; 10 means you agree completely with the statement on the right; and if your views fall somewhere in between, you can choose any number in between. Incomes should be made more equal . . . We need larger income differences as incentives for individual effort.	1 = Agree completely on equality 10 = Agree completely on need for incentives
Government ownership of business and industry	Private ownership of business and industry should be increased . . . Government ownership of business and industry should be increased.	1 = Agree completely on private ownership 10 = Agree completely on government ownership
People should provide for themselves	The government should take more responsibility to ensure that everyone is provided for . . . People should take more responsibility to provide for themselves.	1 = Agree completely on government responsibility 10 = Agree completely on individual responsibility

Environmental Issues

Protect environment over economic growth	Here are two statements people sometimes make when discussing the environment and economic growth. Which of them comes closer to your own point of view? Protecting the environment should be given priority, even if it causes slower economic growth and some loss of jobs. Economic growth and creating jobs should be the top priority, even if the environment suffers to some extent.	1 = priority to protecting the environment 2 = priority to the economy
Reduce income to prevent pollution	I would give part of my income if I were certain that the money would be used to prevent environmental pollution.	1 = strongly agree 2 = agree 3 = disagree 4 = strongly disagree
Increase taxes to prevent pollution	I would agree to an increase in taxes if the extra money were used to prevent environmental pollution.	1 = strongly agree 2 = agree 3 = disagree 4 = strongly disagree

Cultural Issues

Gender equality index	On the whole, men make better political leaders than women do. A university education is more important for a boy than for a girl. On the whole, men make better business executives than women do.	Factor scores computed for three questions

(continued)

A4.1. Continued

Variable	Question wording	Coding
Support democracy	Having a democratic political system is ... 1) very good to 4) very bad. Having a strong leader who does not have to bother with parliament and elections ... Having the army rule ...	Measures support for democracy versus either of the two autocratic alternatives: 3=democracy strongly preferred to - 3=autocracy strongly preferred
National pride	How proud are you to be [nationality]?	1=very proud 2=proud 3=not very proud 4=not at all proud
Social tolerance	Could you please mention any that you would not like to have as neighbors? —people of a different race —people of a different religion. Could you tell me for each whether you trust people from this group completely, somewhat, not very much or not at all? —people of another religion —people of another nationality.	Factor scores computed for these four questions.

Notes

1. Jacques Thomassen, Empirical research into political representation. In M. Kent Jennings and Thomas Mann, eds, *Elections at Home and Abroad*. Ann Arbor: University of Michigan Press, 1994; Paul Abramson, John Aldrich, and David Rohde, *Continuity and Change in the 2008 Elections*. Washington, DC: CQ Press, 2009, ch. 6; Roy Pierce, Mass-elite issue linkages and the responsible party model of representation. In Warren Miller et al., *Policy Representation in Western Democracies*. Oxford: Oxford University Press, 1999.

2. Philip Converse, The nature of belief systems in mass publics. In David Apter, ed., *Ideology and Discontent*. New York: Free Press, 1964; Michael Delli Carpini and Scott Keeter, *What Americans Know about Politics and Why it Matters*. New Haven, CT: Yale University Press, 1996.

3. Bryan Caplan, *The Myth of the Rational Voter: Why Democracies Choose Bad Policies*. Princeton, NJ: Princeton University Press, 2007; Donald Green, Bradley Palmquist, and Eric Schickler, *Partisan Hearts and Minds: Political Parties and the Social Identities of Voters*. New Haven, CT: Yale University Press, 2002; Thomas Poguntke and Paul Webb, eds, *The Presidentialization of Politics: A Comparative Study of Modern Democracies*. New York: Oxford University Press, 2005.

4. For example, Bernd Aardal and Pieter van Wijnen, Issue voting. In Jacques Thomassen, ed., *The European Voter*. Oxford: Oxford University Press, 2005; Paul Abramson, John Aldrich, and David Rohde, *Change and Continuity in the 2008 Elections*. Washington, DC: CQ Press, 2009; Harold Clarke, et al., *Performance Politics: The British*

Voter. New York: Cambridge University Press, 2008; Pieter van Wijnen, *Policy Voting in Advanced Industrial Democracies: The Case of the Netherlands 1971–1998*. Enschede: University of Twente, the Netherlands, 2001.

5. The CSES planning group discussed including an issue battery in the questionnaire for the third module. Several of the European researchers proposed a typical battery of questions about the welfare state, social-cultural issues, environmental quality, and cultural diversity. At this point, the member from Namibia said he could include these questions in his survey if the Europeans asked a question on elephants in theirs (What should be done to limit elephants from eating farmers' crops?). He said this issue was as relevant to Europe as the European questions on the welfare state were relevant to Namibia. In stark terms, this illustrates the complexity of issue comparisons across nations. CSES III did not include a standardized issue battery because of these considerations.

6. Michael McDonald and Ian Budge, *Elections, Parties, Democracy: Conferring the Median Mandate*. Oxford: Oxford University Press, 2005; Ian Budge, Party policy and ideology: Reversing the 1950s. In Geoffrey Evans and Pippa Norris, eds, *Critical Elections*. Newbury Park, CA: Sage, 1999.

7. Converse, The nature of belief systems in mass publics; Delli Carpini and Keeter, *What Americans Know about Politics and Why it Matters*.

8. Michael Lewis-Beck et al., *The American Voter Revisited*. Ann Arbor: University of Michigan Press, 2008, p. 279.

9. David Butler and Donald Stokes, *Political Change in Britain*. New York: Wiley, 1969.

10. Anthony Downs, *An Economic Theory of Democracy*. New York: Wiley, 1957, p. 98; also see Dieter Fuchs and Hans-Dieter Klingemann, The Left–Right schema. In M. Kent Jennings and Jan van Deth, eds, *Continuities in Political Action*. Berlin: de Gruyter, 1989; William Jacoby, Liberal-Conservative thinking in the American electorate. In Michael Delli Carpini, Leonie Huddy, and Robert Shapiro, eds, *Research in Micropolitics*. Greenwich, CT: JAI Press, 2002.

11. Martin Kroh, The ease of ideological voting: Voter sophistication and party system complexity. In Hans-Dieter Klingemann, ed., *The Comparative Study of Electoral Systems*. Oxford: Oxford University Press, 2009.

12. Russell Dalton, Social modernization and the end of ideology debate: Patterns of ideological polarization, *Japanese Journal of Political Science* (2006) 7: 1–22.

13. Ronald Inglehart, *Culture Shift in Advanced Industrial Society*. Princeton, NJ: Princeton University Press, 1990; Oddbjørn Knutsen, Left–Right party polarization among the mass publics. In H. Narud and T. Aalberg, eds, *Challenges to Representative Democracy*. Bergen: Fagbokforlaget, 1990; Hans-Dieter Klingemann, Political ideology. In Samuel Barnes, Max Kaase et al., *Political Action*. Beverly Hills, CA: Sage, 1979.

14. Elisabeth Noelle-Neumann and Renate Köcher, *Allensbacher Jahrbuch der Demoskopie 1998–2002*. Munich: K.G. Saur, 2002, p. 706.

15. Ronald Inglehart and Hans-Dieter Klingemann, Party identification, ideological preference and the Left–Right dimension among Western mass publics. In Ian Budge, Ivor Crewe, and Dennis Farlie, eds, *Party Identification and Beyond*. New York: Wiley, 1976; Inglehart, *Culture Shift in Advanced Industrial Society*; Dalton,

Social modernization and the end of ideology debate; Oddbjørn Knutsen, Left–Right materialist value orientations. In Jan van Deth and Elinor Scarbrough, eds, *The Impact of Values*. Oxford: Oxford University Press, 1995.

16. Inglehart, *Culture Shift in Advanced Industrial Societies*, p. 273.

17. Kenneth Benoit and Michael Laver, *Party Policy in Modern Democracies*. New York: Routledge, 2006; Russell Dalton, Economics, environmentalism and party alignments, *European Journal of Political Research* (2009) 48: 161–75.

18. Gary Cox, Centripetal and centrifugal incentives in electoral systems, *American Journal of Political Science* (1990) 34: 903–35; Knutsen, Left-right party polarization among the mass publics. Thomassen goes one step further and argues that contemporary party competition in advanced industrial democracies is becoming more unidimensional which makes the Left–Right framework even more valid: Jacques Thomassen, Empirical research into political representation. In M. Kent Jennings and Thomas Mann, eds, *Elections at Home and Abroad*. Ann Arbor: University of Michigan Press, 1994.

19. The Japanese and Taiwanese surveys used a Progressive/Conservatives scale as an equivalent to Left–Right. We corrected coding errors in the Chilean Left–Right variables in the CSES release of module 2. There are two German surveys, and we use the telephone sample as more representative.

20. However, in the 1995 and 2005 World Values Survey over 90 percent of the Taiwanese respondents positioned themselves on the Left–Right scale.

21. Dalton, Social modernization and the end of ideology debate. Nineteen nations were included in module 2 of CSES and the fifth wave of the World Values Study. On average, 89 percent of these publics positioned themselves on the Left–Right scale in the CSES, and 85 percent in the WVS.

22. Using module II of the CSES, locating oneself on the Left–Right scale is correlated with education (tau-b=.20), and political knowledge (tau-b=.15). The correlation with turnout in the election is .13. For complementary analyses based on the World Values Survey see Willy Jou, The Left–Right schema among contemporary electorates, PhD Thesis, University of California, Irvine, 2011.

23. For a more extensive discussion of South Korea and the other East Asian nations see Russell Dalton and Aiji Tanaka, The patterns of party alignment in East Asia. *Journal of East Asian Studies* (2007) 7: 203–23.

24. These analyses are based on democracies included in the fifth wave of the World Values Survey. The list of nations is presented in Figure 4.4.

25. Seymour Martin Lipset, *Political Man: The Social Bases of Politics*. Baltimore: Johns Hopkins University Press, 1981, p. 230.

26. See Oddbjørn Knutsen, *Class Voting in Western Europe: A Comparative Longitudinal Study*. Latham, MD: Lexington Books, 2006; Terry Nichols Clark, Seymour Martin Lipset, and Michael Rempel, The declining political significance of class. *International Sociology* (1993) 8: 291–316.

27. Russell Dalton, Ideology, partisanship and democratic development. In Larry LeDuc, Richard Niemi, and Pippa Norris, eds, *Comparing Democracies 3*. Thousand Oaks, CA: Sage Publications, 2009; Ian McAllister, Social structure and party support in the East Asian democracies, *Journal of East Asian Studies* (2007) 7: 225–49; Andre

Freire, Bringing social identities back in: The social anchors of Left–Right orientations in Western Europe, *International Political Science Review* (2006) 27: 359–78.

28. See Dalton, Ideology, partisanship and democratic development and Pippa Norris and Ronald Inglehart, *Sacred and Secular: Religion and Politics Worldwide*. New York: Cambridge University Press, 2004.

29. Ronald Inglehart and Pippa Norris, *A Rising Tide: Gender Equality and Cultural Change around the World*. New York: Cambridge University Press, 2003; Donley Studlar, Ian McAllister, and Bernadette. Hayes, Explaining the gender gap in voting: A cross-national analysis. *Social Science Quarterly* (1998) 79: 779–98.

30. See Sabrina Ramet, *Whose Democracy? Nationalism, Religion, and the Doctrine of Collective Rights in Post-1989 Eastern Europe*. Lanham, MD: Rowman & Littlefield, 1997.

31. Downs, *An Economic Theory of Democracy*.

32. Fuchs and Klingemann, The Left–Right schema; Oddbjørn Knutsen, Value orientations, political conflicts and Left–Right identification: A comparative study, *European Journal of Political Research* (1995) 28: 63–93; Dalton, Social modernization and the end of ideology debate.

33. Inglehart, *Culture Shift in Advanced Industrial Societies*; Knutsen, Value orientations, political conflicts and Left–Right identification; Russell Dalton, Economics, environmentalism and party alignments.

34. Herbert Kitschelt et al., *Post-Communist Party Systems: Competition, Representation, and Inter-Party Cooperation*. New York: Cambridge University Press, 1999; Hubert Tworzecki, *Learning to Choose: Electoral Politics in East–Central Europe*. Stanford: Stanford University Press, 2003.

35. Daniel Bell, The resumption of history in the new century. In Daniel Bell, *The End of Ideology*, rev. edn. Cambridge, MA: Harvard University Press, 2000.

36. Dalton, Social modernization and the end of ideology debate; Aie-Rie Lee, Value cleavages, issues and partisanship in East Asia, *Journal of East Asia Studies* (2007) 7: 177–84; Inglehart and Norris, *A Rising Tide*. Also Jou, *The Left–Right schema among contemporary electorates*.

37. On environmental attitudes, the strongest associations are seen in the developed democracies such as Australia, New Zealand, and Sweden, where strong Green parties have emerged; the association is weakest in the new democracies of Eastern and Central Europe, such as Bulgaria and Romania.

38. Oddbjørn Knutsen, Left–Right party polarization among the mass publics; Knutsen, Value orientations, political conflicts and Left–Right identification; Fuchs and Klingemann, The Left–Right schema; Liesbet Hooghe, Gary Marks, and Carole Wilson, Does Left/Right structure party positions on European integration? *Comparative Political Studies* (2002) 35: 965–89. Also see sources in note 4.

39. See Inglehart and Klingemann, Party identification, ideological preference; Butler and Stokes, *Political Change in Britain*.

40. See Inglehart and Klingemann, Party identification, ideological preference, p. 245.

41. Ian McAllister, The personalization of politics. In Russell Dalton and Hans-Dieter Klingemann, eds, *The Oxford Handbook of Political Behavior*. Oxford: Oxford University Press, 2007.

42. Mair, Left-Right orientations, p. 208. Peter Mair, 'Left-Right Orientations.' In Russell J. Dalton and and Hans-Dieter Klingemann, eds, *The Oxford Handbook of Political Behavior*. Oxford: Oxford University Press, 2007, p. 208.

43. The somewhat moderate position for these partisans might be because the parties are defined by their extreme stance on a few high-profile issues, such as immigration and multiculturalism, but the overall policy views of their supporters are more mixed. However, the locations of party families from the CSES show a clearer Left–Right differentiation of these parties; see Chapter 5.

44. In statistical terms, we included each subset of predictors in a multiple regression analysis separately for each nation and saved the predicted Left–Right scores. This allows the weight of each variable to vary across nations, and each set of variables yields predicted scores. The predicted Left–Right scores then became the independent variables in the models in Table 4.2. Some nations do not have full information on one or the other subsets, so to maximize information we used pairwise deletion for the models in Table 4.2.

45. We used the question of current voting preference. The coding of party families is taken from the CSES macro-datasets, with additional coding provided by the authors.

46. This is from the "Sentry's Song" in *Iolanthe*. This observation about the public is then followed by a criticism that politicians blindly follow ideological and partisan cues: "When in that House M.P's divide, If they've a brain and cerebellum too, They've got to leave that brain outside, And vote just as their leaders tell 'em to." See William S. Gilbert, Sir Arthur Sullivan, *The Works of Sir William Gilbert and Sir Arthur Sullivan*. New York: Kessinger, 2005, p. 101.

5

Party Images and Party Linkage

The American Voter Revisited described how different voters think about the candidates and the parties in the 2000 US presidential election.[1] When asked about the political parties, one voter said:

> (*Likes about the Democrats*): Lots of things. They are trying to help middle class families. They want to do some things that will make us a better America. We need government and people together to make it work.
>
> (*Dislikes about the Democrats*): Sometimes they get a little carried away, and they need to be reined in. It would help if they were just a little more conservative in their views and programs.
>
> (*Likes about the Republicans*): Sometimes I like the fact that they are a little conservative. Still, I don't really agree with them on most issues.
>
> (*Dislikes about the Republicans*): They don't have a clue about what America is all about. All they think about is themselves.

Although most people are not as articulate as this individual in expressing their likes and dislikes about political parties, they do have opinions about the issues that are important to them—and views about the parties' positions on these issues. The party linkage model should provide a method for citizens to find an expression for their views through a political party that shares their preferences, which then transmits their preferences into the policymaking process.

Therefore this chapter examines the second presumption of the policy-voting theory (see Chapter 4): that citizens are able to judge the positions of the political parties relative to their own policy preferences. We begin by asking whether most people can locate the major political parties on the Left–Right continuum. Then we assess whether citizen perceptions are reasonable estimates of party positions by comparing our findings with those of other party research projects.

Placing Parties on the Left–Right Scale

If one's Left–Right position summarizes what a person wants from politics, then the second step in the party linkage process is to find a party or politician who represents these views. In other words, just as a consumer looks for the closest store that meets their needs when they are making a purchase, so people look for a party that is nearest to their political position when they are deciding on their vote. In the political case, however, distances are not measured in miles but in issue or ideological terms—much as the individual expressed nearness or distance to the Democratic and Republican Parties at the beginning of this chapter.

The party linkage model thus assumes that people can reasonably recognize the parties' positions using the Left–Right scale in order to know which party shares their position. As we discussed in Chapter 4, some researchers question the meaningfulness of the public's own understanding of Left–Right terminology, and there are even more doubts about the public's ability to accurately recognize the political parties' positions. Many people have only a limited interest in political matters, so their knowledge of even the major parties and candidates is modest. A substantial minority of the public does not follow politics and remains uniformed on the pressing issues of the day. In addition, political parties (and even individual campaign organizations) are complex entities, and it can be difficult even for well-informed citizens to summarize a party's policy views in terms of a single Left–Right position. As in the example at the beginning of the chapter, people can view a party as more moderate on one issue, and too conservative (or liberal) on another. Doing the math to summarize these policy positions could be a daunting task. Unless voters can make such judgments, however, the workings of party linkage through the Left–Right scale are largely moot.

Previous research yields mixed results on the ability of contemporary publics to correctly identify the positions of political parties. For instance, Abramson, Aldrich, and Rhode showed that about three-quarters of the US public could position the two presidential candidates on a variety of issue scales in 2004,[2] but barely half correctly identified Kerry as more liberal than Bush. Wouter van der Burg found that the public's Left–Right perceptions of the major Dutch political parties were reasonable and relatively stable over the 1974–1994 time span, and attributes this to the parties' adherence to core ideologies.[3] Similarly, the Swedish public has held fairly consistent views of the parties' Left–Right orientations, and has reacted when a party noticeably shifts its political orientation.[4] British citizens also recognized the Labour Party's shift to the center under Tony Blair's New Labour campaign.[5] There is thus considerable evidence that citizens as a whole can reasonably describe the broad Left–Right orientations of political parties.

In contrast, several early representation studies found that the Left–Right positions of party elites differed systematically from the perceptions of the public.[6] Other research has questioned the consistency of citizen and elite perceptions of political phenomena.[7] At issue, in part, is the question of how to measure the accuracy of public perceptions of parties.

Locating the Parties

To determine citizen perceptions of the political parties' broad political orientations, the CSES asked respondents to place the major parties on the same Left–Right scale as that used in Chapter 4. The project guidelines called for the surveys to ask for the locations of up to six parties, or more if there were additional significant parties. The number of parties evaluated differs across nations, ranging from three parties in the United States to nine parties in France and the Netherlands.

To describe people's general awareness of parties' Left–Right positions, we compare the percentage who give a Left–Right location for the two largest parties in each nation. This comparison of the two largest political parties partially adjusts for the differences in the number of parties across nations. For instance, it is presumably easier for Americans to place their two large established parties than for the French to position all nine parties evaluated in the survey. This focus on two parties is still only an approximation of public awareness across different party systems. In nations with a large number of parties, the two largest parties will represent a smaller proportion of the overall electorate, which may make identification more difficult. In addition, in a highly diverse system the public may not feel the need to follow all the parties closely, only those in the range of their likely choice set. For example, a German leftist may pay more attention to the positions of the Linke, Greens, and Social Democrats (SPD), than to the position of the Christian Democrats (CDU) and Free Democrats (FDP).

Figure 5.1 displays the percentage of the public in each nation who can position the two largest parties on the Left–Right scale.[8] Across this wide range of old and new democracies, a relatively high percentage can position these two parties (82 percent). Taiwan is a clear outlier where only a minority use the Left–Right scale for themselves or the parties. However, in the next lowest case, Romania, two-thirds of Romanians can locate the two largest parties on the scale. Even in multiparty systems, a strikingly large percentage of the public can position some of the minor parties. For instance, the Dutch survey asked people to position nine parties; most people can locate the three smallest parties in this set: D66 (96 percent), Christian Union (89 percent), and the Political Reformed

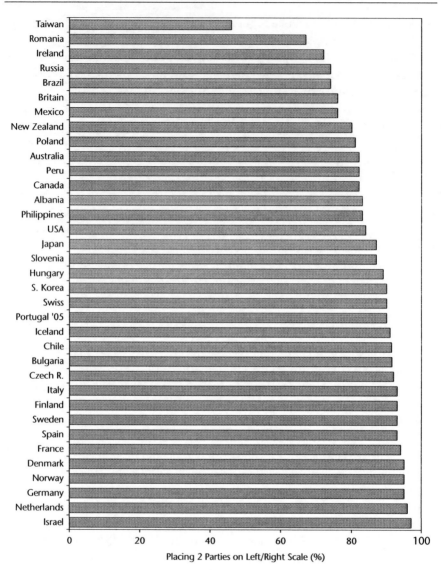

Figure 5.1. Positioning the Two Largest Parties on the Left–Right Scale
Source: CSES module 2.
Note: The figure displays the percentage of the public in each nation who can position both of the two largest parties on the Left–Right scale.

Party (87 percent). Similarly, most of the French public can position the Greens (95 percent), the Liberal Democracy (84 percent), and the Communist Party (PCF) (95 percent), even though each of these parties garnered less than 5 percent of the vote in the 2002 legislative elections. And if we exclude non-voters, the percentage who can locate the parties generally increases.

Party Positions

When people can locate the parties along the Left–Right scale, this provides a basic structure for political competition, as Downs and other spatial modelers have described. A few examples can illustrate how these perceptions define the party space. (The party positions for each nation are listed in the chapter appendix.) Figure 5.2 presents the public's perceptions of the political parties in Britain and Sweden. Each party's position is determined by *the entire public's average placement of the party on the Left–Right scale.* We present party positions in CSES module 1 (below the line in each panel) and the module 2 results (above the line). The black arrows in the figure denote the public's average self-placement. The size of the arrow for each party is roughly proportionate to its vote share in the election.

The top panel in Figure 5.2 displays perceptions of the British parties in 1997 and again in 2005. In the 1997 survey Britons recognized the historic Left–Right alignment of the parties. People positioned Labour toward the left end of the scale, reflecting its ties to the labor unions and its advocacy for leftist economic and welfare policies. In contrast, the Conservative Party is located on the right of the political spectrum because of the party's policy positions during the Thatcher and Major governments. By the 2005 survey Britons viewed the Labour Party as very close to the center of the party

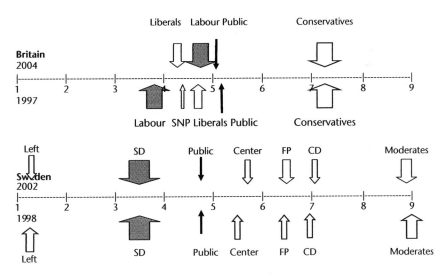

Figure 5.2. Citizen Placement of Parties on the Left–Right Scale in Britain and Sweden

Source: CSES modules 1 and 2.

Note: Figure entries are the entire public's mean placements of the political parties and the public's mean self-placements on the Left–Right scale. The major governing party after the election is noted by a shaded arrow.

spectrum, because of Blair's moderate "New Labour" policies and his support of the Iraq war. This is nearly a full point shift in the party's perceived position along the 0–10 Left–Right scale. At the same time, people saw the Liberal Democratic Party as moving to the Left, presumably because of its strong opposition to the Iraq war and its advocacy of environmentalism and other leftist causes. These programmatic shifts in party positions are commonly cited as an explanation for Labour's victories in 1997, 2001, and 2005—and the British public clearly perceived these shifts.[9]

The lower panel of Figure 5.2 displays Swedish perceptions of the parties in the 1998 and 2002 elections. The Swedish party system is more typical of multiparty systems where a large number of parties cover a wide range of the Left–Right scale. In 1998 the public saw a system polarized between the Left Party at one extreme and the Moderate Party at the other. With each of the six parties occupying its share of the political landscape, party positions appear relatively stable from 1998 to 2002.

These are two examples of the Downsian logic embedded in the party linkage model described in Chapter 1. Prospective voters survey the party landscape to determine which parties broadly represent their policy preferences as summarized in their Left–Right position. The nearest party or parties should garner greater support from citizens who vote on such policy-based terms—although we recognize that other factors, such as candidate image and other dimensions of party evaluation, are also part of the electoral calculus. For instance, a British leftist should be more likely to support the Labour Party in 1997, but the Liberal Democrats should garner an increased share of the leftist vote in 2005. Or, Swedish conservatives have four rightist parties that compete for their support, and therefore their vote should be split between these parties. This linkage between voters and party perceptions is the focus of Chapter 6.

Of course, a number of caveats apply to the spatial comparisons of Figure 5.2. As we noted in Chapter 4, there are good reasons to question whether contemporary party competition can be summarized by a simple one-dimensional space. Other research demonstrates that the Left–Right ordering of parties can vary by the nature of the policy controversy.[10] The parties perceived Left–Right order on social welfare policies can differ from party rankings on environmental or social-moral policies. Other research on European parties argues that the European Union and issues of globalization have produced cross-cutting policy dimensions.[11] A one-dimensional Left–Right scale oversimplifies the complexity of party choice by merging different meanings of Left and Right into a single scale.

We also treat parties as located at a single point on the Left–Right dimension. In reality, people probably think of parties as occupying a range along the scale, since party positions differ across many issues and party leaders typically disagree on exactly which policy position to favor. This means that assessing the closest party may be an imprecise calculation. More fitting would be to accept that party ranges can overlap, so voters can choose meaningfully between multiple parties that share their own position. In practical terms, however, we want to identify the center of each range, so we use point estimates of Left–Right positions in our comparisons of parties and voters.

In addition, one might ask what is the correct basis of assessing a party's "true position" on the Left–Right scale. We rely on the entire electorate in Figure 5.2, but one might use the self-location of party identifiers or party voters to estimate party positions. These are reasonable alternatives that might yield significant differences in a few instances—often very intriguing cases such as the positioning of extremist parties. Our initial exploration of these alternatives showed high consistency in party locations across these alternative methods. For instance, we compared the Left–Right placement of 115 parties in CSES module 2 for both the public at large and those who voted (or partisans) for each party; the two measures are very strongly correlated (.95).[12] In summary, despite the ongoing debates about the public's understanding and meaning of the Left–Right framework, the citizenry as a whole can describe the political parties in their nation in Left–Right terms.

Verisimilitude

Most people in most CSES nations can attribute a Left–Right position to themselves and to the major parties competing in elections. Yet the question of *verisimilitude* remains. To what extent can we consider public perceptions of the parties as an accurate assessment of the parties' political positions?

One answer is that these perceptions *are a reality* to the voters if they use them in making their electoral choices. However, there are several criticisms about the accuracy of these evaluations in more objective terms. Those who doubt the public's own ability to express their views in Left–Right terms would understandably question the public's ability to summarize political party positions. Public perceptions also can be manipulated in election campaigns, creating false choices. In addition, party images are sometimes a projection of the individual's own partisan biases rather than an objective judgment of party positions. Thus, before accepting the public's perceptions of party positions we should consider the general accuracy of these perceptions. But how?

Previous empirical studies have used three other methods to estimate party Left–Right positions:

Party Manifestos. The Comparative Manifestos Project (CMP) has systematically coded the issue content of party manifestos over the past several decades for a large set of established and new democracies.[13] In many electoral systems, manifestos are formal blueprints for party positions in the legislature, providing an authoritative source on a party's policy intentions. The CMP coded the salience of various issues in the party's electoral manifesto, and then combined these codes to construct a measure of each party's overall Left–Right position. This measure has the advantage in that it is based on the parties' official programs for each election, and there is an extensive time series for most of the CSES nations. No other data source has the historical breadth of the CMP.

The disadvantage of the CMP is that the salience of issues can be distinct from actual positions on these issues, and thus some critics have questioned whether the CMP measure of Left–Right is effectively measuring party positions.[14] There is also a potential gap between what a party states weeks or months before an election campaign, and the actual policy content of the election. Election campaigns do matter, and their content is not always equivalent to the presentation of the manifesto. The voter comments at the beginning of the chapter reflect the typical mix of impressions that voters use in making their decisions, with only indirect reference to the formal statements that might appear in the party platforms. In addition, the CMP Left–Right measure is invariant over time and nations, and thus is not sensitive to potential changes in the meaning of Left–Right over time and space.[15]

Expert Evaluations. An alternative method asks academic experts in each nation to position the parties along a Left–Right scale (and often other policy dimensions). This methodology has gradually expanded to a large set of nations and a larger range of policy issues.[16] The experts summarize the totality of the parties' position, including manifestos as well as the content of campaigns and the policy activities of the parties. Moreover, this methodology is flexible as the nature of the political debate changes; it allows the meaning of Left–Right to shift with the issue positions of the parties. At one time the economy may predominate, but the next year politics may revolve around social or non-economic matters. There are extremely high intercorrelations between party placements in various expert surveys.[17]

In contrast, skeptics of expert studies criticize the diffuse nature of these evaluations.[18] Neither the time frame nor the policy content of Left–Right is defined precisely, which allows different experts to apply the method in varying ways. It also appears that expert judgments are more stable over time because they average together a broad array of evidence, and thus may not reflect the specifics of an election with different issues taking center stage or party positions shifting during a campaign. Expert surveys, typically, are not linked to a specific election campaign. These problems can be magnified in cross-national comparisons where the content of elections is likely to vary even more widely. Because expert studies depend on a relatively small number of coders, the accuracy of results can be strongly influenced by a few outliers.

Elite Positions. The third option is to ask party elites to position themselves (or their party). Because elites are representatives of the party, and elected by the voters, one can make a strong claim that elite positions define the party identity. The collective views of the party elites can be treated as synonymous with the party as presented to the voters. Indeed, elite studies have been central to many previous studies of political representation.

Yet elite studies also have potential limitations. One difficulty is that large cross-national elite studies are rare, so elite data to match the CSES surveys are incomplete. In addition, the definition of elites can also vary. Should one define the party by all the members of the national legislature, some smaller group of senior party elites or cabinet officials, or by the chief executive? (Similarly, one could ask elites to position themselves, the party, or the party voters on the Left–Right scale, and each measure would reflect a different reality of the party.) Even if one could agree on the definition of elites, elite surveys have problems similar to the expert studies: neither the precise time frame nor policy content of Left–Right is predefined, allowing different elites to apply the method in different ways. Furthermore, elite surveys pose additional measurement problems since elites, typically, are less accessible and may not be forthright in responding to an interviewer.

Because of the importance of this topic, several recent studies have compared methodologies.[19] At one level, there is a basic consistency across methods. For instance, Kenneth Benoit and Michael Laver find a strong correlation for Left–Right party positions using the manifesto data and their most recent expert survey (Pearson r=.63).[20] We should expect such high congruence because the Left–Right terminology is so central to contemporary political debate. It is not very difficult to realize that communist (or reformed democratic socialists) are located at the left end of the Left–Right scale, and nationalist parties at the right end.

However, the degree of agreement is important in judging the strength of the party linkage between citizens and parties. Even the strong correlation between expert judgments and manifesto scores explains only 40 percent of the variance in party positions on the other indicator. Furthermore, most prior research has not included citizen perceptions as part of these comparisons. This is a critical omission because citizen perceptions are likely the most directly related to the choices citizens make in elections.

Therefore we want to systematically compare all four methods to determine the consistency of evaluations, and thus assess the accuracy of citizen perceptions:

- Citizens' perceptions of Left–Right party positions derived from the CSES.
- Left–Right scores from the Comparative Manifest Project for the same election as the CSES survey, or the election most proximate to the CSES

survey. A total of 144 parties overlap with the CSES set of parties. Most of these pairs are from West European or other advanced industrial democracies, but the CMP also includes democracies from East Europe and East Asia.

- Expert assessments of party positions are from the 2002–03 Benoit and Laver study. Twenty-seven nations are in both of these studies, yielding 168 party comparisons. These pairs are concentrated in Europe, with some additional advanced industrial democracies.
- Political elite data come from two coordinated elite studies in the European Union member states in the mid-1990s.[21] One survey interviewed candidates in the 1994 European Parliament elections (CEPs). A second survey interviewed members of the national parliaments (MNPs) for a smaller set of nations in 1996. Each survey asked elites to place themselves, their party's voters, and their national party on the Left–Right scale.[22] The MNP study is closest to our theoretical goal of measuring the location of each party in its respective nation, since the national legislative delegation is a central element of political parties.

As an introduction to our methodological comparisons, Figure 5.3 presents the Left–Right location of the major Swedish parties using citizen placements from the CSES, the Benoit and Laver expert survey, and the Comparative Manifesto Project Left–Right party positions.[23] The top two panels in Figure 5.3 show a basic consistency between public perceptions of the parties and the judgments of party experts—citizens are answering immediately after the 2002 election and experts are answering substantially after the 2002 election. However, there is a noticeable difference between the public and expert positions of the parties when compared to the manifesto coding for the 2002 election. The manifesto data produce a substantially different Left–Right ordering of the Liberal People's Party (FP), the Christian Democrats (CD), and the Center party (C). The CMP also positions the Green party to the far left of the scale, while experts locate the Greens closer to the center of the continuum. In addition, the manifesto data locate the Social Democrats further left than either the public or elites do.

Figure 5.4 presents the Left–Right location of the major Swedish parties using the citizen placements from the CSES and the MNP and CEP elite surveys. We see a striking similarity in the ordering of parties and their locations on the Left–Right scale, even though the surveys span different elections (citizens in the 1998 Riksdag election, MNPs interviewed in 1996, and candidates from the 1994 European Parliament election). For example, the Social Democrats (SD) are positioned at 3.5 by the Swedish public, 3.8 by SD members of the Riksdag, and 3.6 by SD candidates for the European Parliament. The reasonable variability in defining the "true" party position can be seen in the

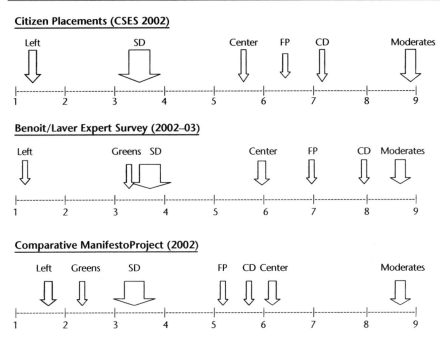

Figure 5.3. Citizens, Experts, and Manifestos Positioning of Swedish Political Parties

Source: CSES Modules 2; Benoit and Laver party expert dataset; Comparative Manifestos Project dataset.

Note: Table entries are mean placements of the political parties by the various projects. The expert survey responses and the CMP scores are adjusted to a common 0–10 scale with the other two surveys.

differences between where these party MNPs and CEPs position themselves, and where they position their own party. Using the SD as an example, SD members of the Riksdag position themselves at 3.2 on the Left–Right scale (top arrows in second panel), significantly to the left of where they place their own party (bottom arrow in this panel). At the other end of the political spectrum, Moderate MNPs position themselves and their party as less extreme than the Swedish public positions them. The public's positioning of the Moderates may reflect a mix of the party's earlier identity as the "Rightist party" and the neoconservative policies that the Moderates pursued under Carl Bildt's prime ministership in 1991–94.[24] For most other Swedish parties, the fit between the public and elite perceptions is quite close.

Sweden is only one nation, yet it illustrates some of the basic patterns in the full dataset and the complications in such comparisons. When we start comparing different data sources, we inevitably are comparing across different electoral contexts. These Swedish comparisons spanned the 1994 European Parliament elections, MNPs interviewed in 1996, the Swedish public

Citizen Placements (CSES 1998)

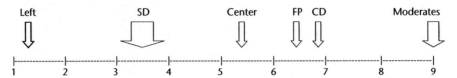

Members of the National Parliament (MNPs 1996)

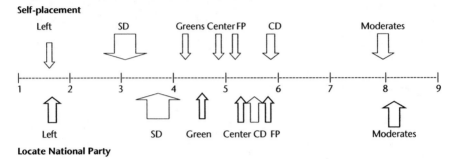

Candidates for European Parliament (CEPs 1994)

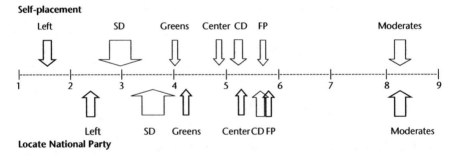

Figure 5.4. Citizens and Elites Positioning of Swedish Political Parties

Source: CSES module 1; 1996 Members of the National Parliament Study; 1994 Candidates for the European Parliament Study.

Note: Table entries are mean placements of the political parties by the various samples. The CEP responses are adjusted to a 0–10 scale similar to the other two surveys.

interviewed after the 1998 and 2002 elections, party manifestos before the 2002 elections, and expert judgments collected the year after the 2002 election. If the parties are changing their positions—as in the British example in Figure 5.1—this makes direct comparisons of different time periods problematic. In addition, it is difficult, if not impossible, to define the "real" party positions because there are several reasonable alternatives. Even with a single elite survey, there is a difference between where party elected officials position themselves and where they locate their own parties (and differences between groups of elected officials such as MNPs and CEPs).[25]

We believe that there is no single definitive source to identify a party's political position. The answer is that it depends on the context and the factors being considered. Still, by comparing these multiple sources we can determine the consistency of party placements with these various measures, which is an indicator of verisimilitude.

We coded the Left–Right position for all the parties that received scores in the CSES module 2 survey. Then we added the Left–Right scores for these parties from four other sources: (1) the Benoit/Laver 2002–03 expert evaluations of parties; (2) the 1996 Members of National Parliament study and the 1997 British representation study, coding the self-placement of party elites and their placement of their own parties; (3) the 1994 Candidates for the European Parliament study, coding self-placement of party elites and their placement of their parties; and (4) the Comparative Manifesto Project coding of party Left–Right position for the same election as the CSES survey.

Table 5.1 presents the intercorrelations between these seven measures of party positions. There is a striking consistency among three of the data sources—public perceptions, expert judgments, and political elites—with very strong correlations. The manifesto data are also consistent with the Left–Right structure from the other sources, but to a weaker degree. Similar to previous research, the correlation between the manifestos and party expert data is only .63, which is similar to the correlation between the manifestos and public perceptions (and elite perceptions) of the parties. This general pattern is seen most clearly in the factor analysis that is in the column on the right side of the table.[26] All six indicators from the public, experts, and elites display very large factor loadings on a first unrotated dimension (in the .89–92 range), while manifesto scores are markedly lower (.59). The party manifesto data are valuable, especially for their cross-national and cross-temporal coverage, but these data appear to yield the least consistent measures of party Left–Right positions.[27]

The largest and most diverse set of parties spans the public–expert comparisons based on 168 parties in 27 nations. One can visualize this strong relationship in Figure 5.5. Although both surveys used Left–Right scales with a different range of responses, there is a tendency for citizens to position more extreme parties on the Left and Right closer to the center than the experts. Thus, the largest discrepancies are for Communist and Green parties on the Left, and extreme right and regional parties on the Right. As we might expect, the level of agreement levels is slightly stronger in the established democracies (r=.92) than in the new democracies (r=.81). There is also somewhat greater agreement in positioning large parties compared with smaller parties. In

Table 5.1. Correlation between Alternative Party Left–Right Measures

Correlations	Public	Experts	MNP Self	MNP Party	CEP Self	CEP Party	Factor Loading
CSES Public							.89
Party experts	.89 (168)						.90
MNP Self-placement	.90 (40)	.88 (55)					.90
MNP Party	.88 (40)	.91 (54)	.95 (59)				.91
CEP Self-placement	.89 (46)	.90 (58)	.85 (46)	.85 (46)			.90
CEP Party	.90 (45)	.90 (56)	.86 (46)	.88 (46)	.98 (60)		.92
Manifestos	.64 (144)	.64 (189)	.70 (53)	.72 (53)	.68 (55)	.67 (55)	.59

Sources: CSES module 2; 2002–03 Benoit and Laver party expert survey; 1996 Members of the National Parliament Study; 1997 British Representation Study; 1994 Candidates for the European Parliament Study; Comparative Manifesto Program coding of manifestos for election closest to CSES survey.

Note: Entries are Pearson r correlations and the (N) of each correlation; the eigenvalue of the factor analysis is 6.0, 85.9% of variance.

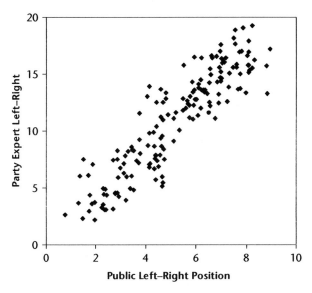

Figure 5.5. Citizen and Party Expert Left–Right Positions of Parties

Source: CSES module 2 and Benoit and Laver expert survey (N=168).

Note: The figure plots the mean Left–Right position of parties from the entire public in the CSES survey (0–10 scale) with the mean party position from the expert survey (0–20 scale).

summary, the consistency of party images between citizens and experts, even across different national contexts, is quite apparent in Figure 5.5.

The accuracy of public opinion may surprise some skeptics of contemporary electorates, but other research displays similar consistency.[28] We have merely strengthened these findings by adding to the breadth of the cross-national evidence and comparing multiple judgments of party positions.

Part of the accuracy of public perceptions comes from the use of aggregate statistics, where individual "errors" balance out so that the collective position-ing of a party is more accurate than the individual judgments. That is, the collective perceptions of a group are normally more accurate than individual evaluations. Some analysts might point to the individual-level variability in citizens' Left–Right scores for a party as a sign of imprecision. Certainly the less engaged and less informed person is more likely to position a party incorrectly as too far Left or Right, or to not position a party on the Left–Right scale.

However, the variability among citizens in positioning a party on the Left–Right scale is not sufficient evidence of the lack of knowledge—it can also arise from legitimate differences in how to evaluate the party position and in the weight attached to specific issues in determining a party's Left–Right position. A party might be considered liberal in terms of economic issues, but more moderate on certain social issues. For example, both voters for the Swedish

Social Democrats and Riksdag representatives of the Social Democrats vary by roughly comparable amounts in their Left–Right positioning of their own party.[29] So variability alone is not evidence that individual voters cannot perceive party positions.

Instead, we lean toward the interpretation that most citizens have a meaningful understanding of political parties that is expressed in their positions on the Left–Right scale. Indeed, voters are exposed to an abundance of information and cues on party positions, and so such summary judgments are not unexpected. For example, party families or party labels alone are a good guide in identifying the political orientation of a party.[30] When a party calls itself "Labour" or "Christian Democratic," its broad orientations are there for everyone to see. When we also accept the idea that many citizens focus their attention on a few issues of personal salience, they can use these issues as a basis for judging party positions. In other words, the public as a whole appears to have a reasonable view of the party choices they face in an election—fulfilling the second step in the party linkage model.

The Varied Content of Left and Right

We have sometimes treated the Left–Right scale as if it were a single dimension with a single meaning. Certainly this is an oversimplification. However, the analytic value of Left–Right is its ability to assimilate different issues into this general dimension of political debate—it can be treated as a "super-issue" that combines the specific policy debates of a nation.

As noted earlier, the term "Left" has a different meaning for a German university student and a German steelworker, or a German feminist. So, when voters say a party is leftist (or rightist), this can also have different meanings. The leftism practiced by the German Greens is different from the policy emphases of the Linke, and different again from the policy emphases of the Social Democrats. And these different issue emphases shape where the party or the public would place themselves on the Left–Right scale. For instance, the Greens and SPD might support the similar policies on preservation of health care benefits, but this is presumably a more important issue to the Social Democrats and thus is more influential in determining their overall political identity. In contrast, the Greens' identity is shaped more directly by their position on the use of nuclear power, environmental taxes, and multicultural issues. Robert Rohrschneider and Stephen Whitefield argue that party diversity in the salience of issues is more varied than actual party positions on these issues, and issue salience is more powerful in shaping the party's overall identity.[31]

The diversity of issue interests across parties can provide an indirect measure of the different meaning of Left–Right to the parties. We can illustrate issue salience with evidence from the Benoit/Laver study of parties in Western democracies and the new democracies of Eastern Europe. In addition to positioning parties on the Left–Right scale and other policy scales, the experts also rated the importance of each policy to the party.[32] The number of policy dimensions varied across nations in an attempt to capture the specific issue controversies in each party system.

We first focus on the established democracies and examine four important policy areas to show how parties vary in their issue emphases.

- Economics—the importance of raising taxes to maintain government services versus cutting services to reduce taxes. This item taps the traditional economic cleavage and is still important in balancing the benefits of social service programs against their costs.
- Religious values—the importance attached to matters such as abortion, homosexuality, and euthanasia.
- Environment—the importance of protecting the environment versus supporting economic growth.
- Immigration—the importance of policies dealing with immigration. This is a new issue of growing importance in the past decade, which has spurred extreme right opposition to multiculturalism or assimilation policies.

We cannot compare effectively the issue agendas of over a hundred parties. Therefore, to illustrate the broad differences in issue salience—and hence the meaning of Left–Right to these parties—we compare nine party families for an aggregated cross-national comparison. The following list presents the party families and their average Left–Right location for the established democracies:[33]

- **Communists**—these include communist or reformed communist parties, such as the PCF in France or the Linke in Germany (Left–Right mean from CSES module 2=2.73).
- **Greens**—explicit environmental parties such as ECOLO in Belgium, or the Verts in France (mean=3.22).
- **Social Democrats/Labour**—includes parties such as the Swedish Social Democrats and the British Labour Party (mean=3.66).
- **New Left/Libertarian**—typically small leftist parties that have moved from socialist programs to New Left identities, such as the Australian Democrats, Radical Venstre in Denmark, or D66 in the Netherlands (mean=3.87).

- **Liberals**—represent the traditional European liberal position of economic conservatism and social liberalism that produces a centrist position on the overall Left–Right scale, such as the German FDP, the Dutch VVD, or the Norwegian Venstre (mean=5.36).
- **Christian Democrats**—often the major rightist party in Catholic nations which combines conservative economic principles with religious-based policies, such as the German CDU/CSU, the Dutch CDA, or the Portuguese CDS (mean=6.22).
- **Right Liberal**—a heterogeneous mix of conservative parties that tend to be less ideological in their policy programs, such as the Canadian Progressive Conservatives and the Irish Progressive Democrats (mean=6.42).
- **Conservatives**—support conservative policies that are oriented toward the middle class and business interests, such as the British Conservatives or the French RPR/UEM (mean=6.97).
- **Extreme Right**—often new parties or reformed conservative parties that advocate nationalist policies and other extreme views, such as the National Front in France, the Danish Progress Party, or the Austrian Freedom Party (mean=7.29).

These nine families include the large majority of parties in these established democracies. More important, they represent the major ideological traditions in Western party systems that historically have given meaning to the Left–Right framework.

Figure 5.6 presents the experts' judgment of the importance attached to each issue averaged across all parties within a party family in the established democracies (the comparable data for new democracies are presented in Figure 5.7). As one might expect, the taxes versus services item receives the high importance rating for all party families. Attention to this issue spans the Left–Right divide; communists, conservatives, and liberals are all seen as stressing this issue because this is a central element of their policy agenda. Welfare state issues generally garner lower attention from Green, Christian Democratic, and extreme right parties because these parties' agendas devote more attention to non-economic issues.

The second column of the figure shows the importance of social issues. Christian Democratic, Green, left-liberal, and extreme right parties display the greatest attention to these issues. This is a very diverse set of parties in Left–Right terms because we are not measuring positions on these issues—just attention to social issues. In other words, Christian Democratic parties have a conservative image due to their opposition to abortion, homosexuality, and other social issues more than to their position on welfare state issues. Green parties' overall leftist position is partially based on their liberal position on social issues (in favor of abortion and supportive of homosexuality) rather

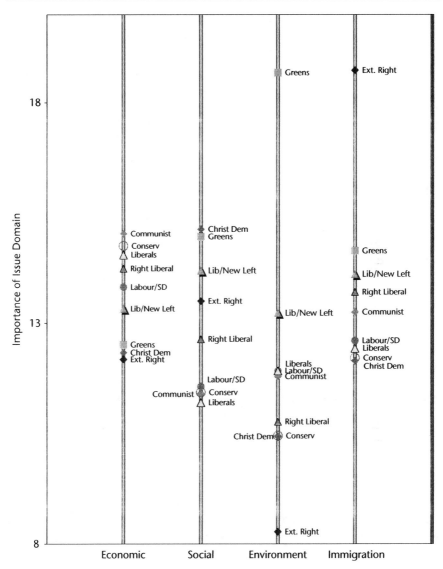

Figure 5.6. Importance of Issue Domains by Party Families in Established Democracies
Source: Benoit and Laver study of party experts (established democracies).
Note: Figure presents the mean importance for each issue for parties within each family.

than on their liberal position on economic issues. Similarly, experts see the parties that are more closely identified with welfare state issues—liberal parties, communists, conservatives, and labor/social democratic parties—as giving less attention to social issues.

The ability of new issue controversies to shape party identities appears in the next two columns of Figure 5.6. Party experts naturally attribute very high importance to environmental issues for Green parties, and immigration for extreme right parties. These are key issues defining the identity of each party family.[34] In comparison, the established parties of the Left and Right tend to cluster together on these new issue controversies, attributing less importance to these new issues than to either economic or social policy. The established parties' lack of attention to these new issues is often cited as a reason why Green and new right parties emerged to address these policies.

We examine the political parties of Eastern Europe separately because the policy challenges there are different, as democratization and marketization dominated politics for much of the 1990s. The issues of EU expansion also have a special relevance for these nations (the expert survey occurred before the 2004 and 2007 EU expansions). In addition, these party systems are still consolidating, which produces a more fluid political landscape where party identities may be less developed. Finally, the mix of parties and party families tends to differ in Eastern Europe. Green and Liberal/New Left parties are less common, and there are more agrarian parties, regional/ethnic parties, and nationalist parties.[35]

Figure 5.7 presents the importance of four policy areas for party families in Eastern Europe: tax and services, social policy and environmental policy—as in the comparisons for Western European parties—and foreign ownership of property to reflect the issues of marketization and participation in an international economic system. There are very few left-libertarian parties in Eastern Europe, so we substitute agrarian parties in these comparisons.

One noticeable contrast between the established Western democracies and the new democracies in Eastern Europe is the generally lower salience of the traditional class and religious cleavages.[36] Not surprisingly, experts also perceive less interest in environmental policy across party families in Eastern Europe. In part, these new party systems are still adjusting to democratic electoral competition and building programs related to these issues, while class and social policies are long-standing elements of party programs in Western democracies. In addition, the nations of Eastern Europe have faced many political challenges accompanying their democratic transitions, which compete with economics, social policy, and environmental protection for political attention. For instance, the issues of EU membership, marketization, and foreign ownership of property are not as salient in Western party systems. We expect that this may be a common pattern for other developing democracies: the salience of the traditional class and social issues is likely to be lower as nations navigate a democratic transition, especially if this is accompanied by major economic restructuring.

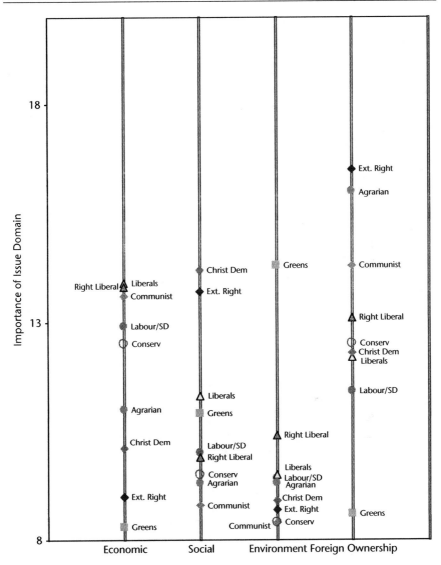

Figure 5.7. Importance of Issue Domains by Party Families in East Europe
Source: Benoit and Laver study of party experts (East European nations).
Note: Figure presents the mean importance for each issue for parties within each family.

When one compares the salience of issues across party families, the ranking of party families in Eastern Europe generally follows the same pattern as for West European parties. The issue of taxes versus services is most salient for communist and liberal parties in Eastern Europe, and least salient for Christian Democratic, extreme right, and Green parties. Christian Democratic parties place an expectedly greater emphasis on social policy matters, and Green parties are the only family to rank environmental issues above the midpoint on the salience scale.

Foreign ownership of land illustrates how the complex issues associated with participation in a European and global economy create new lines of political cleavage in Eastern Europe. The highest salience for this issue is assigned to agrarian parties because land purchases often involve farmlands, and to extreme right parties who frame this issue in nationalistic terms. Communist parties are ranked high in salience because they are hostile to foreign direct investment and other aspects of the capitalist market. On average, the issue of foreign investment generates more overall attention than the other three examples.

In summary, when citizens and parties use the terms "Left" and "Right," these terms do not have a single constant meaning but can take on varied meanings across time and nations. Similarly, experts perceive that party families attach different importance to various political issues, and a leftist party can imply different meanings as well. Although Left–Right captures a diversity of meanings, it still provides a common metric for our analyses using the Left–Right scale. Just as there is a broad congruence in the Left–Right party placements by citizens, experts, and elites, we believe there is a similar congruence in the meaning they attach to these terms.

Citizens and Parties

Democratic accountability requires that citizens understand the choices available to them, either directly or through heuristic cues. Only then can they make meaningful choices based on their own preferences. We do not disagree with those who cite evidence of the limited information of many people on many issues. However, the party linkage model frames this question differently: do citizens have policy preferences expressed in Left–Right terms, and can they judge the parties' positions in these same terms?

The Left–Right scale acts as a summary of the issues of salience to the individual—compressed or combined into a single political dimension. Chapter 4 showed that people can position themselves on this scale, although they might attribute different meanings to the terms Left and Right. This chapter demonstrates that the content of parties' Left or Right identities also varies. Thus, the Left–Right dimension subsumes the controversies of salience to an individual or to a political system. On the one hand, this makes our comparisons more complicated because the meaning of Left and Right is not constant. On the other hand, we are looking for a single metric that allows us to compare the policy views of citizens and parties across time and nations. For instance, a question on candidate affect may reflect different sources of affect for different candidates and across different nations, but we can still use the candidate affect question to make meaningful comparisons of candidate popularity and the impact of this popularity on citizen voting positions. For our comparative analyses, the Left–Right scale is exceptionally valuable because it provides a common framework for analysis by positioning voters and parties along this dimension.

This chapter also asks whether citizens as a whole can accurately perceive a party's Left–Right position as a basic requisite of making meaningful electoral choices. If voters are disinterested or ill-informed, or define Left–Right in idiosyncratic terms, then there should be little congruence between citizen perceptions and more "objective" measures of party positions. Indeed, political scientists who are skeptical of mass publics' political sophistication would predict only weak agreement.

We find a strikingly high degree of congruence between citizen perceptions of the parties' Left–Right positions, the perceptions of political experts, and the self-location of party elites. In fact, if political scientists studying parties are really party experts, then there is remarkable agreement between academic experts and the ordinary public. Ordinary people view most political parties at almost the identical Left–Right positions as a sample of political science PhDs from the same nation. Maybe citizen perceptions of the parties lack verisimilitude, but if they do, the same applies to the experts.

There are several likely reasons why the public's perceptions of political parties so closely match experts' judgments. One factor is the breadth of Left–Right orientations in comparison with specific policy issues. Most people have a Left–Right position and generally understand these terms. This allows them to position themselves and the parties on the Left–Right dimension as they perceive it. In contrast, only a subset of people is interested in any single policy issue, and thus many people may not have clear opinions on an issue or perceptions of a party's position on this issue. This would be apparent in comparing perceptions of party positions on specific issues, where the accuracy of perceptions is probably lower and varies as a function of the salience of the issue and the size of the relevant issue public. So the broad relevance of the Left–Right framework contributes to accurate perceptions.

Citizens also have access to an abundance of information in the political environment and the cues provided by others. Political campaigns are recurring civics lessons, where parties and their representatives debate intensely the parties' political positions. The media coverage of campaigns, and politics in general, often gives a predominate place to political parties as central actors. Thus we found that public–expert congruence is slightly higher in established democracies than in new democracies. In addition, research on the public's understanding of "Left" and "Right" demonstrates that many people think of these positions in group terms. The Left may mean support for unions and the working class, so voters with these orientations may identify leftist parties in terms of their appeal to these groups. Even the names of parties—Labor, Christian Democrat, Green, etc.—provide a guide to their Left–Right position. Except for the party names, Left and Right (or liberal and conservative) may be the most ubiquitous terms in political discourse.

Another factor explaining the public's perceptions of party positions is the power of aggregation. There is inevitably some inaccuracy in party perceptions of individual citizens (and there is some inaccuracy in the perceptions of party experts as well). However, when we average the perceptions of all citizens (or all experts) these inaccuracies tend to diminish, which yields a more accurate aggregate estimate. If people bring meaningful information to their decisions, which overall is unbiased, then aggregation improves the overall estimates of party positions.[37] We observe the effects of aggregation here, and in the voter–party dyad comparisons in Chapter 6. In simple terms, a large group generally makes a better estimate than a single individual.

In summary, electorates as a whole broadly fulfill this second aspect of the party linkage model for electoral choice. First, most voters have meaningful issue positions which define their own Left–Right positions. Second, they can also position the political parties on this Left–Right scale. We thus need to consider the third step in this linkage process: to what extent do voters' positions and perceptions shape their electoral decisions?

Appendix

This appendix lists the parties in each CSES nation for which the survey measured the public's mean Left–Right placement of the party. The table also lists the vote percentage for the party in the election.

Table A5.1. Party Positions on the Left-Right Scale

Party	Left/ Right	Vote %
Albania 2005		
Democratic Party (PD)	8.8	7.6
Socialist Party (PS)	1.5	8.8
Republican Party (PR)	7.8	19.9
Social Democrats (PSD)	2.9	12.7
Socialist Movement of Integration (LSI)	2.8	8.4
New Democratic Party (PDR)	7.3	7.4
Agrarian Party (PAA)	3.4	6.5
Democratic Alliance (PAD)	4.1	4.7
Christian Democrats (PDK)	6.5	3.2
Australia 2004		
Australian Greens (G)	3.2	7.2
Australian Labor Party (ALP)	4.3	37.6
Australian Democrats (D)	4.4	1.2

One Nation (ONE)	5.9	1.2
National Party of Australia (N)	6.6	5.9
Liberal Party of Australia (LIB)	7.0	40.5
Belgium 2003*		
Flemish Liberals and Democrats (VLD)	7.1	15.4
Social Progressive Alternative (SP.A)	2.9	14.9
Christian, Democratic and Flemish Party (CD&V)	6.0	13.3
Socialist Party (PS)	1.7	13.0
Flemish Bloc (VB)	9.6	11.6
Reformist Movement (MR)	6.2	11.4
Humanist Democratic Centre (CDH)	5.1	5.5
New-Flemish Alliance (NVA)	7.1	3.1
Ecologists Confederated for the Organisation of Original Struggles (ECOLO)	1.1	3.1
Brazil 2002		
Workers' Party (PT)	3.5	18.4
Brazilian Social Democracy Party (PSDB)	6.3	14.3
Liberal Front Party (PFL)	6.3	13.4
Brazilian Democratic Movement Party (PMDB)	6.2	13.4
Brazilian Progressive Party (PPB)	—	7.8
Brazilian Socialist Party (PSB)	—	5.3
Democratic Labour Party (PDT)	6.3	5.1
Brazilian Labour Party (PTB)	4.8	4.6
Liberal Party (PL)	—	4.3
Bulgaria 2001		
National Movement Simeon the Second (NDSV)	6.5	42.7
United Democratic Forces (ODS)	8.8	18.2
Bulgarian Socialist Party (BSP)	1.7	17.2
Movement for Rights and Freedoms (DPS)	5.1	7.5
George's Day Movement (G)	5.8	3.6
Canada 2004		
Liberal Party of Canada (LPC)	5.1	36.7
Conservative Party of Canada (PC)	6.2	29.6
New Democratic Party (NDP)	3.4	15.7
Bloc Québécois (BQ)	3.7	12.4
Chile 2002		
Independent Democratic Union (UDI)	9.0	23.5
Christian Democrats (PDC)	5.2	21.3
Party for Democracy (PPD)	3.9	15.9
National Renewal (RN)	8.3	15.2
Socialist Party (PS)	2.9	10.5
Communist Party (PC)	1.1	5.5
Czech Republic 2002		
Czech Social Democratic Party (CSSD)	2.7	30.2
Civic Democratic Party (ODS)	8.2	24.5
Communist Party of Bohemia and Moravia (KSCM)	0.8	18.5
Christian Democratic Union—Czechoslovak People's Party (KDU-CSL)	5.7	10.0
Freedom Union—Democratic Union (US-DEU)	6.9	4.3
Denmark 2001		
Liberal Party of Denmark (V)	7.3	31.2
Social Democratic Party (SD)	4.4	29.1
Danish People's Party (DF)	8.1	12.0
Conservative People's Party (KF)	7.0	9.1
Socialist People's Party (SF)	2.8	6.4
Danish Social Liberal Party (RV)	4.6	5.2
Unity List—The Red-Green Coalition (E)	1.5	2.4
Christian People's Party (KrF)	5.5	2.3

(continued)

Table A5.1. Continued

Party	Left/ Right	Vote %
Finland 2003		
Centre Party C	6.2	24.7
Social Democratic Party of Finland (SDP)	4.7	24.5
National Coalition Party	7.5	18.6
Left Alliance	2.3	9.9
Green League	4.7	8.0
Christian Democrats (KD)	5.9	5.3
Swedish Peoples' Party (SFP)	6.1	4.6
France 2002 (Presidential)		
Rally for the Republic (RPR)	6.7	33.3
National Front (FN)	7.9	11.3
Socialist Party (PS)	3.6	24.1
Union for French Democracy (UDF)	6.4	4.9
Workers' Struggle (LO)	2.3	1.0
Citizen and Republican Movement (MRC)	4.6	1.2
The Greens (Verts)	3.6	4.5
Liberal Democracy (DL)	5.9	1.0
French Communist Party (PCF)	2.4	4.8
Germany 2002		
Social Democratic Party of Germany (SPD)	3.5	38.5
Christian Democratic Union (CDU)	5.9	29.5
Christian Social Union of Bavaria (CSU)	6.4	9.0
The Greens (G)	3.1	8.6
Free Democratic Party (FDP)	4.8	7.4
Party of Democratic Socialism (PDS)	2.3	4.0
The Republicans (REP)	7.6	1.0
Schill Party (Schill)	7.0	0.5
Great Britain 2005		
Labour Party (LAB)	4.8	35.2
Conservative Party (CON)	7.1	32.3
Liberal Democrats (LibDem)	4.3	22.1
Hungary 2002		
Hungarian Socialist Party (MSZP)	1.9	42.1
Fidesz—Hungarian Citizens' Party (Fidesz-MPP)	8.1	35.0
Alliance of Free Democrats (SZDSZ)	2.9	5.6
Hungarian Justice and Life Party (MIÉP)	7.9	4.4
Centre Party (C)	4.2	3.9
Hungarian Democratic Forum (MDF)	7.7	6.0
Iceland 2003		
Independence Party (S)	8.3	33.7
Social Democratic Alliance (SF)	4.1	31.0
Progressive Party (F)	6.0	17.1
Left-Green Movement (VG)	2.3	8.8
The Liberal Party (FF)	5.5	7.4
Ireland 2002		
Fianna Fáil—The Republican Party (FF)	6.4	41.5
Fine Gael—The United Ireland Party (FG)	6.0	22.5
The Labour Party (LAB)	3.6	10.7
Sinn Féin (SF)	3.1	6.5
Progressive Democrats (PD)	6.2	4.0
Green Party (G)	4.4	3.8
Israel 2003		
Likud	7.8	29.4
Israeli Labour Party	2.9	14.5
Shinui	4.9	12.3

Shas	7.0	8.2
National Union	8.2	5.5
Meretz	1.8	5.2
Italy 2006		
Forza Italy (FI)	7.6	23.6
Democrats of the Left (DS)	3.2	17.1
National Alliance (AN)	8.1	12.0
Daisy—Democracy is Liberty (DL)	3.8	10.7
Union of Christian and Center Democrats (UDC)	5.7	6.7
Communist Refoundation Party (PRC)	2.0	5.7
Japan 2003		
Japanese Communist Party (JCP)	2.4	12.6
Social Democratic Party (SDP)	4.7	2.2
Democratic Party of Japan (DPJ)	5.2	10.6
New Komeito Party (NKP)	5.9	28.0
Liberal Democratic Party (LDP)	7.6	38.6
Korea (South) 2004		
Democratic Labor Party (DLP)	3.2	13.0
Yeollin Uri Party (UP)	3.7	38.3
Millennium Democratic Party (MDP)	6.3	7.1
United Liberal Democrats (ULD)	7.2	2.8
Grand National Party (GNP)	7.3	35.8
Mexico 2003		
National Action Party (PAN)	6.3	30.7
Institutional Revolutionary Party (PRI)	5.6	23.1
Democratic Revolution Party (PRD)	3.9	17.6
Mexican Green Ecological Party (PVEM)	4.2	4.0
Labor Party (PT)	2.6	2.4
Democratic Convergence (CD)	2.5	2.3
Netherlands 2002		
Christian Democratic Appeal (CDA)	6.3	27.9
Pim Fortuyn List (LPF)	7.6	17.0
People's Party for Freedom and Democracy (VVD)	7.0	15.4
Dutch Labour Party (PvdA)	3.4	15.1
GreenLeft (GL)	2.3	7.0
Socialist Party (SP)	2.4	5.9
Democrats '66 (D66)	4.4	5.1
Christian Union (CU)	6.6	2.5
Political Reformed Party (SGP)	6.8	1.7
New Zealand 2002		
Green Party of Aotearoa New Zealand (G)	2.4	7.0
Alliance (ALL)	2.7	1.3
Progressive Party (P)	3.0	1.7
New Zealand Labour Party (NZLB)	3.8	41.3
United Future New Zealand (UF)	5.6	6.7
New Zealand First (NZFP)	6.5	10.4
New Zealand National Party (NP)	7.0	20.9
ACT New Zealand (ACT)	7.5	7.1
Norway 2001		
Norwegian Labour Party (DNA)	4.6	24.3
Conservative Party (H)	8.0	21.2
Progress Party (FrP)	8.1	14.6
Socialist Left Party (SV)	2.8	12.5
Christian Democratic Party (KrF)	5.9	12.4
Centre Party (Sp)	4.5	5.6
Liberal Party of Norway (V)	4.4	3.9

(continued)

Table A5.1. Continued

Party	Left/ Right	Vote %
Peru 2006		
Union for Peru (UPP)	3.4	21.2
Aprista Peruvian Party (APRA)	5.2	20.6
National Unity (UN)	5.9	15.3
Alliance for the Future (AF)	4.6	13.1
Center Front/Popular Action (FDC)	4.5	7.1
National Restoration (RN)	3.7	4
Possible Peru (PP)	4.0	4.1
Philippines 2004		
Lakas-Christian Muslim Democrats (Lakas-CMD)	5.5	40.0
Nationalist People's Coalition (NPC)	5.0	36.5
Liberal Party of the Philippines (LP)	4.9	0.0
Struggle of Democratic Filipinos (LDP)	5.2	10.9
Democratic Action (AD)	5.0	6.5
Rise up, Philippines (BPM)	5.3	6.2
Poland 2001		
Democratic Left Alliance (SLD)	1.4	41.0
Civic Platform (PO)	6.3	12.7
Self-Defence of the Republic of Poland (SRP)	4.7	10.2
Law and Justice (PiS)	6.6	9.5
Polish People's Party (PSL)	4.3	9.0
League of Polish Families (LPR)	7.2	7.9
Solidarity Electoral Action of the Right (AWSP)	8.0	5.6
Freedom Union (UW)	6.1	3.1
Portugal 2002		
Socialist Party (PS)	4.6	30.4
Social Democratic Party (PPD/PSD)	7.3	40.1
People's Party (CDS-PP)	7.7	7.5
Unitarian Democratic Coalition (CDU)	1.9	7.0
Left Bloc (BE)	1.7	2.7
Communist	2.0	0.6
Portugal 2005		
Socialist Party (PS)	4.4	45.0
Social Democratic Party (PPD/PSD)	6.9	28.8
People's Party (CDS-PP)	7.3	7.5
Unitarian Democratic Coalition (CDU)	2.1	7.2
Left Bloc (BE)	1.7	6.4
Romania 2004		
Social Democratic Party (PSD)	4.14	32.0
National Liberal Party (PNL)	6.86	15.8
Democratic Party (PD)	6.77	15.8
Greater Romania Party (PRM)	3.76	13.0
Democratic Alliance of Hungarians (UDMR)	4.81	6.2
Humanist Party (PUR)	4.67	4.8
Christian Democratic National Peasant (PNTCD)	4.70	1.8
Russia 2004 (Presidential)		
United Russia (UR)	6.9	38.0
Communist Party (KPRF)	2.4	12.8
Liberal Democrats (LDPR)	4.1	11.7
Homeland People's-Patriotic Union (RNPS)	4.7	9.2
Union of Right Forces (SPS)	7.0	4.0
Russian Democratic Party (RDPY)	5.6	4.4
Slovenia 2004		
Slovenian Democratic Party (SDS)	7.0	29.1
Liberal Democracy (LDS)	3.2	22.8
United List of Social Democrats (ZLSD)	3.5	10.2

New Slovenia—Christian People's Party (NSi)	7.0	9.0
Slovenian People's Party (SLS)	6.1	6.8
Slovenian National Party (SNS)	5.3	6.3
Democratic Party of Pensioners (DeSus)	4.5	4.0
Spain 2004		
Spanish Socialist Workers' Party (PSOE)	3.3	42.6
People's Party (PP)	7.8	37.7
United Left (IU)	1.9	5.0
Convergence and Union (CiU)	4.6	3.2
Sweden 2002		
Swedish Social Democratic Party (S)	3.5	39.9
Moderate Party (M)	9.0	15.3
Liberal People's Party (FP)	6.5	13.4
Christian Democrats (KD)	7.1	9.2
Left Party (V)	1.3	8.4
Centre Party (C)	5.7	6.2
Swiss 2003		
Swiss People's Party (SVP/UDC)	8.1	26.7
Social Democratic Party of Switzerland (SP/PS)	2.9	23.3
Free Democratic Party of Switzerland (FDP/PRD)	6.2	17.3
Christian Democratic People's Party (CVP/PDC)	5.5	14.4
Green Party of Switzerland (GPS/PES)	2.9	7.4
Taiwan 2001		
Taiwan Solidarity Union (TSU)	4.2	7.8
Democratic Progressive Party (DPP)	4.6	33.4
New Party (NP)	5.2	2.6
People First Party (PFP)	5.3	18.6
Chinese Nationalist Party (KMT)	5.9	28.6
Taiwan 2004		
Taiwan Solidarity Union (TSU)	5.1	8.3
Democratic Progressive Party (DPP)	4.9	37.9
New Party (NP)	4.4	0.1
People First Party (PFP)	5.2	14.7
Chinese Nationalist Party (KMT)	5.6	34.9
USA 2004		
Republican Party (Rep)	6.6	49.9
Democratic Party (Dem)	4.2	47.4
Reform Party (Ref)	4.3	0.1

Source: CSES module 2; additional election results compiled by the authors. The Belgian party estimates were calculated from the Benoit and Laver party expert study because the party Left–Right question was not included in the CSES survey.

Notes

1. Michael Lewis-Beck, Helmut Norpoth, William Jacoby, and Herbert Weisberg, *The American Voter Revisited*. Ann Arbor: University of Michigan Press, 2008, ch. 10.
2. Paul Abramson, John Aldrich, and David Rhode, *Continuity and Change in the 2004 Elections*. Washington, DC: CQ Press, 2005, p. 148.
3. Wouter van der Brug, *Where's the Party? Voters' Perceptions of Party Positions*. Amsterdam: University of Amsterdam, 1996, pp. 38–40. He finds that the parties' relative Left–Right positions are quite stable over time, but there is some gradual convergence toward the center.

4. Peter Esaiasson and Sören Holmberg, *Representation from Above: Members of Parliament and Representative Democracy in Sweden*. Aldershoot: Dartmouth Publishing, 1996.

5. Harold Clarke et al., *Political Choice in Britain*. Oxford: Oxford University Press, 2004; Harold Clarke et al., *Performance Politics: The British Voter*. New York: Cambridge University Press, 2008.

6. Russell Dalton, Party supporters and party elites in nine nations, *Comparative Political Studies* (1985) 18: 267–99; Esaiasson and Holmberg, *Representation from Above*.

7. Philip Converse, Some mass-elite contrasts in the perception of political spaces, *Social Science Information* (1975) 14: 49–83; Donald Granberg, An anomaly in political perception, *Public Opinion Quarterly* (1985) 49: 504–16.

8. The question read: "In politics people sometimes talk of left and right. Where would you place [Party A] on a scale from 0 to 10 where 0 means the left and 10 means the right?"

   In most nations we considered only those who were coded as "have not heard of the party" or "don't know" as not knowing a party's position; not ascertained and undifferentiated missing data were excluded from the calculation of percentages. However, Australia, Bulgaria, and Canada had only the single undifferentiated missing data category (code 99), and so we based the calculations on this category.

9. Clarke et al., *Political Choice in Britain*; Clarke et al., *Performance Politics*.

10. Kenneth Benoit and Michael Laver, *Party Policy in Modern Democracies*. New York: Routledge, 2006; Russell Dalton, Economics, environmentalism and party alignments: A research note on partisan change in advanced industrial democracies, *European Journal of Political Research* (2009) 48: 161–75.

11. Robert Rohrschneider and Stephen Whitefield. Representation in new democracies: Party stances on European integration in post-communist Eastern Europe, *Journal of Politics* (2007) 69: 1133–46; Cees van der Eijk and Mark Franklin, Potential for contestation on European matters at national elections in Europe. In Gary Marks and Marco Steenbergen, eds, *European Integration and Political Conflict*. New York: Cambridge University Press, 2004; Gary Marks, Lisbeth Hooghe, and Carol Wilson, Does left–right structure party positions on European integration? *Comparative Political Studies* (2002) 35: 965–89.

12. These analyses are based on parties where at least eighteen respondents were coded as partisans so there are at least a modest number of cases.

13. Hans-Dieter Klingemann, Richard Hofferbert, Ian Budge, and Hans Keman, eds, *Parties, Policies, and Democracy*. Boulder, CO: Westview Press, 1994; Ian Budge et al., *Mapping Policy Preferences: Estimates for Parties, Electors and Governments 1945–1998*. Oxford: Oxford University Press, 2001.

14. Elias Dinas and Kostas Gemenis, Measuring parties' ideological positions with manifesto data: A critical evaluation of the competing methods, *Party Politics* (2010) 16: 427–50; Martin Ejnar Hansen, Back to the archives? A critique of the Danish part of the manifesto dataset, *Scandinavian Political Studies* (2008) 31: 201–16; Michael Laver and J. Garry, Estimating policy positions from political texts, *American Journal of Political Science* (2000) 44: 619–34; Matthew Gabel and John Huber, Putting parties in their place: Inferring party left–right ideological positions from party manifestos data, *American Journal of Political Science* (2000) 44: 94–103.

15. See Hermann Schmitt and Cees van der Eijk, On the changing and variable meaning of left and right. Paper presented at the XXI World Congress of the International Political Science Association, Santiago de Chile, July 2009.

16. Michael Laver and W. B. Hunt, *Policy and Party Competition*. New York: Routledge, 1992; John Huber and Ronald Inglehart, Expert interpretations of party space and party locations in 42 societies, *Party Politics* (1995) 1: 73–111; Benoit and Laver, *Party Policy in Modern Democracies*; Marco Steenbergen and Gary Marks, Evaluating expert judgments, *European Journal of Political Research* (2006) 46: 347–66; Robert Rohrschneider and Stephen Whitefield, Understanding divisions in party systems: Issue position and issue salience in 13 post-communist democracies, *Comparative Political Studies* (2009) 42: 280–313.

17. Michael McDonald and Silvia Mendes, The policy space of party manifestos. In Michael Laver, ed., *Estimating the Policy Positions of Political Actors*. London: Routledge, 2001.

18. Ian Budge, Expert judgments of party positions: Uses and limitations in political research, *European Journal of Political Research* (2000) 37: 103–13.

19. Dinas and Gemenis, Measuring parties' ideological positions with manifesto data; Michael McDonald, Silvia Mendes, and Myunghee Kim, Cross-temporal and cross-national comparisons of party left–right positions, *Electoral Studies* (2007) 26: 62–75; Hans Keman, Experts and manifestos: Different sources—same results for comparative research? *Electoral Studies* (2007) 26: 76–89; Kenneth Benoit and Michael Laver, Estimating party policy positions: Comparing expert surveys and hand-coded content analysis, *Electoral Studies* (2007) 26: 90–107; Andrea Volkens, Strengths and weaknesses of approaches to measuring policy positions of parties, *Electoral Studies* (2007) 26: 108–20.

20. Benoit and Laver, Estimating party policy positions, p. 97. This is based on 114 parties appearing in both the 2002 Benoit and Laver survey and in the CMP database. To convert the MNP and CEP scores to the same metric as CSES we used the following formula: ((Elite-5.5)/0.9)+5. Keman finds similar correlations comparing three expert surveys and the 2001 Manifesto coding of Left–Right: Keman, Experts and manifestos, p. 82.

21. Richard Katz and Bernhard Wessels, eds, *The European Parliament, National Parliaments, and European Integration*. Oxford: Oxford University Press, 1999; Hermann Schmitt and Jacques Thomassen, eds, *Political Representation and Legitimacy in the European Union*. Oxford: Oxford University Press, 1999. Although not formally part of the MNP study, we also include data from the 1997 British Members of Parliament Study because it asked the same Left–Right questions (available from www.pippanorris.com). A third elite survey sampled members of the European Parliament, but there are too few cases in each party to yield reliable estimates.

22. The questions were as follows: "In political matters some people talk about 'left' and 'right'. Where would you place yourself and others on this scale? Your position. Your party's voters. Your party's MPs." Respondents replied in terms of a 1–10 Left–Right scale.

23. These other studies use a different metric for the Left–Right scale, which we converted to match the CSES 0–10 scale. For the Benoit and Laver data we first centered

the scale values around the midpoint, and then divided these values by the different range of their scale: LR = ((BenoitLaver-10.5)/1.82)+5. For the manifesto data we divided the values from the 1998 Left–Right estimates by ten, and then added five: LR = (Manifesto/10)+5. Since the manifesto data do not have minimum and maximum values, this adjusts approximately to the range from the CSES and expert surveys.

24. Esaiasson and Holmberg, *Representation from Above*; Sören Holmberg, Polarizing political parties. In Hanne Marthe Narud and Anne Krogstad, eds, Elections, Parties and Political Representation. *Tidskrift for Samfunnsforskning* (2004) 2.

25. Van der Brug for instance, compares the Left–Right positioning of Dutch parties by their voters, members, sub-leaders, and top-leaders. He finds broad consistency in party positions: van der Brug, *Where's the Party*, pp. 142–45.

26. This is based on the first dimension of an unrotated principal components analysis. The first dimension had an eigenvalue of 5.95 and explained 85.4 percent of the variance.

27. We noted a host of anomalous results in the manifesto coding as we collected these data; for instance, all the parties in some nations are scored on the Left (New Zealand) or Right (Australia) end of the scale, presumably because the standardized scoring was not consistent with the national policy debates. Similarly, the differential patterns of party polarization for Sweden displayed in Figures 5.3 and 5.4 appeared in other nations.

28. Steenbergen and Marks demonstrated similar agreement on citizen and expert judgments of party positions toward European integration: Steenbergen and Marks, Evaluating expert judgments; Dinas and Gemenis, Measuring parties' ideological positions with manifesto data, compare experts' and citizens' perceptions from the European Social Surveys; Esaiasson and Holmberg, *Representation from Above*, compare the public and elites in Sweden over time.

29. Using the 1996 MNP survey of SD members of the Riksdag, 70 percent placed the party on the Left end of the scale (0–4), 24 percent at the midpoint (5) and 6 percent to the Right (6–10). By comparison, 75 percent of SD voters positioned the party to the Left, 13 percent at the midpoint, and 12 percent on the Right. The fact that elected Social Democrat parliamentarians generally match the public Left–Right perceptions speaks to citizenry's ability to make meaningful judgments.

30. An eight-category party family variable is very strongly related to public perceptions of party Left–Right positions (eta=.77) and expert perceptions of the parties (eta=.84). By comparison, the party manifesto coding of Left–Right is more weakly related to public or expert scores (see Table 5.1).

31. Rohrschneider and Whitefield, Understanding divisions in party systems. Also see Herbert Kitschelt et al., *Post-Communist Party Systems*. New York: Cambridge University Press, 1999, ch. 5.

32. Benoit and Laver, *Party Policy in Modern Democracies*, ch. 5; respondents judged the relative importance of the dimension for each party on a scale from 1 (not important at all) to 20 (very important).

33. The classification of party families is taken from the CSES module 2 codings of the parties, and the authors classified some additional parties. The Left–Right mean is

based on the public's average position of parties on the Left–Right scale in CSES module 2 for the established democracies. The number of parties within each family in the established democracies is as follows: communist 13, green 17, social democrat/labor 38, new left-libertarian 11, liberal 23, Christian democrat 21, right liberal 7, conservative 15, extreme right 11. See Chapter 4 for comparable evidence of the positions of party families from the World Values Survey.

34. We do not present the data, but a similar pattern emerges for the decentralization of administrative and policy decision-making; this is seen as being much more important to regional parties than to any of the other party families.

35. For the East European democracies the number of parties within each family is as follows: communist 6, green 2, social democrat/labor 25, liberal 13, Christian democrat 14, right liberal 7, conservative 17, extreme right 7, agrarian 7.

36. Taxes versus services had a mean salience score of 13.2 for parties in the West, and 12.0 for parties in the East; social policy salience was 12.4 in the West and 10.6 in the East; environmental policy salience was 11.5 in the West and 9.3 in the East.

37. This is the essence of the Condorcet Jury Theorem; see Bernard Grofman and Scott Feld, Rousseau's general will: A Condorcetian perspective, *American Political Science Review* (1988) 82: 567–76.

6

Voter Choice and Partisan Representation

The day of the election has arrived. In most parliamentary systems, people face an apparently easy choice to pick a single party or candidate to represent them in the national legislature. But this is anything but an easy choice. In the 2002 French election, for example, the Socialists, the Union for French Democracy (UDF), and the National Front had extensive, complex programs running to several thousand words; the Union for a Popular Movement (UMP) and the Greens were only slightly less verbose. Only the Communist Party had a terse platform of several hundred words, but it called for a radical restructuring of French politics and economics with little detail to explain how this might be effected. Then there were the party and candidate statements and media commentary on the content of the campaign, overlapping with the 2002 presidential election a few months earlier. Was it even possible for the average voter (or the average PhD in political science) to be fully informed on the parties' policy positions and make the correct, rational choice?

Elections allow citizens to evaluate the policies of the incumbent parties and make judgments about the desired course of government in the future. Indeed, in the midst of campaigns the parties ask the voters to give them a mandate to implement their programs, and claim such a mandate when the votes are counted. Whether it is Barack Obama requesting a mandate for change, or the Communists campaigning against existing government policies in France, elections are the vehicle for such policy debates and choices. Thus, a policy-centered view of electoral choice is closely linked to the theoretical concept of responsible party government and democracy.

But faced with a complex choice, and other things to do besides studying party programs, voters seek simplifying mechanisms to help make their electoral choices.[1] Such satisficing behavior is common in many life decisions. Anthony Down's theoretical framework of ideological voting suggests that the Left–Right dimension and similar summary dimensions can provide a basis for making reasonable, satisficing choices.[2] A voter's own policy preferences are summarized by their Left–Right position (Chapter 4); voters can also summarize the parties' overall orientations in the same Left–Right terms (Chapter 5). Therefore, the Left–Right framework can provide a way to make broad policy choices, and thus choose which of the myriad French parties running in the 2002 election are reasonable fits to a voter's broad preferences.

This chapter extends the party linkage model by examining how citizens' Left–Right orientations influence their voting choices—the third step in the electoral linkage process described in Chapter 4. Even if many voters lack the political sophistication that political theorists and electoral scholars expect,[3] the basic fact is that people do make choices when they cast their ballots. Political judgments about government programs past and future should be part of this calculus. Thus, we ask to what extent Left–Right positions shape these voting choices and how the level of Left–Right voting varies across nations.[4]

However, the process of party linkage is not just an individual relationship between a voter and his or her political party. Political representation is also a collective process. In the United States and a few other single member district systems, representation may be judged by the fit between the constituency opinion and the selected legislator. In most parliamentary systems, representation is a collective process between party voters in a nation and the party in parliament.[5] In many nations, people vote directly for a party list (see Chapter 2). Thus, we also examine the aggregate congruence between voters and parties as the next link in the party government chain.

This chapter proceeds in three steps. First, we describe the empirical relationship between Left–Right orientations and vote in the CSES nations. As one should expect based on previous research, Left–Right orientations typically display a strong relationship with vote choice in most nations. We also describe how contextual factors affect this relationship, facilitating or attenuating policy-based voting. Second, we shift our analyses to party aggregates to consider how well the political orientations of party voters as a bloc are matched by the position of the party they support. The results describe the extent to which parties represent the voters who elected them to parliament, at least in Left–Right terms. Third, we discuss the implications of the findings from Chapters 4–6 for the party government model.

Policy Preferences and Left–Right Voting

We assess the impact of political preferences on voting behavior by examining the relationship between Left–Right attitudes and vote. As we have noted previously (Chapter 4), the political content of Left–Right orientations can vary across time, space, and individuals. Historically, the terms Left and Right were most commonly linked to contrasting positions on economic and social class issues. A leftist citizen generally supported more extensive social services, a larger role for government in managing the economy, and policies to ensure the well-being of the working class. The Right was synonymous with smaller government, modest social programs, and the advocacy of middle-class economic interests. To some voters the terms signify positions on issues derived from religious and moral conflicts. Yet other voters think of the new political issues of advanced industrial societies, such as environmentalism, gender equality, and multiculturalism.

Electoral research has regularly demonstrated a strong relationship between citizens' Left–Right orientations and their voting intentions; the existence of a strong relationship is not at question.[6] Indeed, in Chapter 4 we argued that partisanship is one of the factors that might influence an individual's position on the Left–Right scale. However, most previous research has focused on voting behavior in established Western democracies and, typically, elections in a single nation. The CSES allows us to describe how Left–Right attitudes correlate with voting in a range of democracies, and consider how the political context might affect the strength of Left–Right voting.

To what degree are people's Left–Right orientations correlated with their party choice? We use two methods to estimate the relationship between citizens' Left–Right orientations and vote. First, we correlate a person's Left–Right position and his or her legislative vote (without making assumptions on the Left–Right ordering of parties).[7] This method includes all parties for the legislative vote choice since vote is treated as a nominal level variable.

Second, we use the public's average Left–Right scores for each party, described in Chapter 5, to order parties along the Left–Right dimension. In France, for example, the Communist Party receives an average score of 2.4 on the Left–Right scale, while the National Front is placed at 7.9. We recode the parties on the legislative vote variable into their Left–Right scores. Then we calculate a Pearson's r correlation between a voter's own Left–Right position and their Left–Right legislative vote. This second correlation makes more demands on the data, presuming an ordered relationship between Left–Right orientations and voter choice; and it excludes those voters who selected minor parties that lacked a Left–Right score.[8] Both of these methods are reasonable alternatives that use different assumptions to assess the relationship between Left–Right orientations and vote. In practical terms, however, they generate very similar cross-national patterns in the level of Left–Right voting.[9]

As many other electoral studies have demonstrated, there is a significant relationship between citizens' Left–Right orientations and their voting choice in most nations. Pooling all CSES nations together, Figure 6.1 presents the relationship between citizens' Left–Right positions along the horizontal axis and their legislative vote on the vertical axis (coded by the party's Left–Right position). Left–Right attitudes are strongly related to party choice as shown by the line in the figure and the correlation, even when combining three dozen separate democracies with their own set of parties and issue concerns.

Figure 6.1 also shows a slight tendency for voters to select a party that is slightly more centrist than their own position, especially at the ideological extremes. People with a leftist self-placement (e.g., 2.0 on the Left–Right scale) on average vote for a party that is more centrist in its orientation (mean of 3.4). Similarly, rightist voters (8.0 on the scale) select parties that are located closer to the center (mean of 6.7). This pattern may reflect the lack of extreme party choices in some nations, or the impact of strategic voting that draws voters to more centrist parties. Yet, there is still a very strong overall relationship between a voter's Left–Right views and their partisan choices.

At the same time, there are striking differences in the strength of this relationship across nations (Table 6.1). The first column in Table 6.1 presents the nominal level Cramer's V correlations without making assumptions about the party's position; the second column are the Pearson r correlations based on the party's Left–Right position (as in Figure 6.1). The magnitude of these correlations differs by a three-to-one or four-to-one ratio across nations. The first column shows that Left–Right orientations have relatively little impact on party choices in Mexico or Taiwan, but there are very strong correlates of voting behavior in nations as diverse as Albania and Sweden.

Furthermore, these simple correlations presumably underestimate the actual degree of congruence. Within each nation, people may reasonably differ from the average Left–Right placement of parties because of their different issue interests. For instance, the British Labour Party and the Liberal Democrats have different positions if one defines Left–Right primarily in terms of traditional social services issues versus environmental policy or the war in Iraq. These different perceptions of the Left–Right positions of political parties are then averaged together in correlations that are based on the entire electorate's positioning of the party. Michael McDonald and Robin Best show that factoring in an individual's own Left–Right location of parties substantially increases the voting correlation.[10] Moreover, voters in multiparty systems typically have more than one party that is close to their own position, and thus can choose between several compatible parties based on secondary factors such as party experience, leadership, or the capacity to govern.[11] Thus, the degree to which voters translate their political views into appropriate party choices is probably stronger than the correlations of Left–Right voting in Table 6.1.

These analyses do not display a perfect relationship between Left–Right orientations and voting choice. However, compared with most social demographic predictors and many other predictors of vote (such as class, religion, or other characteristics), Left–Right orientations are routinely a much stronger

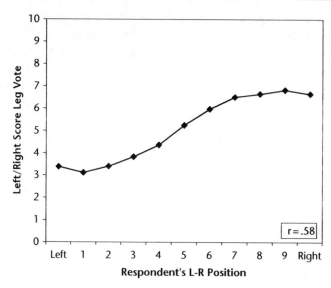

Figure 6.1. The Relationship between Individuals' Left–Right Position and Left–Right Vote

Source: CSES, module 2.

Note: The figure presents the mean Left–Right vote in legislative elections by the survey respondents' Left–Right self-placement.

predictor of vote choice—as we would expect if they represent the policy concerns of voters.

In other research, we examined these cross-national differences in some detail.[12] Electoral systems research often stresses the importance of institutional factors, but we find that characteristics of the electoral rules and institutions have only limited impact on the strength of Left–Right voting. For instance, there is a modest tendency for Left–Right voting to be stronger in proportional representation systems (r=.31) or electoral systems with a larger district magnitude (.14). In contrast to common expectations in the electoral studies literature, the number of electoral or legislative parties has little relevance for the strength of Left–Right voting (r=.02 for both counts).

Instead, characteristics of the party system have a clearer impact on the strength of Left–Right voting. The degree of ideological polarization in the party system strongly affects levels of Left–Right voting (r=.67). In addition, drawing upon the descriptions of electoral processes presented in Chapter 2, we find that Left–Right voting is stronger in party-centered systems (r=.30) and where citizens vote directly for parties at the ballot rather than candidates (r=.37). In short, the clarity of party choice substantially improves voters' ability to cast a policy-based vote derived from their Left–Right position.

Table 6.1. The Strength of Left–Right Legislative Voting by Nation

Nation	Nominal Correlation (Cramer's V)	Interval Correlation (Pearson's r)
Albania	.29	.78
Australia	.20	.50
Belgium	.19	.40
Brazil	.21	.29
Bulgaria	.37	.70
Canada	.18	.37
Chile	.27	.59
Czech Republic	.35	.83
Denmark	.30	.63
Finland	.27	.54
France	.34	.64
Germany	.19	.46
Hungary	.33	.67
Iceland	.36	.68
Ireland	.20	.36
Israel	.32	.75
Italy	.36	.79
Japan	.18	.32
Korea, South	.24	.46
Mexico	.12	.14
Netherlands	.28	.68
New Zealand	.24	.58
Norway	.31	.68
Peru	.13	.21
Philippines	.14	.06
Poland	.25	.65
Portugal '02	.38	.67
Portugal '05	.28	.54
Romania	.21	.33
Slovenia	.32	.57
Spain	.32	.74
Sweden	.35	.71
Switzerland	.26	.66
Taiwan	.12	.16
United Kingdom	.27	.46
United States	.33	.39
Average	.26	.52

Source: CSES, module 2.

Note: The table displays the relationship between respondents' Left–Right self-placement and their legislative vote choice. Vote is coded as nominal categories in the first column (Cramer's V correlation), and as quasi-interval Left–Right positions in the second column (Pearson's r correlation).

Left–Right orientations are more likely to influence voting in established democracies and nations with stable party systems. These societies have more sophisticated electorates who are more likely to vote on the issues and candidates of a campaign. Partisan choices are more strongly related to Left–Right in established democracies compared with new democracies (r=.24).[13] Apart from possessing less politically sophisticated electorates, the party systems in new democracies are more fluid, so voters are not presented with consistent choices at elections. As a consequence, the ability of voters in new democracies to determine the Left–Right positions of the parties is curtailed. In short, a nation's history of democratic elections may affect the level of Left–Right voting.[14]

These results may seem unsurprising and inevitable: Left–Right orientations are strongly related to party choice in most nations. However, for those critics who doubt the meaningfulness of citizens' Left–Right orientations or the public's understanding of the party choices available to them, the strength of this relationship demonstrates that most voters are making reasonable choices based on their political preferences. In addition, with clearer electoral choices, voters can translate more effectively their Left–Right orientations into a party preference. If democracy is about voters making political choices, then the party system that offers meaningful choices to voters is most likely to produce strong policy voting.

Partisan Representation

To this point, we have shown that voters use their Left–Right orientations to guide their partisan choices at election time. However, the process of representation and the party government model in general is a collective one. Much of the classic literature on representation in the United States focused on the link between district opinion as a collective and the individual legislator from each district, often framed in terms of delegate and trustee models of representation.[15] In contrast, in parliamentary systems the legislators are selected as members of a partisan slate and representation occurs through the party group in parliament.[16] In this party government model, a group of voters selects a party to represent them in the legislature and make public policy consistent with their views as voters (also see Chapter 7). In the words of Giovanni Sartori: "citizens in Western democracies are represented *through* and *by* parties. This is inevitable" (italics in original).[17]

The party government model thus directs the voters' attention to parties as political representatives rather than individual legislators. Indeed, Chapter 2 described how many people vote directly for a party list rather than individual candidates in many nations. And when party legislators are elected, they typically act as a united bloc representing their party's voters within the nation.[18] Political representation in most democratic systems is thus based more on a *voters–party* model than a district–legislator model. The voter half of the voters–party dyad is composed of all party supporters in a nation (even if there are geographic electoral districts); the elite half is composed of the party as an institution or party officials as a collective. If the party government model holds, we should expect a close match between the policy views of party voters and those of party elites taken as collectives.

The process of aggregating voters' positions within a party also addresses the persistent critiques about the ability of citizens to make informed electoral choices. We should judge democracy by its collective outcomes as well as by the individual choices that make up these outcomes. The collective decisions that come from elections are often better than the judgments of any single individual because they cumulate the knowledge of the whole community. Some voters might be biased in one direction, some in the opposite direction; some are well informed, others pay only limited attention to politics. However, when cumulated together, the total information brought to the collective decision should improve the outcome over single individuals. For instance, James Surowiecki's *The Wisdom of Crowds* is full of fascinating examples of how collective decisions are better than those of the individuals who contributed to the decision—ranging from guesses about how many jellybeans are in a jar to who should be president.[19]

This approach builds on the Condorcet Jury Theorem, which predicts such outcomes if certain conditions are fulfilled.[20] If individuals make imperfect but reasonable choices, then the average of their decisions will well represent their collective view. The reasonableness of citizen Left–Right orientations and perceptions has been demonstrated by the previous two chapters. In addition, the accuracy of their choices can be determined by studying voting outcomes—much like testing the theorem by comparing estimates of jellybeans in a jar to the actual number. In this case, we compare party voters' average Left–Right position to the Left–Right position of their party vote. Thus, the question is not simply how individual voters make their voting choices, but do the collective preferences of a party's voters closely match those of the party?

Of course, the answer to this question is: it depends. We expect that party voters generally match the party position on most issues, but to varying degrees.[21] In addition, since parties offer a package of policies in different domains, it is normal for people to vote for a party they generally agree with, but differ on some subset of issues. Furthermore, one can easily imagine conditions that will widen the gap between voters and parties: party identifiers may habitually vote for their preferred party even if it distances itself from their political views, voters may be attracted to a party because of a charismatic leader who outweighs policy congruence, or some voters might simply not make well-informed choices.

An additional factor that has to be taken into account is that party representatives may make vague or even conflicting statements on a policy issue, so the party's precise position may be difficult to assess. This is especially likely in parties with decentralized decision-making and multiple elites who claim to be party representatives. It is also more likely to occur in new democracies where parties have short histories or operate as factions, with ever-changing memberships and policy prescriptions. Ultimately, however, the degree of congruence is a measure of the strength of this link in the party government chain, even if voter–party congruence is inevitably imperfect.

We cannot compare all the parties on all issue controversies. However, we can again turn to the Left–Right scale as a summary measure of congruence— comparing the average Left–Right position of party voters with the entire electorate's average Left–Right placement of the party. Philip Converse and Roy Pierce, for instance, suggested that the Left–Right framework provided a means of representation and popular control even when specific policy positions were ill-formed.[22] A host of other representation studies included the Left–Right dimension as a key basis of judging voter–party agreement.

The horizontal axis in Figure 6.2 plots the average Left–Right position of each party's voters; the vertical axis plots the entire public's average Left–Right placement of the party. These two coordinates define a party's location in the figure. The 45-degree line represents perfect intraparty agreement: when the opinions of party elites exactly match those of their supporters. We study parties that have a minimum of twenty-five voters in the CSES survey.

The voters–party dyads display a strikingly high level of congruence, with a .92 correlation across these 185 parties. On average, the absolute difference

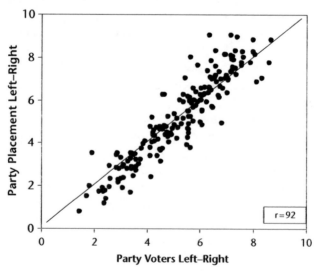

Figure 6.2. Congruence between Party Voters and Perceptions of Parties' Left–Right Position

Source: CSES, module 2.

Note: The figure plots the mean Left–Right position of party voters with the electorate's mean Left–Right placement of each party. N=185 party dyads.

between party voters' Left–Right position and the total public's Left–Right location of the party is barely half a point (.59) on the Left–Right scale. Given the potential sampling variability in both aspects of the party dyad, this level of congruence is strong confirmation that aggregate party linkage in Left–Right terms functions very well in contemporary democracies—voters as a group find a political party that represents their broad orientations quite closely and parties have voters who share their broad political orientations.

Figure 6.2 also presents a pattern of voter–elite differences that are commonly found in representation studies: political parties are more polarized than their voters. Leftist parties are more leftist than their voters (below the 45-degree line) and rightist parties are more rightist than their voters (above the line). For instance, the average voter for the French Communist Party (PCF) locates themselves at position 3.4 on the Left–Right scale, but the entire public locates the PCF as more leftist at position 2.4. Similarly, National Front voters position themselves at 7.8 on the scale, but the French public locates the party as slightly more rightist (7.9). Thus, parties generally accentuate the political differences existing within the electorate.[23]

Voter–party agreement can also vary across parties because of different party characteristics or characteristics of the party-electoral systems. Indeed, Figure 6.2 shows that agreement decreases at both ideological poles as parties hold positions more extreme than those of their average voter.[24] In addition, there is some variation by party family as depicted in Figure 6.3. Disagreement is greater for communist parties and for extreme right parties; but since overall agreement is so high, these gaps are still only modestly above the average for all parties. Regional parties show the largest gap, but this is based on only four parties.

We explored a range of other factors that might affect the degree of agreement, but found only small differences. For instance, established and new democracies differ only marginally in the size of the voter–party gap. Similarly, the size of the voter–party gap is essentially unrelated to the size of the political party. There is a tendency for this gap to be larger when the Left–Right positioning of the party varies more among members of the public (r=.16), which suggests that the clarity of party cues might improve congruence when voters can identify the party's position more easily. In essence, however, the voter–party dyad relationship is so strong that there is little systematic variation left to explain.

One might question whether the close relationship between voters and party positions is a by-product of using citizen perceptions from the CSES rather than an objective measure of party positions. When the entire public is asked to position a political party, they may ascribe a position that they identify with the typical party voter rather than party elites or the party as an institution. In this case, it would not be surprising that the average

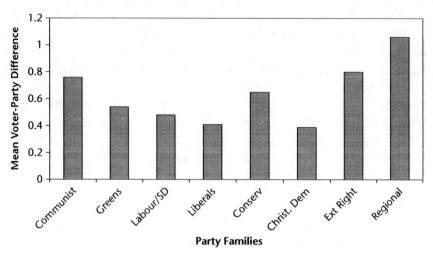

Figure 6.3. Level of Voters–Party Dyadic Difference by Party Family

Source: CSES, module 2.

Note: The figure plots the mean difference between the mean Left–Right position of party voters and the electorate's mean Left–Right placement of each party for different party families. N=117 party dyads.

Left–Right position of party voters matches the electorate's placement of the parties. However, Chapter 5 demonstrated that the public's Left–Right positioning of the parties is essentially the same as the positions given by panels of party experts and by party elites themselves. So the relationship in Figure 6.2 is not a circular by-product of comparing party voters' positions and the entire public's perceptions of party positions.

In addition, while we occasionally speak in causal terms—voter opinions presumably influence party positions—we recognize that the causal flow works in both directions. Voters influence parties, as parties try to persuade voters. The essence of the democratic marketplace is that like-minded voters and parties search out each other. Even if one cannot determine the direction of causal flow, the similarity of opinions between party voters and party elites is a meaningful measure of the representativeness of parties. Across the vast diversity of nations and parties included in our analyses, the dominant finding is that democratic elections achieve this congruence between party voters and their parties.

Furthermore, our results are consistent with other recent studies comparing the Left–Right position of party voters and their respective political parties. Jacques Thomassen and Hermann Schmitt found a very high level of agreement between party voters and elites based on the 1994 European Parliament Election Study.[25] Our comparison of party voters from the CSES module 1 and the Left–Right position of each party's Members of the National Parliament also finds strong dyadic agreement (data not shown). Similarly, a comparison of public and MP attitudes across several representation studies generally found the greatest congruence for Left–Right attitudes.[26]

In summary, these results speak to the importance of aggregation in ensuring democratic outcomes and the process of party linkage. At the individual level, there is substantial cross-national variation in the degree to which voters can link their own Left–Right orientations to their voting choices. When we aggregate voters into a party collective, the fit between party voters and their preferred party is extremely close—even in party systems where individual-level Left–Right voting correlations are very modest.[27] The aggregate party level comparisons replace the idiosyncrasies and variability of individual voters by the average position of all party voters, which matches the Left–Right position of the party very closely. Democracy begins with individual choice, but it functions as a collective decision-making process.

Party Choice and Democratic Politics: Conclusion to Part II

It is easy to imagine the complexity facing a voter as an election approaches. Many nations have several viable parties, and numerous others appear on the ballot paper. The parties' campaigns and the media deluge citizens with information—and much of this information is contradictory. Friends, neighbors, and family have their own political views, and often can see the same "fact" in different terms. The not so simple act of voting expects that citizens can sort through this information and identify a party that shares their view. Then, these choices have to be for political parties that reasonably represent the political views of their supporters. This is the essence of democratic representation.

The ability of voters to make informed political choices through elections is a major part of the party linkage model. Democracy requires that elections provide the means for citizens to make party choices that reflect competing programs of government and thus represent their voters in the governing process. Chapters 4–6 examined this assumption through the mechanism of Left–Right voting. We began with the presumption that several conditions must be fulfilled in order for citizens to connect these links of the chain in the party government model:

- Voters have policy views (Left–Right orientations);
- They accurately perceive the Left–Right choices being offered by the political parties;
- Voters use their Left–Right orientations as a major factor in voting choice.

Despite persisting skepticism of the public's ability to use an abstract concept such as Left–Right orientations, Chapter 4 found that such attitudes are widespread in contemporary democracies. Most people in most nations can locate themselves on the Left–Right scale. These positions are also meaningfully correlated with social characteristics and policy opinions.

Chapter 5 then addressed the question of whether citizens can clearly perceive the choices among the parties competing in elections, and whether these appear to be informed perceptions. Certainly many individuals do have biased or inaccurate political opinions (as do many political elites). However, we found strong evidence that people as a collective can accurately identify the Left–Right positions of political parties. In overall terms, the public's perceptions of political parties' Left–Right positions are very strongly correlated with the judgments of academic experts in each nation, as well as the self-placement of elected party officials.

This agreement in party perceptions is a striking contradiction to the literature discounting the abilities of democratic electorates. In part, the agreement arises because of the power of aggregation. While individual citizens may differ in their Left–Right placement for reasonable and unreasonable terms, the collective judgment of an electorate comes very close to other "expert" estimates of party positions. In addition, we think previous research has often focused on the examples of the public's political shortfalls, without giving equal attention to the positive traits of the citizenry. This ability to identify party positions fulfills the second of our criteria for meaningful Left–Right voting.

As many previous studies have demonstrated, this chapter has shown that Left–Right orientations are a strong predictor of individual vote choice in most elections in most nations. One might question whether this relationship is overstated because we have not controlled for other predictors of vote such as candidate image or party identification. However, in terms of policy-based voting, the direct relationship between Left–Right orientations and vote is the essential measure, even if part of this relationship is then mediated by factors such as candidate image or partisanship. Our analyses show that policy voting is a substantial part of the electoral calculus for contemporary electorates.

Even more directly related to the party linkage model, we aggregated our analyses to party dyads based on party voters and the entire public's perceptions of party positions. There is extremely close agreement between the average Left–Right position of party voters and the total electorate's perception of the Left–Right position of the party. This agreement is so strong that there is little variation in congruence across parties or party systems.

Although this level of voter–party congruence is impressive evidence of the broad functioning of representative democracy, there are some caveats to these findings. Left–Right is the best summary measure for comparing the political positions of citizens and parties, but the actual agenda of politics involves specific policy issues. In practice, this means that the agreement between voters and their parties is more varied.[28] This is to be expected, because parties must take positions on a range of issues and it is unlikely that they please all of their voters on all of these issues. In addition, specific policy agreement must be judged in terms of which issues are salient to the voter and the party—congruence on salient issues is more important than on less salient issues. As contemporary electorates become more issue-oriented in their electoral choice, these policy differences may be masked by broad Left–Right comparisons.

In addition, we suspect that the congruence between voters and parties has changed over time, but we are not sure how.[29] On the one hand, the erosion of long-standing class and religious cleavages may have blurred voter perceptions of the parties' positions. In addition, voter interests have become more fragmented as new issues have entered the political agenda. Among European democracies, for example, new issues of immigration, multiculturalism, and European integration have unsettled party alignments and voter–party congruence.[30] It was probably more valid to claim that there was a single Left–Right dimension in Western democracies during the 1950s–1960s than it is today. On the other hand, because contemporary electorates are more educated and cognitively mobilized, the ability to understand politics and select parties on their policy positions may have increased. Similarly, party elites now know more about their potential voters and their preferred policies because of the advent of polling and sophisticated research on public opinion.

Accepting these caveats, Chapters 4–6 have assembled the evidence to describe this part of the party linkage model. If the goal of elections is to enable voters to select a party that shares their political views, then the electoral process functions relatively well across the set of democratic elections we have studied. Like-minded voters and parties search out each other, and form a linkage that continues the process of party government. Certainly there are often gaps in this representation process, for reasons sometimes due to changing voter sentiment and sometimes to party positions, or differences on specific issues in a party's political program. Often electoral analyses focus on these gaps, especially when considering one country or one election. The electoral process is complex. Yet, we have shown that contemporary elections work as an effective means of democratic representation as embodied in the party government model.

Notes

1. Arthur Lupia and Mathew McCubbins, *The Democratic Dilemma: Can Citizens Learn What They Need to Know?* New York: Cambridge University Press, 1998; Richard Lau

and David Redlawsk, *How Voters Decide: Information Processing During Election Campaigns*. New York: Cambridge University Press, 2006.

2. Anthony Downs, *An Economic Theory of Democracy*. New York: Harper and Row, 1957; James Adams, Samuel Merrill III, and Bernard Grofman, *A Unified Theory of Party Competition: A Cross-National Analysis Integrating Spatial and Behavioral Factors*. New York: Cambridge University Press, 2005.

3. We realize, of course, that there is continuing academic debate on the public's understanding of public policy and thus the role of factors such as Left–Right as a basis of electoral choice. For example, *The American Voter* declared that the electorate "is almost completely unable to judge the rationality of government actions; knowing little of the particular policies and what has led to them, the mass electorate is not able either to appraise its goals or the appropriateness of the means chosen to secure these goals": Angus Campbell, Philip Converse, Warren Miller, and Donald Stokes, *The American Voter*. New York: Wiley, 1961, p. 543. Also Bryan Caplan, *The Myth of the Rational Voter: Why Democracies Choose Bad Policies*. Princeton, NJ: Princeton University Press, 2007.

4. For instance, the extent of Left–Right voting varies as a function of the political and institutional context of elections; see Russell Dalton, The quantity and quality of party systems, *Comparative Political Studies* (2008) 41: 899–920; Cees van der Eijk, Hermann Schmitt, and J. Binder, Left–Right orientations and party choice. In Jacques Thomassen, ed., *The European Voter*. Oxford: Oxford University Press, 1998.

5. Warren Miller et al., *Policy Representation in Western Democracies*. Oxford: Oxford University Press, 2000; Russell Dalton, Political parties and political representation: Party supporters and party elites in nine nations, *Comparative Political Studies* (1985) 18: 267–99.

6. See van der Eijk, Schmitt, and Binder, Left–Right orientations and party choice; Martin Kroh, The ease of ideological voting: Voter sophistication and party system complexity. In Hans-Dieter Klingemann, ed., *The Comparative Study of Electoral Systems*. Oxford: Oxford University Press, 2009; Romain Lachat, The impact of party polarization on ideological voting, *Electoral Studies* (2008) 27: 687–98; Oddbjørn Knutsen, Left–Right party polarization among the mass publics. In H. Narud and T. Aalberg, eds, *Challenges to Representative Democracy*. Bergen: Fagbokforlaget, 1990.

7. The Japanese survey was based on the upper house election, while surveys of other nations are for the lower house. The French CSES survey was conducted before the 2002 legislative elections so legislative vote was not included in the CSES release. We acquired the original French survey to analyze legislative vote intention for 2002.

8. On average, the relationship based on the Left–Right coding of parties includes 91 percent of the cases from the basic nominal relationship. However, in a few highly fragmented party systems (e.g., Brazil, the Czech Republic, and Israel) the percentage drops below 80 percent because Left–Right scores are not available for many smaller parties. The Philippines presents a special case because of the highly fragmented system and extensive non-partisan voting in legislative elections; the percentage for included cases drops to 47 percent of the nominal relationship. In several nations a coalition of parties ran as a single slate in the election (e.g., Hungary, Italy, and

Romania); in these cases we coded the coalition as the average of the constituent parties.

9. The Left–Right voting correlations for both measures in Table 6.1 are strongly related (r=.85).

10. Michael McDonald and Robin Best, The role of party policy positions in the operation of democracy. In Russell Dalton and Christopher Anderson, *Citizens, Context and Choice: How Context Shapes Citizens' Electoral Choices*. Oxford: Oxford University Press, 2011.

11. See Russell Dalton, Left–Right orientations, context and voting choice. In Russell Dalton and Christopher Anderson, eds, *Citizens, Context and Choices*. Oxford: Oxford University Press, 2011. He finds that two-fifths of the public have more than one party within a single point of them on the Left–Right scale.

12. Dalton, Left–Right orientations, context, and voting choice. The correlations in the next three paragraphs are based on the strength of Left–Right voting using the less-restrictive Cramer's V correlations. Also see van der Eijk, Schmitt, and Binder, Left–Right orientations and party choice; Kroh, The ease of ideological voting; Lachat, The impact of party polarization on ideological voting.

13. Herbert Kitschelt et al., *Post-Communist Party Systems*. New York: Cambridge University Press, 1999; Kay Lawson, Andrea Römmele, and Georgi Karasimeonov, eds, *Cleavages, Parties, and Voters: Studies from Bulgaria, the Czech Republic, Hungary, Poland, and Romania*. Westport, CT: Praeger, 1999; Hubert Tworzecki, *Learning to Choose: Electoral Politics in East-Central Europe*. Stanford: Stanford University Press, 2003.

14. In a stepwise regression to determine which aggregate characteristics had an independent impact on Left–Right voting, only two-variables entered the regression analysis as statistically significant (p<.05): party system polarization (ß=.68) and established/new democracy (ß=.28). Combined they explained 51 percent of the overall variance in Left–Right voting across nations. See Dalton, Left–Right orientations, context, and voting choice.

15. Warren Miller and Donald Stokes, Constituency influence in Congress, *American Political Science Review* (1963) 57: 45–56. Also see the related representation studies: Samuel Barnes, *Representation in Italy*. Chicago: University of Chicago Press, 1977; Barbara Farah, Political representation in West Germany. PhD dissertation, University of Michigan, 1980; Philip Converse and Roy Pierce, *Political Representation in France*. Cambridge, MA: Harvard University Press, 1986.

16. Roy Pierce, Mass-elite linkages and the responsible party government model of representation. In Warren Miller et al., eds, *Policy Representation in Western Democracies*. Oxford: Oxford University Press, 1999; Soren Holmberg, Collective policy congruence compared. In Warren Miller et al., eds, *Policy Representation in Western Democracies*. Oxford: Oxford University Press, 1999; Jacques Thomassen and Hermann Schmitt, Policy representation, *European Journal of Political Research* (1997) 32: 165–84; Dalton, Political parties and political representation.

17. Giovanni Sartori, Representational systems. In David Sills, ed., *International Encyclopedia of the Social Sciences*. New York, Macmillan, 1968, vol. 13, p. 471.

18. See Chapters 3 and 7 in this volume. Also see Shaun Bowler, David Farrell, and Richard Katz, eds., *Party Discipline and Parliamentary Government*. Columbus: Ohio

State University Press, 1999; Shaun Bowler, Parties in legislature: Two competing explanations. In Russell Dalton and Martin Wattenberg, eds, *Parties without Partisans* Oxford: Oxford University Press, 2000.

19. James Surowiecki, *The Wisdom of Crowds: Why the Many are Smarter than the Few and How Collective Wisdom Shapes Business, Economies, Societies, and Nations*. New York: Doubleday, 2004; also see Howard Rheingold, *Smart Mobs: The Next Social Revolution*. Cambridge, MA: Perseus Press, 2002; Cass Sunstein, *Infotopia: How Many Minds Produce Knowledge*. Oxford: Oxford University Press, 2006.

20. On the Condorcet Jury Theorem, see Bernard Grofman and Scott Feld, Rousseau's general will: A Condorcetian perspective, *American Political Science Review* (1988) 82: 567–76.

21. Russell Dalton, *Citizen Politics: Public Opinion and Political Parties in Advanced Industrial Democracies*, 5th edn. Washington, DC: CQ Press, 2008, ch. 11.

22. Philip Converse and Roy Pierce, *Political Representation in France*. Cambridge, MA: Harvard University Press, 1989, pp. 772–74.

23. The simple regression analysis quantifies this pattern. The slope for the relationship in Figure 6.3 is b=1.13, and the intercept is a=−.74.

24. We also modeled this as a non-linear relationship, but this was not statistically significant.

25. Hermann Schmitt and Jacques Thomassen, eds, *Political Representation and Legitimacy in the European Union*. Oxford: Oxford University Press, 1999.

26. Pierce, Mass-elite linkages and the responsible party model, pp. 20–3.

27. For example, in the four nations with the weakest Left–Right voting in Table 6.1 (Mexico, Peru, Philippines, and Taiwan), the average gap between voters and party is only a tenth of a scale point greater than the overall average.

28. Pierce, Mass-elite issue linkages and the responsible party government model of representation; Soren Holmberg, Dynamic representation from above. In Martin Rosema, Bas Denters, and Kees Aarts, eds. *How Democracy Works: Political Representation and Policy Congruence in Modern Societies*. Amsterdam: Amsterdam University Press/Pallas Publications, 2011.

29. Two insightful studies compare party voters and Members of Parliament over time for Sweden and the Netherlands. They find evidence that voter–party congruence on the overall Left–Right scale has improved over the past few decades, even while new issues have entered the political agenda. See Holmberg, Dynamic representation from above. Jacques Thomassen, The blind corner of representation. Paper presented at the conference on Comparative Perspectives on Political Representation, Simon Fraser University, Vancouver, July 2010.

30. Liesbet Hooghe, Gary Marks, and Carole Wilson, Does Left/Right structure party positions on European integration? *Comparative Political Studies* (2002) 35: 965–89; Hanspieter Kriesi et al., Globalization and the transformation of the national political space: Six European countries compared, *European Journal of Political Research* (2006) 45: 921–56.

III. Parties in Government

7

Government Formation and Democratic Representation

On November 22, 2006 Dutch voters went to the polls to elect a new parliament.* The election produced a shift toward the left (the Socialist Party nearly tripled its vote share), which yielded a rough balance between left and right. Because of the Netherlands' highly proportional electoral system, the parties' vote shares in the election were closely translated into their seat shares in the House of Representatives. Ten parties won seats in the parliament. On November 30 the new parliament took office—and negotiations about who would form the government began. Because of the diversity of the party system, there were several possible ways that a new majority government might be formed. Party leaders met with an *informateur*, whom Queen Beatrix appointed to explore cabinet options and share information across party groups. These discussions continued in several rounds until the end of December. In early January formal negotiations on forming a new government began in earnest, but party negotiations continued for another month. In early February the CDA, PvdA, and CU finally reached a coalition agreement, and Queen Beatrix appointed a *formateur* to implement the coalition agreement. Queen Beatrix appointed the new cabinet on February 22, 2007. Since the previous minority cabinet had called for new elections in June 2006, this caretaker cabinet had governed for nearly eight months.

This example demonstrates that elections oftentimes do not decide the government in multiparty systems. In this case, the government was decided not by the voters, but through the negotiations of party elites three months after the election. This post-election coalition process raises several questions about whether the resulting government is congruent with the broad Left–Right preferences of the Dutch public.

The previous chapters discussed the voters' deliberations and choices between the parties in elections. This chapter continues examining the chain of party government by tracking the process after the votes have been counted. As the Dutch example shows, elections in multiparty systems often require coalition negotiations to form a new government—and we briefly describe this process. If the outcome of elections is not direct and controlled by the public, then this raises the question of the public's ability to use elections as an instrument of democratic control. Indeed, an author of the classic study of political representation in the United States concluded: "few serious students of government are convinced the connection between elections and acts of government is sufficiently close to allow the mere existence of a formal system of government to stand as a test of the empirical premises of the system."[1]

The theoretical literature on representation provides the foundation for the research presented here.[2] However, we offer a different perspective on how elections produce democratic representation and accountability. We suggest that party-based democracy works through a process of ongoing, dynamic representation that occurs through a comparison of the past and the future across repeated elections. In other words, elections are not simply a method of collective political choice at election time, *but act as a dynamic method of steering the course of government.*

This chapter proceeds in four steps. First, we briefly review the literature on government coalition formation, and illustrate these processes with the nations from the CSES. Second, we review the previous literature on political representation and offer a dynamic extension of this literature. Third, we examine the empirical correspondence between citizens and their government as a test of the dynamic model and explain how dynamic representation occurs. The concluding section discusses the implications of our findings for our framework of party-based governance.

Government Formation

One of the leading electoral researchers in Germany often said, "voters don't decide election outcomes in Germany, the FDP decides."[3] This is because no single party holds a majority of seats after the election in many multiparty systems, and so parties must negotiate with others to form a majority governing coalition. In Germany the small Free Democratic Party (FDP) often holds enough parliamentary seats to produce a majority if it aligns itself with either of the two major parties.

This coalition process applies to many of the nations in the CSES (Table 7.1). In more than two-thirds of these nations, a multiparty coalition formed the government. This is the common outcome in electoral systems with proportional representation (PR) and many parties competing in elections. On average, about 2.5 parties are represented in the governing cabinets, with the

Table 7.1. Absolute and Effective Number of Governing Parties

Country	Absolute Number of Parties	Effective Number of Parties
Albania	5	1.88
Australia	2	1.32
Belgium	4	4.00
Brazil	5	3.30
Bulgaria	3	2.08
Canada	1	1.00
Chile	3	–
Czech Republic	3	1.87
Denmark	2	1.53
Finland	3	2.28
France	1	1.00
Germany	2	1.43
Hungary	2	1.22
Iceland	2	1.84
Ireland	2	1.20
Israel	4	2.42
Italy	7	–
Japan	3	1.32
Korea, South	1	1.00
Mexico	1	1.00
Netherlands	3	2.79
New Zealand	2	1.08
Norway	3	1.99
Peru	1	1.00
Poland	3	1.58
Portugal '02	2	1.27
Portugal '05	1	1.00
Romania	3	1.75
Russia	1	1.00
Slovenia	4	2.43
Spain	1	1.00
Sweden	1	1.00
Switzerland	4	3.74
Taiwan '01	3	1.97
Taiwan '04	3	1.76
United Kingdom	1	1.00
United States	1	1.00

Source: CSES, module 2, macro datafile.

Albanian and Italian cabinets overflowing with five and seven parties respectively. In contrast, most single-member plurality electoral systems produce single-party governments (Canada, Britain, and the United States) because the electoral system encourages majoritarian outcomes.

Table 7.1 also shows that in many instances one dominant party aligns with one or more smaller parties. This is seen by the substantially lower effective number of governing parties in the second column of the table.[4] In the German example, the 2002 elections produced a government of the Social Democratic Party and the Greens. The Social Democrats won 42 percent of the parliamentary seats in the election, and depended on the Greens' 9 percent to gain a majority. Such unbalanced coalitions are common, typically based around a dominant Left party or dominant Right party, and its coalition allies.

The formation of government can be an evolving process. One option in multiparty systems is to form a pre-election alliance and campaign with a formal or implicit commitment to form a government with the parties in the alliance—typically such coalitions are based on ideologically compatible parties.[5] In the highly fragmented Italian party system, for example, two broad electoral alliances formed before the 2006 parliamentary elections. The House of Freedoms coalition included at least nine conservative parties, with Silvio Berlusconi as the prime ministerial candidate. The Union was a leftist coalition of another nine parties, including the Olive Tree which was itself a coalition of three parties. The Union won a narrow victory, and Romano Prodi became prime minister with a cabinet including the parties from the Union coalition. In other instances, the pre-electoral coalitions are more implicit but their composition is still signaled to the voters. In the 2002 Irish elections, the incumbent Fianna Fáil party and the Progressive Democrats indicated their intention to form a post-election government if they won sufficient votes, but both parties ran independent campaigns to court the voters.

The thirty-eight cases in Table 7.1 span a variety of outcomes. Eleven elections resulted in single-party majorities. In nine elections there were formal pre-election coalitions that formed the post-election majority (in three of these cases this required the addition of a minor party to produce a majority of seats). In four additional elections there was an implicit coalition comprised of the incumbent parties who ran to re-elect the government although each party ran an independent campaign. Finally, in thirteen nations the election resulted in multiparty governments where a pre-election agreement was lacking, and so coalition formation began after the election.

Pre-election coalitions serve many purposes. For the voters they simplify what might otherwise appear as a bewildering array of parties competing in the election. Instead of viewing the 2006 Italian ballot as a choice between several dozen parties that might actually win parliamentary seats, the coalitions of the Union and the House of Freedoms made the broad programmatic choices more identifiable for voters. Bingham Powell shows how such identifiability improves voters' ability to collectively hold political parties in a coalition accountable for past actions and policy statements.[6] Equally important, such identifiability allows voters to control more clearly the formation of the post-election government so that elections decide governments and not post-election elite bargaining as in the Dutch example at the start of this chapter. With pre-election coalitions, voters know in advance that these parties would combine to form a government. Even when a coalition falls short of a majority and must gain an additional party to govern, the pre-election coalition, typically, defines the framework for a post-election governing program. So at first appearance, multiparty governments may weaken the clarity of political representation and accountability, but pre-election coalitions lessen this possibility.

If a government does not result from a single party or coalition winning a majority, then a post-election coalition process is required. The determination of the governing majority is often a complex process involving informal norms (such as the largest party has the first opportunity to form a government) and formal rules and procedures (such as the role of a separate head of state in identifying the new government).[7] The complexity of the options, such as the number of parties and the number of issues being addressed, affects the ease of coalition formation and the stability of the resulting government. Negotiations are also complicated when there is uncertainty about party preferences and strategies. Among West European democracies in the later twentieth century, the typical post-election coalition took slightly more than five weeks of negotiations after the election, but many took months to resolve.[8]

Even with the complexity of negotiation among multiple parties, the dominant factor in determining which parties form a government is their ideological (or policy) compatibility.[9] Comparisons linked to Left–Right positions are omnipresent throughout this process. Parties form pre-election coalition agreements because they share a general view of what government should do. After the election, parties are more likely to coalesce into a majority coalition if they have such shared policy visions. Other factors certainly come into play, but if parties do not broadly agree on the course of government it is difficult to agree to govern together.

Coalition researchers generally describe such ideologically compatible coalitions in terms of their positions on the Left–Right dimension or in a multidimensional space, and a "connected coalition" consists of parties that are adjacent to each other on the dimension and which together hold a majority of parliamentary seats.[10] For instance, the two broad pre-election coalitions in the Italian 2006 elections were largely defined in terms of left and right blocs. Similarly, after the 1998 Swedish elections the Social Democrats lacked a majority, and formed a coalition with the Left Party and the Greens, which were immediately adjacent to it on the Left–Right scale (see Figures 5.4 and 5.5). There are, of course, exceptions to connected coalitions: the 2003 Belgian elections produced a disconnected "purple coalition" uniting parties of the left and right in the hope of producing national unity through the incorporation of both blocs.[11] The most unusual case is Switzerland, where until 2008 the four major parties routinely agreed to a post-election power-sharing agreement, and garnered more than three-quarters of the seats in the National Council.

We cannot formally test for ideologically connected coalitions across the CSES nations because we have a relatively small number of multiparty coalitions and we are missing Left–Right placements for some coalition partners.

However, when we pool the available party data for roughly two dozen coalition governments where we have sufficient information, about two-thirds of these coalitions are composed of parties that are essentially ideologically adjacent on the Left–Right scale. In a few cases a regional or ethnic party is included in the government for reasons separate from Left–Right agreement, such as the Swedish People's Party in Finland or the Agrarian Party in Bulgaria. The major deviations are the purple coalition in Belgium, the Likud-led coalition that emerged from the 2003 Israeli elections, and the Grand Coalition in Switzerland.

In summary, forming a multiparty governing coalition is another discrete link in the process of party government in most democracies. Coalition negotiations among political parties can weaken the link between citizens and their government if the resulting coalitions are not representative of electoral outcomes or are distorted by elite priorities in the negotiations.[12] Yet, the constraints of Left–Right ideology run through this entire process, from the development of pre-election coalition agreements to post-election coalition negotiations that create governments of ideologically connected parties. It is inevitable that governing parties do not agree on all issues, and even MPs within a single-party government will disagree. But the Left–Right framework seems to provide the connecting mechanism that defines the governments formed after elections.

Conceptualizing Representation

As we have just noted, the coalition formation process occurring between elections and the investiture of the government may blur the process of political representation because elections that do not yield a single victor can have ambiguous outcomes. Thus, a core question is: how well are voters' preferences actually represented by the government that emerges following elections? This section lays the foundation for our empirical analyses by discussing two questions that are central to this issue: who is represented and how they are represented?

Who is Represented?

How do we assess political representation in a democracy? Modern empirical research offers three different answers to this question, evolving from studying the representativeness of individual legislatures, to political parties, to the government overall. First, the early Michigan representation studies focused on the linkage between an electoral district and its legislator. This followed from the long-standing debate over trustee–delegate models of representation in a single-member plurality (SMP) electoral system.[13] This research compared opinions of voters in an electoral district with those of the legislator elected from the district, and yielded mixed empirical results especially in the party-dominated European cases.

In a second phase, research focused on the linkage between voters and their preferred parties rather than individual legislators. The partisan model seems more relevant for parliamentary systems with strong political parties.[14] In these nations, parties rather than candidates are the prime vehicles for representing their voters. The party government model thus compares agreement between voters and their selected party.

To an extent, Chapter 6 addressed this point by comparing the Left–Right positions of party voters and the parties themselves. We demonstrated strikingly high congruence between these voter–party dyads in terms of their Left–Right positions. The correlation was almost perfect (r=.92) across the CSES module 2 nations. Thus, democracy generally works to unite voters and parties that share a common political orientation as the basis of having their views represented in the legislature.

However, the previous section in this chapter discussed how electing parties is only an intermediate stage to electing a government in most multiparty parliamentary systems. And selecting a government is the ultimate goal of elections. Many democratic governments cannot even claim to represent a majority of the voters because of distortions introduced by electoral rules. So a broader definition of representation focuses on the extent to which governments represent the citizenry. But who does government represent among the citizens?

The broadest perspective maintains that government exists to represent all the people. John Stuart Mill and other liberal philosophers argued that only a government that represents all the people is truly democratic. Otherwise, they maintain that a government either distorts the public's preferences or could trample the rights and interests of the minority. Contemporary scholars have similarly stressed that a true democratic process should be judged by how well it represents the median citizen.[15] Perhaps one of the clearest recent examples is Barack Obama's stress during the 2008 campaign that the distinctions between blue states and red states were superficial and he would represent the United States. Indeed, such rhetoric is common from politicians *after* they have won election.

Reflecting this logic, G. Bingham Powell was one of the first to compare empirically the Left–Right position of the *median citizen* (from public opinion surveys) with the Left–Right position of the governing parties (from expert surveys) for a large set of established Western democracies.[16] He found broad congruence, which varied with the clarity of government responsibility and other contextual factors. Since then, several studies have used the

Comparative Manifesto Project data to compare the median citizen's Left–Right position with the position of the government.[17] Much of this research has considered how electoral system rules might affect the degree of congruence between citizens and their government in Western democracies.[18] Recent studies have expanded the comparisons to include new democracies in Eastern Europe and East Asia. In broad terms, these studies of citizens–government congruence found high levels of agreement—evidence that democracy works.[19]

One can make an equally valid argument that parties campaign to represent those who place them in office: *the electoral majority*. This is typically the rhetoric of candidates and parties *during* a campaign as they appeal to their supporters. Indeed, the principle of majority rule seems central to the democratic creed ranging from Bentham's philosophical advocacy of majority rule to modern public choice arguments that only majority rule ensures political equality and accountability.[20] And through the alternation of majority governments of different perspectives, the public's overall interests are represented in cumulative terms.[21] Yet, empirical research on representation has typically focused on the views of the entire electorate and not the majority.

There is some evidence that politicians think about their mandate primarily in terms of their own supporters. Bernhard Wessels has shown that MPs in several European parliaments are almost equally likely to state that they represent all the people in the country as that they represent party voters.[22] Representation studies in Australia, France, Italy, Norway, and Sweden similarly found that parliamentarians primarily define their role in terms of representing their party.[23]

In addition, even in terms of representing a geographic constituency, previous research has demonstrated that the fit between legislators' political positions and those of their party supporters is much closer than for the constituency as a whole. In one such comparison in Italy, Samuel Barnes concludes: "it is apparent that the mean opinion of all the respondents in the constituency explains very little [of elite responses]. Party, on the other hand, raises the strength of these relationships tremendously."[24] We therefore should consider the congruence between the government and the median Left–Right position of its supporters as another definition of representative government.

How Representation Occurs

Previous research typically examined representation as a static cross-sectional relationship between citizens and parties/government based on a single point in time. Do voters in an election get a government that is generally congruent with their overall policy preferences—which is the essence of democratic representation? This literature debates the time frame of representation.

Does representation function through voters evaluating alternatives prospectively and providing governments with a mandate for future action, or do voters judge the performance of past governments retrospectively and hold them accountable at election time?[25] This is a reasonable starting point, but we believe that this approach creates a false dichotomy and misspecifies the actual nature of democratic representation.

Democracy is not a single event, but an ongoing process. Voters typically face a competition structured by one set of parties that is right of the median citizen, and another set that is to the left of the median citizen. The alternatives may overlap with the median citizen, but the governing options normally draw election outcomes away from the moderate median citizen. The clearest example is in the United States, where voters face a choice between a Democratic administration to their left and a Republican administration to their right. Often the alternation of government is the most feasible way to produce long-term representation of public preferences, even in proportional representation systems with multiparty governments.[26]

Furthermore, people judge parties not just by what they said in the campaign, but by how they actually govern and by the decisions they take that affect people's lives. Sometimes the gap between campaign rhetoric and the reality of governing can be large. George H. W. Bush's "read my lips, no new taxes" comes to mind, followed by a tax increase once he won re-election. Helmut Kohl followed the same script following the 1990 German elections. Parties and governments also campaign on a large range of issues, and the attention given to each may change overall public perceptions of government performance because the public's agreement with the governing parties on specific issues should naturally vary. Between elections new parties or political leaders emerge, so citizen decisions might shift with a new choice set. In fact, given the complexity of politics, it is almost inevitable that some voters (and expert analysts) are surprised by some of the actions of government once it takes office. Democratic governance is as much about selecting governments that are representative of the public, as it is about voting out governments that are not responsive to public preferences.

Thus, rather than a single decision, the representative aspect of elections is more like a repetitive decision process or repetitive game. The example of navigating a sailboat might be a useful, albeit imperfect, analogy. The public (the captain) makes the best choice in directing the ship of state (the government) at the moment. But one cannot sail into a headwind in a direct line (assume the objective is to represent the median citizen), and must tack to make progress. If a government moves too far in one direction while in office, the next election provides a mechanism to shift direction back toward the public's collective preferences. If the public oversteers in one election, perhaps influenced by a charismatic personality or an intense issue controversy, they can correct the government's policy course at the next election. And if conditions in the world change, elections can also steer a new course in response to these changes. In short, representative democracy is a repetitive decision-making process that provides a method for the citizenry to adjust the course of government, correcting discrepancies in direction that arise from the actions of the incumbent government or new political developments.[27]

In fact, we might argue that democracy's primary strength is its ability to enter such feedback into the political process. Prospective voting on a party or government's election manifesto is only likely to generate meaningful representation if there is accountability at the next election. Retrospective evaluations of a government's performance have greater meaning if considered in terms of the government's initial policy goals. To dichotomize accountability and representation misses the key point that both can function meaningfully only in a process where they are both considered on an ongoing basis across elections.

There is partial empirical evidence supporting this framework in the research literature. McDonald, Mendes, and Budge argue that while governments might deviate from the median citizen in the short run, in reaction to events of a campaign or other reasons, democracy works to ensure that citizen preferences are taken into account in the long run.[28] This dynamic perspective appears in time-series research linking public opinion and government policy outputs.[29]

This chapter provides a partial empirical test of this dynamic hypothesis. The comparison of citizen and government positions across nations and across time is a difficult empirical challenge because of the data requirements it imposes. We therefore present a simple first test of the dynamic hypothesis. We ask whether citizen agreement with a newly elected government is greater than with the pre-election government. *If representation is a dynamic process, then post-election congruence generally should be greater than pre-election congruence, as citizens steer the ship of state back in the direction to reach their broad policy goals.*

The Evidence on Representation

The standard methodology in examining the representativeness of government compares the position of the median citizen or voter, with the position of the government. The degree of congruence indicates the extent to which elections generate a democratic government that reflects public preferences.

As in other chapters in this volume, we begin by assuming that party competition is structured along a Left–Right dimension, which we now apply to the study of representation.[30] For each nation we calculated the *median Left–Right score for the entire public* among those who expressed a Left–Right position. If government is to represent everyone, then this is the standard of reference. In addition, we calculated the *median Left–Right score for the voters who supported a party that entered the post-election government* (held seats in the cabinet). This is a definition of representation based solely on a government's electoral constituency.

The median citizen position and the median position of voters for the governing parties are theoretically and empirically distinct. One is comprised of all the public, the other of only half (or less). As we might expect, government voters are sometimes significantly to the left of the public overall, and sometimes they are to the right.[31] One can think of the American or British case, where elections produce a government to the left or right of the median citizen because the party choices are more polarized than the electorate itself, such as Obama versus McCain in 2008 or Brown versus Cameron in 2010. At the same time, there is a very strong correlation between the Left–Right positions of the median citizen and the median government supporter across all thirty-six CSES nations (r=.72). This may initially seem counterintuitive if some governments are to the left of center and some to the right. But this pattern occurs because of the cross-national variation in the overall Left–Right distribution of citizens. When the majority of the public positions itself on the left, both the median citizen and a majority of government voters are typically to the left of center. In nations where the majority locate themselves on the right, both the median citizen and the median government supporter are generally to the right. Such consistency in Left–Right views is only apparent in cross-national comparison.

The next step estimates the position of the government in Left–Right terms. We begin with the public's positioning of political parties on the Left–Right scale from Chapter 5. When parliamentary systems produce a multiparty governing coalition, we combine scores for the parties in the governing coalition. We follow the standard methodology to define the government's Left–Right position as the average of the governing parties weighted by each party's share of cabinet portfolios.[32] This gives greater weight to large parties that exercise more influence in setting government policy. And naturally, in a single-party government the government's position is synonymous with this party. We use this method to estimate a Left–Right score for both the pre-election government and the post-election government.

There are, of course, many caveats and conditions that precede such a comparison.[33] The use of a single Left–Right dimension to summarize citizen and government positions has both advantages and disadvantages in capturing political reality, especially when used to compare citizens and governments across very diverse democracies. The broad Left–Right dimension undoubtedly overestimates the agreement on specific policy issues because it averages together divergent issue positions. In addition, the weighted combination of parties in the governing cabinet might not fully reflect the power of each party in defining government actions. And in some instances, information is missing which can bias our estimates. Consequently, we approach these analyses with modest expectations.

Citizens and Governments

The challenge of democratic governance is to aggregate the interests of millions of individuals, across a vast potential array of issues, into a government that broadly represents the public. One could imagine that even a benign dictator would find this a difficult challenge because of the complexity of the task. What does the public really want? How does one reconcile conflicting issue interests, such as for economic growth and environmental protection? And presumably some politicians and political parties have their own less than altruistic motivations for seeking government. So a central question of our party government model is: how well does government represent its citizens? We approach this in two steps paralleling our theoretical discussion above: first we examine who is represented, and then the process of representation.

Who is Represented?

We begin with the broadest possible measure of representation: that government should represent all the citizenry, even those who voted for an opposition party or did not vote. This involves comparing the Left–Right position of the median citizen and the Left–Right position of the newly elected government. Figure 7.1 depicts a strong congruence between citizens and their elected governments. Leftist publics generally select leftist governments, and similarly on the right. One way of summarizing this is to note that only four of the thirty-six nations lie in the two off-diagonal quadrants that indicate a government is significantly out of synch with its public.[34] In overall terms, the congruence in Figure 7.1 provides strong evidence that democratic representation works even over this varied set of established and new democracies—as noted by the .60 correlation between these variables.

As we might expect, the scores for the citizens cluster near the center of the Left–Right scale (between 4.0 and 6.0), since there is a bell-shaped distribution of the public's Left–Right attitudes in most nations. The Left–Right positions of governments are more varied, with a standard deviation that is three times larger than for the citizen scores. This means that *governments accentuate differences between electorates by roughly a two-to-one ratio*. In other words, a

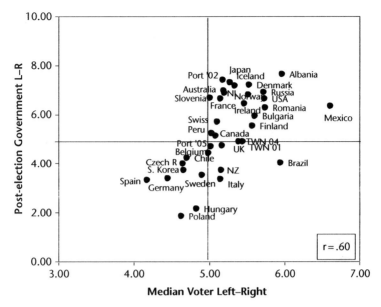

Figure 7.1. Comparing Median Citizen and Post-Election Government on Left–Right Scale

Source: CSES, module 2.

Note: The figure plots the median Left–Right position of the public and the average post-election government position (party scores weighted by shares of cabinet seats) for each nation. N=36.

one-point difference in the median position of the public overall predicts a two-point change in the composition of the government.[35] In addition, the government was selected by only half the public, and thus it typically leans more to the left or right than the public as a whole.

Another alternative is that governments attempt to represent their own voters more so than the public overall—which is a reasonable strategy for electoral success. We examine this definition of representation by comparing the median Left–Right position of those who voted for a governing party with the Left–Right position of the government bloc (Figure 7.2). This figure provides striking evidence that contemporary democratic governments are congruent with their own voters. Given the potential imperfections in our empirical measures, the .91 correlation between voters and their government is as close to perfect as we are likely to see. Or expressed in other terms, the public overall differs over one point from its governments on the Left–Right scale across these thirty-six nations; the average gap between voters and their government is less than half a point.

The degree of congruence between citizens and their governments is an essential measure of the meaningfulness of democratic representation and

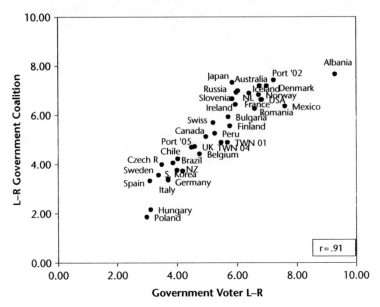

Figure 7.2. Comparing Median Voter for Government Parties and Government on Left–Right Scale

Source: CSES, module 2.

Note: The figure plots the median Left–Right position of the voters for the governing parties and the average post-election government position (party scores weighted by shares of cabinet seats) for each nation. N=36.

accountability. This led us to ask if there are institutional factors that facilitate congruence, perhaps differentially for our two measures of citizen opinions. For instance, previous literature compares the representation gap across different characteristics of the electoral system that might facilitate representation. Initial evidence suggested greater congruence in proportional representation systems, but this relationship seems to have narrowed in recent elections.[36] We also might expect that new democracies experience greater fluidity and volatility as the party system is being established, which would suggest greater congruence in established democracies. Furthermore, Powell's most recent research indicates that the level of party system polarization along the Left–Right continuum is even more strongly related to congruence between government and the median citizen than are electoral system characteristics.[37]

We measured the representation gap as: (1) the absolute difference between the government's Left–Right position and that of the median citizen, and (2) the absolute difference using the median supporter of the governing parties. Figure 7.3 correlates these two representation measures with several national characteristics. Consistent with other recent research, the nature of the

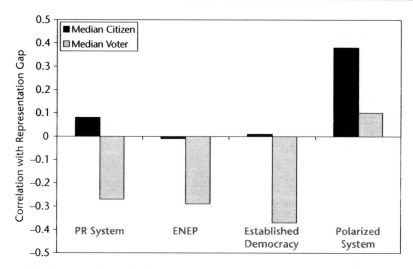

Figure 7.3. The Correlates of Public–Government Congruence

Source: CSES, module 2.

Note: The figure plots the Pearson r correlation between the representation gap (the difference between the public's and the government's Left–Right position) and each national characteristic. We calculate the gap separately using the median position of all citizens and the median position of those who voted for a party in the post-election government. N=36.

electoral system—either a majoritarian/PR system or the effective number of electoral parties—is now essentially unrelated to the representation gap based on the median citizen.[38] However, these same two characteristics are significantly related to the representation gap between governments and their own voters. PR systems and those with a larger number of parties produce a substantially smaller gap between governments and their own voters. This is because parties in PR systems are less subject to the centrifugal and centripetal forces that pull parties away from their supporters in majoritarian systems, where parties often engage in competition for the median voter.

The two other contextual variables also display significant, albeit varied, effects on the representation gap. New and established democracies do not differ in the gap between government and the median citizen, but established democracies are more successful in lessening the gap between governments and their own supporters. Finally, party systems that are highly polarized along the Left–Right dimension produce a larger representation gap between governments and the median citizen.[39] This is because a polarized system presents the public with stark partisan options, and an elected government is more likely to be distant from non-supporters. At the same time, polarization has little impact on congruence with a government's own supporters because only the subset of government voters is being compared.

175

These findings suggest that elections broadly produce governments that represent the position of the median citizen, and even more clearly reflect the Left–Right preferences of their voters. Although there have been frequent claims that the structure of the electoral system affects these relationships, we find that PR/majoritarian systems are about equally effective in representing the median citizen. Identifying who is being represented makes more difference than how they are represented.

How Representation Occurs

Most analyses of political representation focus on the evidence just presented in the previous section. The basic and important question is: how well does government represent its citizens? This framing of the question focuses on a single dyadic comparison.

However, an equally important question is: how does this congruence occur? Our dynamic model of representation implies that democratic elections should provide the power to remove governments that are not consistent with public preferences while retaining governments that share the public's political views. This requires that we compare the congruence between citizens and governments over time and across changes in government. We do this by comparing the public's Left–Right congruence with both pre-election governments and post-election governments.

We might expect a broadly similar relationship between citizen Left–Right positions and those of pre- and post-election governments because of the incumbency advantage and the persistence of government. When incumbents are re-elected, there is no change. Therefore, we might hypothesize that most changes in government are incremental rather than dramatic, especially in multiparty PR systems. But a theory of meaningful democratic representation and accountability would predict that congruence should generally be greater for the post-election comparison if elections generally provide a method to steer government back on course. This is a basic assumption about accountability in democratic theory.

Figure 7.4 compares the Left–Right position of the median citizen and the Left–Right position of the government in office immediately before the CSES election. This figure is strikingly different from Figure 7.1. For the exact same set of nations there is only a weak and statistically insignificant relationship between citizens and the pre-election government (r=.06). In this comparison, about a third of the nations are in the two off-diagonal quadrants. Spain and Poland, for example, had pre-election governments that the public perceived as much more conservative than the median citizen, while the Albanian and Romanian governments were seen as much more liberal than the median citizen. Moreover, this is not because the public changed its position (it is the

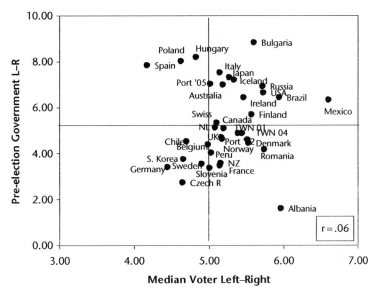

Figure 7.4 Comparing Citizens and Pre-Election Government on Left–Right Scale

Source: CSES, module 2.

Note: The figure plots the median Left–Right position of the public and the average pre-election government position (party scores weighted by shares of cabinet seats) for each nation. N=36.

same in both Figures 7.1 and 7.4), nor because the public changed its Left–Right placement of individual parties (the same party scores are used in both figures to calculate the government position). Another way to express this pattern is to compare the absolute difference in the Left–Right positions between the median citizen and the pre-election and post-election governments. This gap decreases from an average difference of 1.39 scale points for the pre-election government to 1.13 for the post-election government.

In other words, by the end of an election cycle some governments are distant from the Left–Right political orientations of the citizenry. This is when electoral accountability can improve democratic representation. In many of the nations where citizens see the pre-election government as out of synch with the public's broad political orientations, elections provide a way to increase congruence—this is how democracy should work.

These results show that elections can change the course of government, either shifting the tiller of state to the right or the left. And yet we might presume that there is a generally persisting pattern of congruence as we have measured it: leftist publics will generally elect leftist governments, and rightist publics will generally elect rightist governments. And most of the time, governments (or the major coalition parties) are re-elected. We can marshal more direct evidence on the ideological changeability of government produced by elections by comparing the pre-election and post-election governments directly in the CSES nations.

Figure 7.5 plots the pre-election and post-election Left–Right positions of the governments. First, about half of the nations in this set (19) had elections that returned the incumbent government to office or produced small shifts in the composition of the cabinets (less than .50 on the Left–Right scale). These nations lie along the 45-degree line indicating the same pre-/post-election position, or very close to the line if a small shift in cabinet seats changed the average for the coalition.

The dynamic effect of elections enters when there is a significant change in government. This is quite apparent in the nations that are located off the diagonal. For instance, the 2004 Spanish election produced a shift from the People's Party-led government of José María Aznar to the socialist government of José Luis Rodríguez Zapatero. This caused a 4.52-point shift in the Left–Right composition of the Spanish government. Similarly, the Democratic Left Alliance victory in Poland produced more than a 6-point leftward shift in the

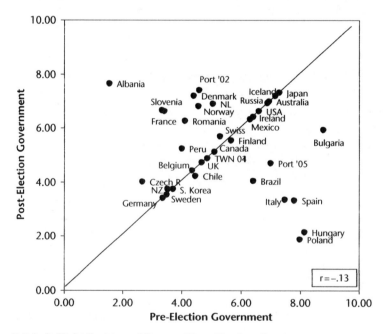

Figure 7.5 Left–Right Position of Pre- and Post-Election Governments

Source: CSES, module 2.

Note: The figure plots the average Left–Right position of governments (party scores weighted by shares of cabinet seats) for each nation. N=36.

government (on a 0–10 scale). Elections in Denmark, the Netherlands, Norway, and Portugal produced sizeable rightward shifts between pre- and post-election governments. These are the political equivalents of seismic shocks, dramatically altering the political landscape.

At least to the authors, this pre-/post-election comparison is a striking pattern. To the extent that these results from the CSES nations are generalizable to other democracies, this means that the composition of a post-election government is essentially independent of the pre-election government (r=−.13)—even factoring in the perfect stability of re-elected incumbents. This might be interpreted as meaning that elections are a random process, with no predictability of what will happen after the votes are counted. However, Figures 7.1 and 7.4 show that this is not a random process, since voters are steering government toward a position more consistent with their median Left–Right preferences.

In addition, there are some systematic patterns in these cross-time comparisons. For instance, the overall Left–Right polarization of the party system is strongly related to the absolute difference in the Left–Right position of pre-/post-election governments (r=.46). This presumably occurs because when voters do change course in highly polarized systems, the available party choices generate a large shift in government positions. The shifts in pre-/post-election governments are also greater in proportional representation systems than in majoritarian electoral systems (Eta=.35). While one might expect PR systems to produce less change because of a smaller shifting of vote shares among parties, the greater diversity of choices and the increased likelihood of alternation in government create more volatility. Even though majoritarian democracies may produce a substantial policy shift when the majority changes, the obvious point is that a change in government occurs less frequently in these systems.[40] Among the six majoritarian elections in our set, only one produced a change in government.

Finally, pre-/post-election shifts tend to be larger in new democracies than in established democracies (Eta=.18). This seems consistent with a pattern of political entropy that suggests greater partisan and government volatility in new democracies which decreases with the institutionalization of the political system and, more specifically, with the development of a stable party system. Yet we also note that some of the largest instances of pre-/post-election volatility occur in established democracies

How Does Congruence Increase?

Although one can provide a *post hoc* explanation for the shifts in government in most of the nations in Figure 7.5, some broader processes must generate these general patterns. Some elections obviously produce governments that deviate from past electoral history, but there is a restorative process that then works to improve congruence over time. This seems like simple Downsian spatial competition at work. However, the actual mechanisms of citizen–government congruence are more complex than implied by the basic Downsian model. This section thus considers how this dynamic relationship between voters and governments functions.[41]

The simplest explanation for a change in government is that the public changes its median position. For instance, an economic recession or a terrorist attack may stimulate individuals to shift their political views. Or popular reactions to government policies may stimulate a rethinking of Left–Right orientations. Governments can lead as well as follow. In addition, there may be differential turnout between groups of voters that will influence the Left–Right position of the electorate as a whole.[42] These processes are likely to produce small aggregate changes in the position of the median citizen because Left–Right orientations are fairly stable. However, often governments change because of a shift in party vote shares of 10 percent or less. For instance, the large shift in Left–Right position of the government after the 2004 Spanish parliamentary elections resulted from only a 6–8 percent swing in vote shares between the major parties.

Another explanation suggests that if voters change their Left–Right images of the parties, this will alter their party choices and estimates of government representation.[43] Voters may perceive parties as acting differently in office in comparison to what they said they would do before the election. When this occurs, a future election permits voters to correct the course of government. The changing salience of political issues between elections may also affect party vote shares, but not the overall Left–Right positions of the parties. For instance, one election may be concerned with the economy, the next about social welfare. By highlighting different issues, a party can change the salience of factors that define the public's Left–Right orientations. Since elections decide a package of policies, it is inevitable that the shifting agenda of government policy action will act like winds buffeting our sailboat of state. As with changes in the Left–Right position of the median citizen, shifts in the Left–Right positions are typically modest between elections since parties represent an established ideological position. Among the 107 parties that the public positioned on the Left–Right scale in the first and second modules of the CSES project, there is very little change in the parties' Left–Right score over time.[44] But modest shifts in vote shares can be enough to produce a change in government.

In a few instances, the parties consciously try to reshape their broad Left–Right position. Such an explanation would apply to the British Labour Party's centrist move under Tony Blair or the large swing in the perceived ideological position of the Korean Millennium Democratic Party from 2000 to 2004 because of changes in party leadership. Party changes such as these draw attention from party researchers, and have the potential to change party fortunes and electoral results dramatically. Longitudinal comparisons do show the dramatic partisan shifts in Britain and South Korea (and a few other cases) that we have just described, but such changes are anomalies in a general pattern of ideological persistence.

Another set of factors might prompt changes in the vote share of the parties separate from their Left–Right orientations. Some of these changes might be based on government performance, such as incumbent governments suffering if political conditions worsen, even if they are not responsible for the events. A political scandal or demonstrated incompetence is another aspect of performance that is not ideologically based, but which could substantially affect a government's electoral fortunes. The entry (or exit) of a charismatic leader onto (or from) the political stage can also shift party fortunes. Such changes may lead people to change their voting preferences independently of whether they agree with the change in Left–Right terms.

When such non-ideological factors come into play in a major way, they can produce what is called a "deviating election."[45] Voters temporarily discount their policy agreement with a party or candidate, and vote for a choice that deviates significantly from the political equilibrium defined by the distribution of Left–Right orientations and the median voter. Such deviating elections have the potential to widen the representation gap substantially. Anzar's election in the 1996 Spanish elections, the victory of the conservative Solidarity Electoral Action of the Right in the 1987 Polish elections, and the 2002 election of the left-leaning PDSR coalition in Romania might all be considered deviating elections in Left–Right terms. In these cases, other non-Left/Right factors in the campaign led the public to elect a government that was not closest to them in Left/Right terms (see below for a discussion of the Spanish and Romanian examples). And because of the incumbency advantage, this pattern may persist across several elections. Eventually, however, the short-term deviating factors should dissipate, and the patterns of elections should converge toward the median citizen—if democracy works in the long term.

Finally, this dynamic process also may involve changes in the array of parties running in elections, and in winning seats in parliament. The list of winning parties often changes significantly between elections, especially in new democracies. Established parties fragment into competing factions, or coalesce with other parties to form a new political alliance. Some parties fail outright, either because of their performance or the loss of a formative leader, and do not compete in subsequent elections. New parties appear to challenge the political status quo, and sometimes they gain significant new votes and parliamentary representation. If the partisan landscape changes, then the public's relative position in this landscape is also likely to change.[46]

Even with the exceptional resources of the CSES, we cannot estimate empirically the effects of these multiple processes with the available data. However, we can illustrate these different mechanisms of representation with two nations that experienced significant changes in the representation gap over time.[47]

Spain presents an insightful example of this dynamic process of representation that we can plot across three electoral cycles (Figure 7.6). As the 1996 election approached, the Socialists (PSOE) and Felipe González had headed the government since 1982. However, González and the party were struggling because of a stagnant economy, charges of governmental corruption, and abuses of power in the campaign against the Basque ETA. In contrast, Aznar had invigorated the organizational base of the People's Party (PP) and offered a fresh perspective to those voters who had lost faith in the PSOE. Despite the left leanings of the Spanish public, noted by the left-of-center location of the median citizen in 1996, the PSOE lost votes and the PP gained enough votes (4 percent) to form a new conservative government. Because of the desire for change after fourteen years of PSOE governance, 1996 was a clear deviating election in Left–Right terms that produced a large representation gap.

The new Aznar/PP government had considerable success in improving the economy and addressing Spain's social and political problems.

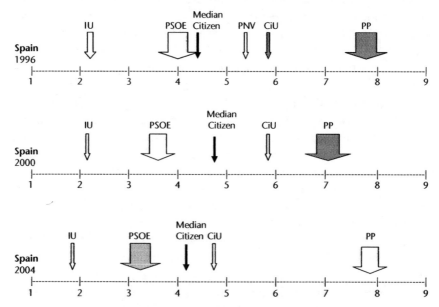

Figure 7.6 Spaniards' Left–Right Self-Placement and Party Placements

Source: CSES, module 1 (1996 and 2000) and module 2 (2004).

Note: The figure displays the entire public's average position for each party, and the median citizen's position. The post-election governing parties are noted in gray.

Unemployment decreased, the economy grew, and budget deficits were trimmed to meet European Union standards. Other reforms privatized state-owned enterprises and the government dealt more effectively with corruption and regional policy. By the 2000 election, voters rewarded the PP with a further 6 percentage point gain in its vote share and an outright majority in the parliament. The governing experience also affected the representation gap in two ways: (1) by 2000 the public saw the PP as located closer to the center (a 0.73 shift on the left) which probably reflects the party's pragmatism and success in dealing with national problems, and (2) the public itself became slightly more conservative (a 0.44 shift to the right). Consequently, the perceived gap between the median citizen and the PP narrowed considerably.

Gradually, however, disenchantment with the PP's conservative policies increased. The economy slowed during Aznar's second term, and many Spaniards opposed his Atlanticist alliance with the Bush administration (including sending troops to Iraq). Also, Aznar chose not to run for re-election, depriving the party of its most visible candidate. Then, just before the election, a Jihadist terrorist attack at Madrid's train station shifted public opinion, partly in response to the attack and partly in response to the government's misstatements about it. Consequently, the 2004 CSES survey shows that the median Spaniard had again moved left. At the same time, the PSOE and the PP became more polarized in their respective Left–Right positions. The result was an 8.5 percent growth in support for the Socialists who re-entered government—and a sharp drop in the representation gap (from 2.31 in 2000 to 0.88 scale points in 2004).

These three elections illustrate the complex dynamics of the representation process that often act in an apparently un-Downsian manner. Spain experienced a deviating election in 1996 as some voters moved away from the Socialists because of their poor policy performance, while still closer to the PSOE in Left–Right terms. The governing experience then changed both the self-location of some citizens and their perceptions of the parties in Left–Right terms. The Left–Right representation gap thus had decreased by 2000 even though the PP continued to govern. However, 2004 was a reinstating election, as voters redirected government back toward the median citizen who generally favored leftist policies. To return to our nautical analogy from earlier in this chapter, the Spanish ship of state tacked to starboard and then back to port to make headway; these shifts might seem random but they were reasonable reactions and counter-reactions to the performance of government and changes in the political context.

Romanian elections offer a contrasting pattern, but one that is similar to other new democracies (Figure 7.7). A governing coalition of socialists and former communists (PDSR) had been slow to enact economic and political reforms, and was increasingly plagued by charges of corruption and

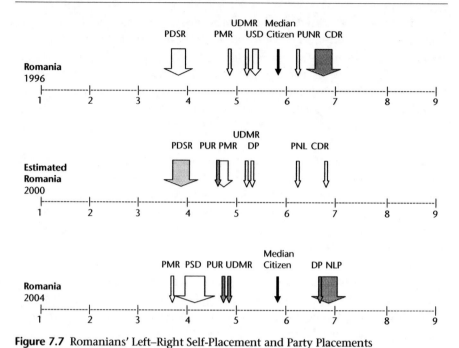

Figure 7.7 Romanians' Left–Right Self-Placement and Party Placements

Source: CSES, module 1 (1996) and module 2 (2004); 2000 is estimated by the authors.

Note: The figure displays the entire public's average position for each party, and the median citizen's position. The post-election governing parties are noted in gray.

malfeasance. Finally, in 1996 the leftist government was defeated by a center-right coalition, the Romanian Democratic Convention (CDR). The CDR won 30 percent of the legislative vote and the separately elected presidency. Since the median Romanian placed themselves closer to the CDR than the outgoing government, this likely improved the fit between citizens and their government.

We do not have survey data for the 2000 elections, but we present party vote shares in Figure 7.7 and our own estimates of the parties' Left–Right positions. The most dramatic change was the collapse of the governing CDR, which garnered only 5 percent of the popular vote and no legislative seats. The coalition had suffered from infighting amongst its members, which hampered government performance and produced a continual turnover of governing officials. Any mandate the CDR had gained from its victory in 1996 had been squandered by inaction and ineffective governance. Without a competent conservative alternative, voters swung back toward the left. The PDSR vote share surged to 36 percent of the poll, gaining nearly half the seats in parliament and forming a minority government. The party's leader and president prior to 1996, Ion Iliescu, was re-elected president a month after the parliamentary election. With the former governing coalition in shambles, this produced a surge of support for the nationalist Greater Romania Party (PRM) (from 4.4 percent in 1996 to 19.5 percent in 2000). In addition, nearly a quarter of the vote was divided among several microparties that gained little representation in parliament.

The CSES resurveyed the public following the 2004 elections. The partisan landscape had changed again. On the left, the National Union was a pre-electoral coalition of the Social Party (which itself was a merger of the former PDSR and the Social Democratic Party, PSDR) and the Humanist Party of Romania (PUR). On the right, the Justice and Truth Alliance was an electoral coalition of the National Liberal Party (NLP) and the Democratic Party (DP). The parties in the Justice and Truth Alliance formed a center-right majority in a coalition with the PUR and the Democratic Union of Hungarians in Romania (UDMR).

The Romanian experience across these three elections contrasts with the logic of a simple, stable Downsian spatial model. By the 2004 election, for instance, the choice of parties had changed so dramatically that only about 10 percent of the vote went to parties that had competed in 1996 under the same name. In three electoral cycles the government had shifted from left to right, to left, and to right. At the same time, the position of the median Romanian citizen is essentially the same in the 1996 and 2004 surveys. It is clear that valence issues, the competence of parties, and the appeal of political leaders can pull voters away from a simple Downsian calculation of the nearest party. This can change party vote shares without changing their basic ideological position. Yet, there is an explainable rationale behind the public's choice, and the representation gap had narrowed substantially following the 2004 election.

Spain and Romania are only two of the nations examined in this chapter, but they provide insightful examples of the representation process at work. Many of the other nations with significant shifts in pre-election governments followed a similar pattern. If we only compare the nine nations that made large changes in the representation gap between the pre- and post-election governments in Figures 7.1 and 7.2 (greater than a 1.0 point change), seven of them had an improvement in representation and only two had a growing representation gap. The pull of the median citizen appears to be a force that restores democracy toward an equilibrium position after non-ideological factors have produced deviating election results.

The Representation Linkage

Theories of representative democracy maintain that elections perform two essential functions. First, they should perform a representation function by ensuring that the legislature broadly reflects the distribution of opinions within the electorate. Second, elections should ensure that governments are accountable for their actions to the citizens who elected them. There are seeming tensions between these two functions. For instance, research suggests that consensus democracies emphasize the representative function by giving voice to many parties and ensuring their proportional representation in the parliamentary process.[48] In contrast, majoritarian democracies supposedly stress the accountability function because they are more likely to produce single-party governments that provide a clearer focus for voter evaluations of the government's performance. In both instances, the ability of democracy to produce both representation and accountability is uncertain.

Our findings provide a more sanguine view of democratic party governance. Accountability is maximized when a single party campaigns as the incumbent, and voters can hold the party accountable for its past actions. However, even in multiparty systems, voters often see pre-election coalition agreements that produce shared responsibility and accountability. And coalition governments that form after elections are also constrained by a need for broad political agreement among parties if the government is to be effective. So accountability and representation may not present such stark contrasts in electoral reality.

Even more significantly, we find that governments are highly representative of their constituents. The diverse set of nations in the Comparative Study of Electoral Systems display a strong congruence between the Left–Right preferences of the median citizen and the Left–Right position of the newly elected government ($r = .60$). Moreover, if we define the government's constituency as their voters, the agreement is exceptionally strong ($r = .91$). Given the vagarious nature of elections and the intervening steps between casting a vote and forming a government, this seems a strong indication that elections do steer the course of government. Even more striking, by comparing pre- and post-election relationships, we found that elections systematically improve the congruence between citizens and their government.

In short, congruence results because democracy is an iterative process of political choice. Rather than elections acting as a discrete, point-in-time choice, as is often discussed in theoretical and empirical studies, there is a dynamic relationship between voters and their government. Democracy's ongoing process of representation and accountability occurs through retrospective as well as prospective evaluations of government performance. People elect a government, and then they have the chance to re-evaluate this decision at the next election. Democracy achieves its long-term success through this dynamic process, even if decisions at one election deviate from what was desired or expected.

In addition, the basic Downsian spatial analysis that is depicted in the theoretical literature on electoral choice seems to be an oversimplification of reality. Some elections produce sizeable deviations from the Left–Right position advocated by the median citizen. Non-ideological criteria, changing issue salience, or perceptions of political competency can regularly produce deviating elections. We identified such deviating elections in Left–Right terms for about a quarter of the CSES election pairs. Deviating elections need not be irrational deviations from Left–Right policy representation; they can also be an effective means of sanctioning a party that strays from its values or performs ineffectively. In other instances, the polarization of parties precludes a stable centrist government congruence with the median citizen—and voters are forced to choose between steering left or right, and then correct the balance at a future election. Small changes in the position of the median citizen produced twice as large a shift in the Left–Right position of the government because of this oversteering. The turnover in political parties and coalition politics provides further variability beyond the basic Downsian model. In the short term, these patterns seemingly distort the democratic process of representation. However, the dynamic aspect of elections and the mechanisms of iterative representation and accountability provide a mechanism to encourage a government to be congruent with the public's Left–Right preferences.[49] The basic Downsian model assumes a simple world of electoral competition, but the world is not so simple.

In summary, our assessment of this stage in the process of party linkage is positive. The dynamic aspect of the representative linkage between citizens and governments is evidence of a feedback process that operates across electoral cycles. In the lead-up to an election, voters may have tired of the government, changed their views, or are unsure which way to turn in the approaching election. The congruence between the two parts of the classic representation dyad may have weakened. The election allows voters to make a correction if desired, and to identify more strongly with the newly incumbent government. This is how democracy should function.

Notes

* We would like to thank G. Bingham Powell for his extensive advice and comments on the material in this chapter.

1. Warren Miller, Majority rule and the representative system. In Erik Allardt and Yrjo Littunen, eds, *Cleavages, Ideologies and Party Systems*. Helsinki: Transactions of the Westermarck Society, 1964, p. 344.
2. Warren Miller and Donald Stokes, Constituency influence in Congress, *American Political Science Review* (1963) 57: 45–56; Warren Miller et al., *Policy Representation in*

Western Democracies. Oxford: Oxford University Press, 1999; Hermann Schmitt and Jacques Thomassen, eds, *Political Representation and Legitimacy in the European Union*. Oxford: Oxford University Press, 1999; Michael McDonald and Ian Budge, *Elections, Parties, Democracy: Conferring the Median Mandate*. Oxford: Oxford University Press, 2005; Ian Shapiro, Susan Stokes, Elisabeth Wood, and Alexander Kirshner, eds, *Political Representation*. New York: Cambridge University Press, 2010.

3. Dieter Roth, Forschungsgruppe Wahlen in personal communication. This observation applies for most postwar elections in Germany.

4. Markku Laasko and Rein Taagepera, Effective number of parties: A measure with application to West Europe, *Comparative Political Studies* (1979) 12: 3–27.

5. Sona Golder, Pre-electoral coalition formation in parliamentary democracies Pre-electoral coalition formation in parliamentary democracies, *British Journal of Political Science* (2006) 36: 193–212.

6. G. Bingham Powell, *Elections as Instruments of Democracy: Majoritarian and Proportional Visions*. New Haven: Yale University Press, 2000.

7. Kaare Strom, Wolfgang Müller, and Torbjörn Bergman, eds, *Cabinets and Coalition Bargaining: The Democratic Life Cycle in Western Europe*. Oxford: Oxford University Press, 2008.

8. Lieven De Winter and Patrick Dumont, Uncertainty and complexity in cabinet formation. In Kaare Strom, Wolfgang Müller, and Torbjörn Bergman, eds, *Cabinets and Coalition Bargaining: The Democratic Life Cycle in Western Europe*. Oxford: Oxford University Press, 2008.

9. Abram de Swaan, *Coalition Theories and Cabinet Formation*. Amsterdam: Elsevier, 1973; Lawrence Dodd, *Coalitions in Parliamentary Government*. Princeton, NJ: Princeton University Press, 1976; Michael Laver and Norman Schofield, *Multiparty Government*. Oxford: Oxford University Press, 1990; Michael Laver and Ian Budge, eds, *Party Policy and Government Coalitions*. New York: St Martin's Press, 1992.

10. We recognize that other factors also come into play. Some minor parties may represent important issues that are not fully integrated into the Left–Right dimension. The number of parties required to generate a majority is another factor, as well as the electoral and governing strategies of party leaders. Many governing coalitions actually represent a minority of voters. However, the basic premise of coalition formation is based on ideological compatibility of participants.

11. John Fitzmaurice, Belgium stays "purple": The 2003 federal election, *West European Politics* (2004) 27: 146–56.

12. For example, some parties and political elites may place office-holding above ideology in negotiating a coalition. Different electoral systems can also distort the seat share of parties compared with their vote share, and this disproportionality creates a legislature that is not fully representative of the party vote shares in the election. Small parties can often "blackmail" a coalition by threatening to withhold the last votes necessary to form a majority coalition, and thereby distort the government's overall policy program. In addition, in both majoritarian and proportional electoral systems, it is common for the government to represent less than a majority of the votes cast. About a third of West European cabinets are minority governments. See Strom, Müller, and Bergman, eds, *Cabinets and Coalition Bargaining*.

13. Miller and Stokes, Constituency influence in Congress; Samuel Barnes, *Representation in Italy*. Chicago: University of Chicago Press, 1977; Barbara Farah, Political representation in West Germany. PhD dissertation, University of Michigan, 1980; Philip Converse and Roy Pierce, *Political Representation in France*. Cambridge, MA: Harvard University Press, 1986; Ian McAllister, Party elites, voters and political attitudes: Testing three explanations for mass-elite differences, *Canadian Journal of Political Science* (1991) 24: 237–68.

14. Jacques Thomassen, *Kiezers en Gekozenen in een Representatieve Demokratie*. Alphen an den Rijn: Samsom, 1976; Russell Dalton, Political parties and political representation, *Comparative Political Studies* (1985) 17: 267–99; Peter Esaiasson and Sören Holmberg, *Representation from Above: Members of Parliament and Representative Democracy in Sweden*. Sudbury, MA: Dartmouth Publishing, 1996; Donald Matthews and Henry Valen, *Parliamentary Representation: The Case of the Norwegian Storting*. Columbus, OH: Ohio State University Press, 1999.

15. James Buchanan and Gordon Tullock, *The Calculus of Consent*. Ann Arbor: University of Michigan Press, 1962; McDonald and Budge, *Elections, Parties, Democracy*; Gary Cox, *Making Votes Count*. New York: Cambridge University Press, 1997, ch. 12.

16. John Huber and G. Bingham Powell, Congruence between citizens and policymakers in two visions of liberal democracy, *World Politics* (1994) 46: 291–326; Powell, *Elections as Instruments of Democracy*.

17. Hans-Dieter Klingemann, Richard Hofferbert, and Ian Budge, *Parties, Policy and Democracy*. Boulder, CO: Westview Press, 1994; McDonald and Budge, *Elections, Parties, Democracy*; Myunghee Kim, G. Bingham Powell, and Richard Fording, Electoral systems, party systems, and ideological representation. *Comparative Politics* (2010) 42: 1–19.

18. Huber and Powell, Congruence between citizens and policymakers in two visions of liberal democracy; Bernhard Wessels, System characteristics matter: Empirical evidence from ten representation studies. In Warren Miller et al., eds, *Policy Representation in Western Democracies*. Oxford: Oxford University Press, 1999; Powell, *Elections as Instruments of Democracy*.

19. G. Bingham Powell, Institutions and the ideological congruence of governments. In Russell Dalton and Christopher Anderson, eds, *Citizens, Context and Choice: How Context Shapes Citizens' Electoral Choices*. Oxford: Oxford University Press, 2010; Matt Golder and Jacek Stramski, Ideological congruence and electoral institutions, *American Journal of Political Science* (2010) 54: 90–106; André Blais and Marc Bodet, Does proportional representation foster closer congruence between citizens and policy makers? *Comparative Political Studies* (2006) 39: 1243–62; G. Bingham Powell, Election laws and representative government, *British Journal of Political Science* (2006) 36: 291–315.

20. Anthony McGann, *The Logic of Democracy: Reconciling Equality, Deliberation, and Minority Protection*. Ann Arbor: University of Michigan Press, 2006; Kenneth May, A set of independent necessary and sufficient conditions for simple majority decisions, *Econometrica* (1952) 20: 680–84.

21. This argument is also made by Paul Warrick, Bilateralism or the median mandate: An examination of rival perspectives on democratic governance, *European Journal of Political Research* (2010) 49: 1–24.

22. Bernhard Wessels, Whom to represent: Role orientations of legislators in Europe. In Herman Schmitt and Jacques Thomassen, eds, *Political Representation and Legitimacy in the European Union*. Oxford: Oxford University Press, 1999, p. 216. MNPs were much more likely to say they represent party voters in Belgium, the Netherlands, and Sweden.

23. Donley T. Studlar and Ian McAllister, Constituency activity and representational roles among Australian legislators, *Journal of Politics* (1996) 58: 69–90; Converse and Pierce, *Political Representation in France*, ch. 21; Barnes, *Representation in Italy*, pp. 128–34; Matthews and Valen, *Parliamentary Representation*, p. 154; Esaiasson and Holmberg, *Representation from Above*, chs. 3–4.

24. Barnes, *Representation in Italy*, p. 122; also Converse and Pierce, *Political Representation in France*, ch. 18; Miller, Majority rule and the representative system.

25. Adam Przeworski, Susan Stokes, and Bernard Manin, eds, *Democracy, Accountability, and Representation*. New York: Cambridge University Press, 1999.

26. James Stimson, Michael Mackuen, and Robert Erikson, Dynamic representation, *American Political Science Review* (1995) 89: 543–65; McDonald and Budge, *Elections, Parties, Democracy*.

27. This analogy is flawed because of principal-agent problems. Even if the public directs government to move in a certain direction, the member of government may choose to act differently. In our nautical jargon, a significant gap between principals and agents might be considered an act of mutiny.

28. Michael McDonald, Silvia Mendes, and Ian Budge, What are elections for? Conferring the median mandate, *British Journal of Political Science* (2004) 34: 1–26.

29. There are a few time-series studies of a single nation that begin to explore the dynamics of representation over time. See Soren Holmberg, Dynamic representation from above. In Martin Rosema, Bas Denters, and Kees Aarts, eds. *How Democracy Works: Political Representation and Policy Congruence in Modern Societies*. Amsterdam: Amsterdam University Press/Pallas Publications, 2011; Jacques Thomassen, The blind corner of political representation. Paper presented at workshop "Comparative Perspectives on Political Representation," Simon Fraser University, Vancouver, 2009. However, the limited number of elections makes it difficult to test models predicting changes in the representativeness of governments. Other research examines the congruence between public policy preferences and government policy outputs over time. See Benjamin Page and Robert Shapiro, *The Rational Public: Fifty Years of Trends in Americans' Policy Preferences*. Chicago, IL: University of Chicago Press, 1992; Stuart N. Soroka and Christopher Wlezien, *Degrees of Democracy: Politics, Public Opinion and Policy*. New York: Cambridge University Press, 2010.

30. For other representation applications see Jacques Thomassen and Hermann Schmitt, Policy representation, *European Journal of Political Research* (1997) 32: 165–84; Klingemann, Hofferbert, and Budge, *Parties, Policy and Democracy*; Dalton, Political parties and political representation; Converse and Pierce, *Political Representation in France*; Roy Pierce, Mass-elite issue linkages and the responsible party

model of representation. In Warren Miller et al., *Policy Representation in Western Democracies*. Oxford: Oxford University Press, 1999.

31. In precise terms, the differences range from government voters being two points (2.05) to the left of the median citizen in Brazil to three points to the right (3.33) in Albania.

32. We want to acknowledge Steffen Blings of Cornell University who calculated these government scores. The list of party positions is in the appendix to Chapter 5.

33. Powell, Institutions and the ideological congruence of governments; Powell, *Elections as Instruments of Democracy*.

34. The deviations are Brazil, Britain, Italy, and New Zealand.

35. A 45-degree line where pubic Left–Right attitudes predict identical Left–Right positions of government would have a slope of 1.0. Our data yield a slope of 2.01, which means that government Left–Right positions tend to accentuate public preferences by a factor of two. This is similar to the pattern in Chapter 5 with parties at the left and right poles being more polarized than their own voters.

36. Powell, Institutions and the ideological congruence of governments; Golder and Stramski, Ideological congruence and electoral institutions; Blais and Bodet, Does proportional representation foster closer congruence between citizens and policy makers?; Wessels, System characteristics matter; Powell, *Elections as Instruments of Democracy*.

37. Powell, Institutions and the ideological congruence of governments.

38. The electoral system is coded 1) majoritarian, 2) mixed, and 3) proportional representation; the effective number of parties uses the standard Laasko-Taagepera formula.

39. See Russell Dalton, The quantity and quality of party systems, *Comparative Political Studies* (2008) 41: 899–920.

40. G. Bingham Powell, Consequences of elections. In Lawrence LeDuc, Richard G. Niemi, and Pippa Norris, eds, *Comparing Democracies 3*. Thousand Oaks, CA: Sage, 2010, table 11.1.

41. For previous attempts to test alternative models of party change see Ian Budge, A new spatial theory of party competition: Uncertainty, ideology and policy equilibria viewed comparatively and temporally, *British Journal of Political Science* (1994) 24: 443–67; James Adams, Michael Clark, Lawrence Ezrow, and Garrett Glasgow, Understanding change and stability in party ideologies: Do parties respond to public opinion or to past election results? *British Journal of Political Science* (2004) 34: 589–610.

42. Georg Lutz and Michael Marsh, The consequences of low turnout, *Electoral Studies* (2007) 26: 539–47.

43. A variant of this process is a change in the composition of a coalition government between elections. Powell suggests that such changes typically improve the representation fit, but there is mixed evidence on this point. See Powell, *Elections as Instruments for Democracy*.

44. Based on the 107 parties that were positioned on the Left–Right scale in both modules, there is a .97 correlation in the public's placement of the parties on the Left–Right scale. Also see Michael McDonald, Silvia Mendes, and Myunghee Kim,

Cross-temporal and cross-national comparisons of party left–right positions, *Electoral Studies* (2006) 14: 1–14.

45. Donald Stokes discussed deviating elections in terms of the distribution of long-term party identification, but the median citizen can have a similar influence in defining a stable partisan equilibrium. Donald Stokes, Party loyalty and the likelihood of deviating elections, *Journal of Politics* (1962) 24: 689–702; Angus Campbell, Philip Converse, Warren Miller, and Donald Stokes, *The American Voter*. New York: Wiley, 1960, pp. 531–38.

46. There is some evidence that party fragmentation and the creation of new parties are increasing for the established democracies. See Anne Wren and Kenneth McElwain, Voters and parties. In Charles Boix and Susan Stokes, eds, *The Oxford Handbook of Comparative Politics*. Oxford: Oxford University Press, 2007; M. Tavits, Party system change: Testing a model of new party entry, *Party Politics* (2006) 21: 99–119.

47. Eight nations had a change of more than 1.0 point in the representation gap in the CSES election of module 2: Albania, Brazil, Bulgaria, the Czech Republic, the Netherlands, Portugal, Romania, and Spain. We selected two countries as examples, Spain and Romania, because they were included in the CSES module 1 to provide data for more than one electoral cycle.

48. Arend Lijphart, *Patterns of Democracy: Government Forms and Performance in Thirty Six Countries*. New Haven: Yale University Press, 1999; Powell, *Elections as Instruments for Democracy*.

49. One caveat is the persistence of a large representation gap in pre-election and post-election comparisons for six nations in our set. These might be deviating elections if we had a longer series of elections to compare. If a large gap persists over time, this may indicate a breakdown of democratic presentation of Left–Right preferences. But even in this instance, the conclusion would depend on what options party elites make available to the voters.

8

Party Policies and Policy Outputs

The *Partido Popular* (PP) had governed Spain since 1996 under the leadership of José María Aznar. After initially taking office, the Aznar government had pursued a variety of conservative policies designed to strengthen the Spanish economy by lowering taxes and cutting government spending. During his first term, Aznar held social spending constant (after adjusting for inflation), which amounted to a 1 percent decrease in social spending as a percentage of the national gross domestic product (GDP). In per capita terms, social spending increased by barely 200 euros per person during the first Aznar term (and actually decreased after adjusting for inflation).[1] The government privatized parts of the economy that had been nationalized by the previous socialist government. When conflict began in Afghanistan and then Iraq, Spain supported US policies as part of Aznar's Atlanticist orientation.

The polls predicted a close result in the 2004 legislative elections. The PP wanted to continue its conservative agenda, under a new party leader. The Spanish Socialist Workers' Party (PSOE), headed by José Luis Rodríguez Zapatero, promised a much different course for the nation: the end to Spanish participation in Iraq, an increase in government investments in housing and education, a liberal social agenda, and greater concern for the needs of average Spaniards. A Jihadist bombing of the Madrid train station a week before the election shifted the outcome. The PSOE won a plurality of parliamentary seats and formed a coalition government. The Spanish public had decided that their nation should follow a different policy course, and handed the reins of power to Zapatero and his party.

Barely a month after taking office, Zapatero announced the withdrawal of Spanish military forces from Iraq. The government also pursued a dramatic break with Spain's conservative religious traditions, with a very liberal policy agenda on social issues. Same-sex marriages were legalized in 2005, and policies affecting divorce were liberalized. Although the economy was struggling and the government faced large deficits, the socialists also sought to increase support for the very needy, expand educational spending, and increase the minimum wage. Between 2004 and 2007, total social spending increased from approximately 4,000 euros per capita to 5,000 euros. Clearly, the Spanish ship of state was following a different course before and after the 2004 elections, because the election had changed its direction.

This example illustrates the final connection in our party linkage model—the extent to which parties deliver policies that appeal to their voters who, in turn, reward them with their support at the ballot box. This question is at the heart of party competition, since parties place their policies before the voters and use them to attract votes. Placed in a comparative context, we would assume that most Social Democratic voters support the party because they prefer its policies over those of its competitors, most Christian Democrats expect their party to pursue a different policy course, and a Green voter has distinct policy expectations. This is the essence of democratic politics.

Despite the apparent simplicity of the relationship, the question of its importance is not an easy one to answer. Governments enact policy in many areas, as the above example shows, thus making a single assessment of a government's policy responsiveness very difficult to estimate. It is almost inevitable that governments perform better (or worse) in some policy areas than others—even from the perspective of their own voters. In the above example, we expect that many Spaniards were positive about Aznar's initial economic achievements, but concerned about some of his social and foreign policies.

A complex range of direct and indirect effects also influence the relationship between control of the government and policy outputs. Interest groups and lobbying organizations press their views on the government, often in conflict with voter preferences. The bureaucracy and the courts are also significant participants in the policy process, albeit in different ways. Past policies also tend to institutionalize programs that persist over time, even when party control of the government changes. Public policies were initially enacted because a constituency supported the program, and thus programs persist over time once established. One frequently hears government leaders pleading to implement a new policy if they can successfully navigate the labyrinth of public policymaking.

Even though Chapter 7 showed that voters generally elect a government that agrees with their broad Left–Right orientations, this does not mean the actions in government match voters' expectations. There are numerous cases where governments followed an unexpected course after taking office, or where external events forced a major change in policy direction. George Bush in 1988 and Helmut Kohl in 1990 promised no new taxes during the election, but then changed direction almost as soon as the votes had been counted. Such deviations are sometimes warranted by the circumstances that new leaders find themselves in, but often they appear to arise from politicians saying one thing to get elected, and then governing on different criteria.[2]

Furthermore, the relationship between voters and government orientations and outputs is a dynamic one, with voters responding to the policies that the parties advance, and parties constantly adjusting their policies to maximize their appeal to voters. For instance, parties understandably changed policies in response to the 2008 global recession, and public sentiments changed as well. Change is an important part of the representation function. By implication, the largest changes in policy should come with substantial changes in the partisan composition of the government.

The policy impact of governments is also influenced by the political context. For instance, economic development and the structure of the economy are strongly related to the extent of social spending in a nation. All else being equal, we expect higher social spending in Sweden than in Mexico, regardless of the partisan composition of the government. In addition, social and economic conditions change, and governments may be constrained to adopt policies that are different from their election promises in order to respond to such socioeconomic conditions.

Consequently, dramatic policy changes, such as the British Labour Party's nationalization of industry in the 1950s (and the subsequent denationalization by the successor Conservative government) or Obama's health care reforms, are unusual occurrences. More typically, Margaret Thatcher entered British government with a strong program of cutting government services, but social spending was relatively unchanged after her first term. As Aaron Wildavsky famously wrote, most policy change is incremental.[3]

These issues of causality present a major challenge in disentangling the link between mass party support and party policies, as we have seen in previous chapters. In theory, parties and coalitions on the political left should deliver redistributive policies by increasing social spending and emphasizing the importance of equality and social protection. In contrast, governments on the political right should reduce spending by stressing the role of market-based solutions and individual enterprise. In practice, however, motivations for more social spending may come less from a desire to redistribute wealth more equally across society than from the need to minimize risk by providing comprehensive social protection. Other policy controversies, such as environmental protection or civil liberties, can generate similar differences between policy supporters and opponents.

This chapter investigates whether party control of government affects policy outputs by examining social spending and relating changes in spending to changes in the partisan composition of the government. The first section describes how the party government model leads to parties functioning like unitary actors that produce nearly unanimous policy voting. The second section outlines the literature on the role that parties can play in shaping policy. The third section looks at how we measure policy and its relationship to voters' and government positions on the Left–Right dimension. Finally, we draw these themes together to see what they can tell us about how parties operate to attract votes, and the role of policy in the electoral equation.

Parties as Policy Actors

In the winter of 2010 a certain Jackie Healy-Rae informed the Irish government that he needed "a hospital and a bypass" (the latter referring to a new road, rather than a medical condition). He was an independent member of the Irish parliament and held a very weak coalition government over a barrel as it needed his support to pass a crucially important budget vote in parliament. Healy-Rae could not have been more explicit in demanding a high price for his support—a demand that the desperate government acceded to, much to the consternation of the members of the two parliamentary parties that were in government.

The ability of a legislator to force the hand of government on a pork-barrel policy arises from time to time in many districted systems; more common still are those instances of legislators voting against their party line in parliamentary votes.[4] "Free mandate" theory might lead us to believe that individual legislators should have a free hand in parliamentary votes; after all, under most electoral systems the legislators are chasing personal votes to maintain their seats. And the right of legislators to vote with their conscience is enshrined in some constitutions. Under the Danish and German constitutions, for example, legislators are bound only by their conscience; the Dutch constitution states that a legislator "shall not be bound by a mandate or instructions when casting their vote."[5]

Even if "the fiction of the fully independent MP is still part of much parliamentary rhetoric,"[6] the reality is that it is the parties, not individual legislators, that decide on policy in parliament. This was one feature stressed by the influential "responsible parties" report issued by the American Political Science Association's Committee on Political Parties in the 1950s, which said that parties should be sufficiently disciplined and cohesive in parliament to implement their election programs. It is also at the core of party government theory.[7]

That parties should have a dominant role in parliamentary assemblies makes intuitive sense. Rational choice approaches theorize that party cohesion is a necessity for a properly functioning parliament. Even if parties did not exist they would emerge naturally from the "primeval slime."[8] Emergent parliamentary systems reveal practical examples of this process of "parliamentarization" in action: whether it's through legislative steps to ban "faction-hopping" by recalcitrant MPs; the institutionalization of a whipping system to keep legislators in line; or even—as in the case of some parties in Slovakia—forcing candidates in advance of the election to sign undated letters of resignation.[9]

The most widely used measure of party unity (i.e., how often legislators vote consistent with the majority of their parliamentary party) is the Rice index of cohesion.[10] It is calculated as the absolute value of the difference between yes and no votes in a parliamentary party on any specific vote. It ranges from zero when the legislators are evenly divided, to 100 when all legislators vote in the same way (yes or no). The figures in Table 8.1 are the average scores over a number of votes, indicating that party-based voting is very high in most democracies. Ireland's score of 100 or the 99 in Australia, Belgium, Denmark, and the UK indicate almost perfect unity in parliamentary party voting in the period.

There are some differences across countries. Newer democracies have lower scores, consistent with the expectation that it takes time for systems to bed down and for the process of parliamentarization to occur. As the various studies have shown, other factors influencing levels of party unity include:

Table 8.1. Measures of Parliamentary Party Unity[11]

Nation	Party unity
Australia	99
Belgium	99
Brazil	75
Canada	82
Chile	82
Czech Republic	87
Denmark	99
Finland	88
France	85
Germany	96
Iceland	96
Ireland	100
Israel	88
Italy	96
Mexico	84
New Zealand	96
Norway	95
Peru	80
Philippines	70
Poland	42
Russia	55
Sweden	96
UK	99
USA	70

Note: Rice index scores of average party unity; based on trends in the late 1990s.

the electoral system, candidate selection rules, and the independent power of parliamentary committees.[12] John Carey develops this at length in his examination of the "competing principals" that legislators face when determining how to vote. As he notes, the parliamentary party leaderships are the main principals, but depending on institutional design, there can be other principals competing for the legislator's vote.

While there may well be differences in levels of party unity across our CSES cases, the more significant finding is just how high the levels of cohesion are across the board: the index records high values in most cases. This is consistent with the findings of other cross-national research of parliamentary parties in a large range of countries: levels of cohesion are high and increasing over time.[13]

Parties, Party Policies, and Elections

As we have argued throughout this book, parties undertake a range of functions that are essential for the operation of representative democracy. At the most basic level, parties aggregate the demands and opinions of the mass electorate, revise and enhance them, and then articulate those opinions within the political sphere. These opinions form the basis of political competition within a democratic society. But beyond refining and channeling popular opinion, do parties ultimately have an impact on public policy? Does the level of spending on certain government responsibilities—health, education, and social services, for example—vary with the political complexion of the party holding office?

This question has preoccupied many political scientists, particularly since the growth of the welfare state in postwar Europe.[14] If the answer to the question is no, then beyond providing symbolic choices for voters, parties have no substantive role to play within the political system, other than managing and regulating government activities. Any programmatic appeal that parties may make to voters is largely irrelevant if the parties are unable to make systematic changes to public policy. If, on the other hand, the answer to the question is yes, then parties become key actors in the policy process, and can shape the trajectory of the societies that they aspire to govern.

One research stream looks at aggregate levels of social spending or cross-system comparisons of other policy outputs. For instance, Thomas Dye, Harold Wilenski, and others concluded that economic growth was the major driver behind public policy across the US states and cross-nationally, and was especially important in determining welfare spending.[15] Countries that enjoyed favorable economic conditions could afford to extend their financial largesse to those who they deemed required it; countries that found themselves in less favorable economic circumstances had to restrict their welfare spending.

The variations in redistributive policies are especially apparent in the wider range of nations surveyed by the CSES. Sweden, for example, devotes about three-tenths of its GDP to social programs, while social spending accounts for only about 6 percent of GDP in Mexico. It is unlikely that party promises in the immediate election or the partisan composition of the government after the election explain these differences. Rather, the socioeconomic circumstances of a nation and its political culture are more important. Yet this research approach found clearer effects of party when the course of policy reform was examined over time.[16]

Institutional arrangements can also influence policy; for example, the structure of the electoral system has implications for whether a party governs alone or forms a coalition with others, which in turn affects the direction of public policy. Torben Iversen and David Soskice claimed that electoral institutions are a key variable in determining redistribution through the way in which they shape coalitions.[17] In PR electoral systems, the most likely outcomes are center-left coalitions that redistribute more of the country's wealth; majoritarian electoral systems are more likely to produce center-right governments that are less dependent on other parties for support and therefore redistribute less.

Additional constraints involve the actors who participate in the policy process, particularly the bureaucracy and the interest groups. Although the role that these groups play in the policy process is widely debated, business and industry have a key role in that they determine the level of investment in the economy which ultimately affects economic growth. The bureaucracy, too, can influence policy by ensuring that legislation meets certain requirements of quality and consistency; when a government's proposed changes fail to meet these standards, it can delay or modify legislation.

Because of such constraints, research that simply links the Left–Right composition of government to policy outputs often finds negligible effects. Louis Imbeau and his colleagues conducted a meta-analysis of published research and concluded that "the average correlation between the party composition of the government and policy outputs is not significantly different from zero."[18] Evelyn Huber and John Stephens found "a sharp narrowing of political differences" on welfare state policies in established democracies during the 1980s that lessened the potential for partisan differentiation and representation.[19] Andre Blais and his colleagues presented an extensive cross-national and cross-temporal comparison of spending patterns for fifteen advanced industrial democracies. Even with their sophisticated statistical analyses, they found only small differences in overall public spending as a function of the partisan composition of government.[20]

In contrast, research that adopts an explicitly dynamic framework is more likely to conclude that parties do make a difference to public policy because such research generally holds contextual factors constant to examine incremental change.[21] One approach has examined the specific policy reforms promised by parties during an election. In his study of British governments in the 1970s, Richard Rose concluded that "both the Conservative and Labour governments act consistently within the manifesto model of governing; in office they do the majority of things to which they pledge themselves in their opposition manifestos."[22] For example, Rose found that the 1970–74 Conservative government implemented 80 percent of its election promises, and adopted an opposite policy on just 1 percent of promises. The proportion of promises acted upon by the 1974–79 Labour government was less—54 percent—but still represented a majority of its manifesto commitments. And like the Conservatives, there were hardly any cases of the Labour government adopting an opposite policy to the one laid out in the party manifesto.

Hans-Dieter Klingemann, Richard Hofferbert, and Ian Budge extended this logic with evidence from the Comparative Manifesto Project.[23] They systematically coded the policy emphases of parties' election manifestos for ten nations over four decades, and then linked these manifesto statements to the policy outcomes of government. Their multivariate models explained more than half the variance in public spending across a range of policy areas. These authors concluded with an optimistic assessment of parties' abilities to translate their stated priorities into policy outcomes.

Another approach to policy representation comes from a set of studies that link public opinion to public policy in a dynamic framework. Benjamin Page and Robert Shapiro conducted a landmark study of policy congruence in the United States.[24] They demonstrated that instances of major policy change were congruent with changes in public sentiment. For instance, when international conditions changed significantly, this was followed by increased public support for defense spending and increased spending on defense. Alan Monroe examined the congruence between public preferences for policy change and actual shifts in US government policy—and found that most cases displayed a congruence between public preferences and policy outcomes.[25]

Stuart Soroka and Christopher Wlezien extended this model to tracking five policy areas in the United States, Britain, and Canada.[26] In each area they found that public preferences for more or less spending in a policy area had a substantial impact on actual government budgets. Other research has replicated this basic model for other democracies.[27] Although these studies linking public opinion to public policy do not explicitly tie this agreement to political parties, they provide strong evidence that policy representation occurs.

The evidence on whether or not governments deliver what they promise is, while extensive, mixed. In the next section we bring our own evidence to bear on this relationship, by relating the partisan composition of government to the policy actions of governments.

Measuring the Impact of Voter Opinions on Government Policies

As we have already indicated, the role of governments in shaping public expenditure in general, and welfare state expenditure in particular, has generated considerable controversy. One interpretation of the party/policy nexus suggests that center-left parties were instrumental in establishing and consolidating the welfare state, but after that was accomplished (generally in the 1960s and 1970s), their role largely ceased.[28] As social protection became a consensus issue between the left and right, and with spending being largely driven by demand (itself contingent on the business cycle), governments have had only a limited role to play in either expanding or reducing welfare spending. This is what is sometimes referred to as the "end of partisanship" claim within the welfare state debate, which posits that parties have only a very limited role in determining welfare spending.[29]

A revisionist view is sometimes called the "politics matters" school; it argues that governments are constrained in how they can redirect spending, because of the huge fixed costs of the welfare state.[30] However, governments do still retain some discretionary influence on spending, in line with their political predispositions. Frank Castles has argued, for example, that the presence of a government of the right has a major effect on social policy.[31]

The situation is further complicated by three factors. First, the expansion of liberal democracy to the former communist countries of Central and Eastern Europe has made the relationship between the political complexion of the government and government expenditure more complex. Margrit Tavits and Natalia Letki showed that with the dual transition to democracy and a market economy in the postcommunist societies, the center-left parties applied fiscal austerity while center-right parties generally spent more on social protection to alleviate hardship.[32] In this situation, the traditional argument that a government of the right will spend less on social spending and that a government of the left will spend more may be turned on its head. The socioeconomic development of a nation can also strongly affect the level of social spending in a nation.

A second issue is the complexity of measuring policy outputs. Most large-scale empirical studies rely on spending as a measure of policy outputs, but spending is an admittedly imperfect indicator of a government's policy goals. Aggregate expenditure data often do not capture "how and on whom the money is spent," which is, arguably, central to understanding the political control of spending.[33] For example, George Bush's "No Child Left Behind" initiative increased federal spending on education, but with a set of goals and procedures that were widely criticized by many Democrats in the US Congress. Because of their differing Left–Right orientations, some governments may want to increase educational spending for primary schooling or apprentice-ships, while other governments may want to increase investments in univer-sity education or science training.

Moreover, costs will ebb and flow in response to changing economic cir-cumstances rather than in response to the political priorities of the party in office. For example, welfare spending increased during the early 1980s' reces-sion in Britain, even though the Conservative government under Margaret Thatcher was committed ideologically to reducing the size of the welfare state. Other types of social spending, such as expenditure on health, exhibit the same problems in ascertaining any political control, in that spending often reflects demand (such as, for example, the demands of an aging population) rather than government policy.

We analyze social spending patterns across the CSES nations, but we are cognizant of the significant limitations of counting just spending. Govern-ment spending is a very blunt measure of what a government actually does, as illustrated in the Spanish example at the start of this chapter. A more exact measure of policy outcomes is the examination of specific policies compared with election promises, such as in the study by Richard Rose, but applying this methodology across a large number of nations over time would be a daunting task.

The third consideration, which complicates analyzing the impact of parties on policy, is the electoral system. Researchers argue that the method of election acts as an intervening variable between the party and the policies it pursues when in government. As Iversen and Soskice put it, "to a very consid-erable extent, redistribution is the result of electoral systems and the class coalitions they engender."[34] They maintain that center-left governments predominate in proportional electoral systems, and thereby produce more distributive policies, while center-right governments predominate in majori-tarian systems, producing less redistribution. In proportional electoral systems in particular, bargaining among coalition partners often places center parties in alliance with the political left, creating an incentive for greater redistribution.

Bearing these added complexities in mind, we begin our examination of the relationship between governments and policy expenditure by identifying three measures of government social expenditure that are expressed as a percentage of a country's gross domestic product: education spending, health spending, and overall social spending. These measures were derived from the Organisation for Economic Co-operation and Development (OECD).[35] We collected data to match the year in which the CSES survey was conducted.

In addition, to isolate the impact of changes in the partisan composition of government on policy, we collected data from approximately three years before and three years after the CSES election.[36] These time comparisons allow us to hold constant the effects of national characteristics that might affect aggregate levels of spending—such as socioeconomic development, cultural traditions, or electoral institutions—and thereby isolate whether a change in partisan composition of government alters spending priorities. This, we believe, is the most direct test of the partisan effects model.

It is particularly difficult to obtain reliable, cross-nationally comparable data for several of the non-OECD countries matched to the election year in which the survey was conducted. These difficulties meant that nine countries— Albania, Brazil, Bulgaria, Peru, Philippines, Romania, Russia, Slovenia, and Taiwan—could not be included in the analyses, leaving twenty-five countries for which we had sufficient data for at least some spending analyses.

Of all the topics examined in this book, the empirical measurement of government policies through spending is probably the least robust measure of our desired goal. Spending is constrained by national conditions which transcend the partisan composition of government. In addition, the content of policy legislation is more important than the size of the budget. So we proceed with modest ambitions, but this comparison of spending patterns can provide useful evidence of whether the partisan composition of government does matter for policy outputs.

Government Political Orientation and Spending Priorities

The core test of the party effects hypothesis is that the Left–Right position of a government influences the policy output with regard to social security expenditures. We measure social spending for education, health, and overall social services spending. This provides a central test of the hypothesis, since social spending is most directly linked to the traditional bases of the Left–Right dimension. For center-left governments, comprehensive social security is the basis for a fair society and places limits on how the market economy can undermine equality of opportunity. For center-right governments, a generous social security system inhibits initiative and individual responsibility, and creates a culture of dependency among a significant minority of the population.

We examine the relationship between the partisan composition of government and policy expenditures in two stages. First, we examine the simple cross-sectional relationship between government composition and spending. Then, to move closer to measuring causal effects, we examine how changes in the Left–Right composition of government can shift a government's spending priorities. Together, these two analyses illustrate the importance of party in this final link of the party government chain.

Cross-sectional Relationships

We examine measures of direct government expenditure on three areas: education, health, and social security. Aside from defense, these sectors have traditionally provided the largest areas of expenditure. The data show that spending varied considerably by country. Iceland had the highest spending on education, at 7.9 percent of GDP, followed by the USA at 7.4 percent, compared with an average of 5.9 percent across the twenty-five countries as a whole. The lowest level of education spending was 4.6 percent in Spain. The USA had the highest level of health spending, at 15.6 percent of GDP, followed by Switzerland at 10.9 percent; this compares with an average of 8.8 percent. At the other end of the scale, South Korea spent just 5.3 percent of GDP on health. And total social security spending varied from a high of 29.5 percent in Sweden, to 6.3 percent in South Korea; the cross-national average was 20.6 percent. These are substantial variations and are, we would predict, at least partly a consequence of the differing policies pursued by the parties holding office.

To estimate policy congruence, we correlated the Left–Right position of the pre-election government (presented in Figure 7.4 in Chapter 7) with government spending in the year of the CSES election.[37] Figure 8.1 displays the relationship between the position of the government and spending on social programs. The figure supports the hypothesis that center-left governments spend more on social programs than center-right governments, with a correlation of -0.22 (rightist governments spend less). However, the small number of cases means that the relationship falls below the usual levels of statistical significance. While the relationship clearly exists, it is relatively weak. South Korea and Mexico are clearly outliers in the figure as new, non-European democracies; excluding them from the analysis, the correlation rises to $-.44$.

The relationship between the political orientation of a government and health expenditures also weakly supports the hypothesis that right-leaning governments spend less than those on the left. However, the relationship is again weak, with a correlation of $-.06$. Similarly, the Left–Right position of the government has the expected relationship with education spending, with a correlation of -0.04 (not statistically significant). Thus, while the relationships between the Left–Right position of the government and expenditure in the areas of education, health, and social security are all as predicted, with the partial exception of social security spending they are all relatively weak.

One can see that enduring national characteristics affect spending levels independent of the composition of a government. For example, social

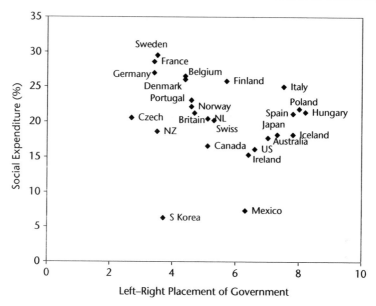

Figure 8.1 Social Spending and the Left–Right Position of the Government

Source: CSES, module 2 for the Left–Right placement of the government; OECD social statistics for social spending in the year of the CSES survey.

Note: The figure plots of twenty-five countries by the Left–Right placement of the government before the election (with 0 representing the most left, 10 the most right) and social spending as a percentage of GDP.

spending is always higher in Sweden than in Mexico, regardless of the parties that are in government. In the next section we extend the analysis to examine social spending over a period of time, and relate that to changes in government in order to better separate partisan effects from longer-term national characteristics.

Cross-temporal Relationships

The government budgeting literature tells us that the best predictor of a nation's spending in a policy sector is what it spent the previous year. This pattern is only incrementally affected by the partisan composition of government because national levels of spending reflect the commutation of national conditions such as socioeconomic development, resources, and policy needs. In addition, changes in spending levels are often linked to changes in social conditions, such as recession or economic growth, rather than the actions of government.

To address these issues, and to test more directly for a causal link between the composition of the government and spending, we turned to the unique resources of the CSES project. Chapter 7 detailed how we can use citizen perceptions of the political parties to estimate the Left–Right orientation of the pre- and post-election governments for the CSES nations. Based on Figure 7.4, we identified a subset of nations that had shifted noticeably to the left as a result of the election (and for which we have expenditure data): Denmark, France, the Netherlands, and Norway, and Portugal in 2002. Another set of nations shifted noticeably to the right: Hungary, Italy, Poland, Portugal in 2005, and Spain. Another large group of nations that lie close to the diagonal in Figure 7.4 did not experience a significant change in the Left–Right composition of government.

If the partisan composition of government matters, we expect that a shift in the composition of government should be apparent in comparing social spending three years before the election and three years after. Furthermore, such a time comparison essentially allows us to remove the effects of long-term national characteristics that affect general levels of spending, such as the broad contrast between affluent and developing economies in the analyses of the last section, by looking at change in spending rather than absolute levels of spending.

Figure 8.2 presents the pre-/post-election differences in social spending as a function of the composition of a government. One obvious pattern is the general growth of all three social spending measures over this time period for

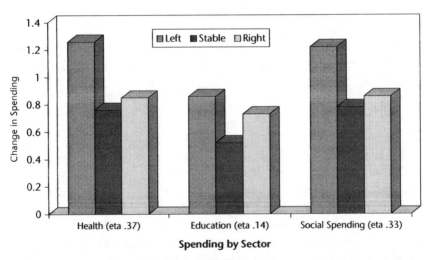

Figure 8.2 Change in Social and Education Spending by Change in Government

Source: OECD social spending statistics. Available at: www.oecd.org/els/social/expenditure

Note: Figure entries are changes in social spending approximately three years prior and three years after the CSES election, compared by the pre-/post-election Left–Right position of the government.

all three government conditions. Over a roughly six-year period, each area increased spending by approximately 0.8 percent of GDP. This is a small change in percentage terms, but it is often a large number when converted to euros, pounds, or dollars. For instance, using these statistics, overall social spending in Germany increased by approximately 15 billion euros between 1999 and 2005 (the six years bracketing the 2002 election), even though the partisan composition of the government was unchanged. Thus, the government's Left–Right orientation may have affected the rate of growth between leftist and rightist governments, but social spending was growing for both in the early 2000s.

Figure 8.2 also presents strong evidence that the Left–Right composition of government does matter for social spending priorities. For instance, overall social spending increases by an average of 1.22 percent of GDP for nations whose government moved decisively to the left after the CSES election, compared with a 0.86 percent growth rate for governments that had shifted to the right. Or, expressed in other terms, the growth rate among left-moving governments is a quarter again greater than among right-moving governments. If these patterns continued over several parliaments, the impact on overall government spending would be substantial. In addition, the same general pattern is observed for more specific spending on education or health.

A closer examination of these statistics also illustrates the complexity of measuring policy priorities by spending. There is considerable variability among all three categories in Figure 8.2 as other factors come into play in determining government social spending. For instance, among those governments whose partisan composition did not change significantly, we still observe a wide range in changes in overall social spending from a decrease of -1.1 percent in New Zealand to an increase of 2.6 percent in Ireland. Britain's experience provides further illustration of the complexity of interpreting even longitudinal spending patterns. The Labour government had a commitment to increase social spending, and this grew substantially (a 1.1 percent increase as a percentage of the GDP) in the years surrounding the 2005 election even though the control of the government did not change. At the same time, Figure 8.2 provides clear evidence that when the Left–Right composition of the government changes, spending policies generally change in a consistent manner.

To what extent, then, does the Left–Right position of a government determine expenditure on social programs? The evidence from our subset of countries analyzed over time suggests that the ideological position of the government does matter. Governments that moved to the left tended to spend more on social programs, while governments that moved to the right tended to spend less. Politics does matter, but only to a modest degree since social spending is driven by a wide range of factors, of which politics is only one. We would expect that a similar exercise conducted in the post-global financial crisis world would show different results, since the bulk of social spending would be driven by the significantly higher rates of unemployment across many advanced societies.

Conclusion

Theory suggests that policy should be affected by the partisan composition of government. In the responsible party government model dominant in countries in the Westminster tradition, parties seek elected office based on a programmatic platform. If elected to government, a party is judged on its record of implementing that platform. This is what is often called the "politics matters" interpretation of welfare spending. The alternative view is the "end of partisanship" interpretation, which suggests that because of structural and other constraints, parties have only a limited role to play in shaping government expenditure.

A prerequisite of party-based policymaking is that parties act as unified actors rather than loose groups of independent legislators. On this point the research literature is clear. Parties in most parliamentary systems function as unified actors in the setting of policy priorities and then in voting on legislation. Caucuses and party discipline limit the degree of individual autonomy for legislators in parliamentary democracies.

The next step is testing the "politics matters" thesis. In practice, many studies testing these two alternative theories often reach contradictory conclusions, even when similar groups of countries are examined over similar periods of time. Part of the inconsistency relates to the problems of reliable measurement; what appears in qualitative studies may often be difficult to measure in quantitative ones, and we have alluded to some of these measurement difficulties in this chapter.

Another explanation is the complexity of the model required to test these hypotheses, and the large number of intervening variables that exist between the party in government and the policy output. And the period under examination has often been highlighted as a major factor in its own right. In a comprehensive meta-analysis of forty-three empirical studies, Louis Imbeau, François Pétry, and Moktar Lamari, find that studies conducted on data collected prior to 1973 show more effects for the "politics matters" interpretation, while studies based on data collected after 1973 are more likely to support the "end of partisanship" interpretation.[38]

The results presented here—limited as they are by the choice of countries and the nature of the available data—mirror much of the recent research on the relationship between party orientation and policy outputs. That is, we find that there is a modest relationship between the Left–Right position of a government and expenditure on social programs. If a government moved to the left or the right, expenditure on social programs moved in the predicted direction. Parties do indeed matter in shaping policy, although they form just one part of the policy repertoire.

Notes

1. The social spending statistics for the PP and PSOE administrations are from the Eurostats database. Available at: http://epp.eurostat.ec.europa.eu/portal/page/ portal/social_protection/data/database.
2. Susan Stokes calculated that nearly a quarter of presidential elections in Latin America were followed by a fundamental economic policy shift from the pre-election campaign. Susan Stokes, What do policy switches tell us about democracy? In Adam Przeworski, Susan Stokes, and Bernard Manin, eds, *Democracy, Accountability, and Representation*. New York: Cambridge University Press, 1999.
3. Aaron Wildavsky, *Politics of the Budgetary Process*. Boston: Little, Brown, 1964.
4. For data on British trends, see http://www.revolts.co.uk/
5. Lars Bille, A power centre in Danish politics. In Knut Heidar and Ruud Koole, eds, *Parliamentary Party Groups in European Democracies: Political Parties Behind Closed Doors*, London: Routledge, 2000; Rudy Andeweg, Fractiocracy? Limits to the ascendancy of the parliamentary party group in Dutch politics. In Knut Heidar and Ruud Koole, eds, *Parliamentary Party Groups in European Democracies: Political Parties Behind Closed Doors*, London: Routledge, 2000.
6. Knut Heidar and Ruud Koole, Parliamentary party groups compared. In Knut Heidar and Ruud Koole, eds, *Parliamentary Party Groups in European Democracies: Political Parties Behind Closed Doors*, London: Routledge, 2000, p. 254.
7. Richard Katz, Party government and its alternatives. In Richard Katz, ed., *Party Government: European and American Experiences*. Berlin: de Gruyter, 1987, p. 7.
8. Michael Laver and Kenneth Shepsle, How political parties emerged from the primeval slime: Party cohesion, party discipline and the formation of governments. In Shaun Bowler, David Farrell, and Richard Katz, eds, *Party Discipline and Parliamentary Government*. Columbus, OH: Ohio State University Press, 1999; Gary Cox and Mathew McCubbins, *Legislative Leviathan: Party Government in the House*, 2nd edn. Cambridge: Cambridge University Press, 2007.
9. Atilla Ágh, The parliamentarization of the East Central European parties: Party discipline in the Hungarian parliament, 1990–1996. In Bowler et al., *Party Discipline and Parliamentary Government*; Manuel Sánchez de Dios, Parliamentary party discipline in Spain. In Bowler et al., *Party Discipline and Parliamentary Government*; D. Malová and D. Siváková, The National Council of the Slovak Republic: Between democratic transition and national state-building. In D. Olson and Philip Norton, eds, *The New Parliaments of Central and Eastern Europe*. London: Frank Cass, 1996.

10. The Rice index, though not perfect, is the most commonly used measure in the literature.

11. John Carey, *Legislative Voting and Accountability*. Cambridge: Cambridge University Press, 2009; Sam Depauw and Shane Martin, Legislative party discipline and party cohesion in comparative perspective. In Daniela Giannetti and Kenneth Benoit, eds. *Intra-Party Politics and Coalition Governments in Parliamentary Democracies*. London: Routledge, 2008; Ulrich Sieberer, Party unity in parliamentary democracies: A comparative analysis, *Journal of Legislative Studies* (2006) 12: 150–78.

12. Shaun Bowler, Parties in legislatures: Two competing explanations. In Russell Dalton and Martin Wattenberg, eds, *Parties without Partisans: Political Change in Advanced Industrial Democracies*. Oxford: Oxford University Press, 2001; Bowler et al., *Party Discipline and Parliamentary Government*; Herbert Döring, ed., *Parliament and Majority Rule in Western Europe*. Frankfurt/New York: Campus Verlag/St Martin's Press, 1995; Heidar and Koole, *Parliamentary Party Groups in European Democracies*.

13. For a general discussion of the issues, see Hans-Dieter Klingemann, Richard Hofferbert, and Ian Budge, *Parties, Policies and Democracy*. Boulder, CO: Westview Press, 1994; Francis Castles, *Comparative Public Policy: Patterns of Post-War Transformation*. Cheltenham: Edward Elgar, 1998; Torben Iversen and Thomas Cusack, The causes of welfare state expansion: Deindustrialization or globalization? *World Politics* (2000) 52: 313–49; Paul Pierson, The new politics of the welfare state, *World Politics* (1996) 48: 143–79; Kenneth Benoit and Michael Laver, *Party Policy in Modern Democracies*. London and New York: Routledge, 2006.

14. Thomas Dye, *Politics, Economics and Pubic Policy*. Chicago: Rand McNally, 1966; Harold Wilenski, *The Welfare State and Equality*, Berkeley: University of California Press, 1975.

15. Peter Flora and Arnold Heidenheimer, *The Development of Welfare States in Europe and America*. New Brunswick, NJ: Transaction, 1981.

16. Torben Iversen and David Soskice, Electoral institutions and the politics of coalitions: Why some democracies redistribute more than others, *American Political Science Review* (2006) 100: 165–81.

17. Louis Imbeau, François Pétry, and Moktar Lamari, Left–right party ideology and government policies: A meta-analysis, *European Journal of Political Research* (2001) 40: 1; Manfred Schmidt, When parties matter: A review of the possibilities and limits of partisan influence on policy, *European Journal of Political Research* (1996) 30: 155–83.

18. Evelyn Huber and John Stephens, *Development and Crisis of the Welfare State*. Chicago: University of Chicago Press, 2001, p. 221. See also Pierson, The new politics of the welfare state.

19. Andre Blais, Donald Blake, and Stephane Dion, Do parties make a difference? Parties and the size of government, *American Journal of Political Science* (1993) 37: 40–62; Andre Blais, Donald Blake, and Stephane Dion, Do parties make a difference? A reappraisal, *American Journal of Political Science* (1996) 40: 514–20.

20. The best work outlining this approach is Blais, Blake, and Dion, Do parties make a difference?; also Imbeau, Pétry, and Lamari, Left–right party ideology and government policies.

21. Richard Rose, *Do Parties Make a Difference?* London: Macmillan, 1980. p. 65.

22. Klingemann, Hofferbert, and Budge, *Parties, Policy and Democracy*; Richard Hofferbert and Ian Budge, The party mandate and the Westminster model: Election programmes and government spending in Britain, 1948–85, *British Journal of Political Science* (1992) 22: 151–82.

23. Benjamin Page and Robert Shapiro, *The Rational Public: Fifty Years of Trends in Americans' Policy Preferences*. Chicago: University of Chicago Press; also see Robert Erikson, Michael MacKuen, and James Stimson, *The Macro Polity*. New York: Cambridge University Press, 2002; Larry Bartels, Constituency opinion and congressional policy making: The Reagan defense buildup, *American Political Science Review* (1991) 85: 457–74.

24. Alan Monroe, Public opinion and public policy 1980–1993, *Public Opinion Quarterly* (1998) 62: 6–28.

25. Stuart Soroka and Christopher Wlezien, *Degrees of Democracy: Politics, Public Opinion and Policy*. New York: Cambridge University Press, 2010.

26. Clem Brooks and Jeff Manza, *Why Welfare States Persist: Public Opinion and the Future of Social Provision*. Chicago: University of Chicago Press, 2007; John Brooks, The opinion-policy nexus in France: Do institutions and ideology make a difference? *Journal of Politics* (1987) 49: 465–80; Franz Brettschneider, Public opinion and parliamentary action: Responsiveness in the German Bundestag in comparative perspective, *International Journal of Public Opinion Research* (1996) 8: 292–311.

27. See Castles, *Comparative Public Policy*; Geoffrey Garrett, *Partisan Politics in the Global Economy*. Cambridge: Cambridge University Press, 1998; Iversen and Cusack, The causes of welfare state expansion.

28. James Allan and Lyle Scruggs, Political partisanship and welfare state reform in advanced industrial societies, *American Journal of Political Science* (2004) 48: 496–512.

29. See in particular Castles, *Comparative Public Policy*.

30. Francis Castles, The impact of parties on public expenditure. In Francis Castles, ed., *The Impact of Parties: Politics and Policies in Democratic Capitalist States*. Beverly Hills, CA: Sage Publications, 1982.

31. Margrit Tavits and Natalia Letki, When left is right: Party ideology and policy in postcommunist Europe, *American Political Science Review* (209) 103: 555–69.

32. Allan and Scruggs, Political partisanship and welfare state reform, p. 498.

33. Iversen and Soskice, Electoral institutions and the politics of coalitions.

34. Organisation of Economic Co-operation and Development, *Social Expenditure Database* (SOCX). Available at: http://www.oecd.org/els/social/expenditure.

35. In some cases, the measures for particular countries were missing, and they were supplemented from individual country sources. In a few cases data were missing for a specific year, and the most appropriate timepoint was used to include the nation in our analyses.

36. One issue is whether to measure the political complexion of the government before or after the election that is being considered. Logically, the timelag in implementing policy means that the political complexion of the government before the election should have a better fit to the independent variables, and that appears to be the case. In three of the four measures of expenditure, the correlations are higher with the government that was in place before the election compared with the government that was in place after the election—as indeed we would expect. For example, for social spending, the correlation with the Left–Right placement of the government is -0.13 for the government before the election and -0.04 for the government after the election.

37. Imbeau, Pétry, and Lamari, Left–right party ideology and government policies. This finding is interpreted as a consequence of the pre-1973 period being characterized by more economic growth, and therefore greater flexibility for parties to exercise their ideological predispositions, relative to the post-1973 period, when growth was lower and inflation higher.

38. Sources: John Carey, *Legislative Voting and Accountability*. Cambridge: Cambridge University Press, 2009, table 5.2; Sam Depauw and Shane Martin, Legislative party discipline and party cohesion in comparative perspective. In Daniela Giannetti and Kenneth Benoit, eds, *Intra-Party Politics and Coalition Governments in Parliamentary Democracies*. London: Routledge, 2009, table 6.1.

Conclusion

9

Party Evolution

From the very first writings on political parties up until the present, the demise of the political party has been predicted in some form or other. As we noted in Chapter 1, even a cursory review of the literature reveals that some of the most common terms applied to parties are "decline," "crisis," and "vulnerability."[1] This leaves the clear impression that the heyday of the political party has long since passed. Yet, for all of this apparent pessimism, political parties remain as central as they ever were to the effective operation of modern democracy—perhaps even more so, given the complexities of modern government.

As we have argued in this book, modern democracy is synonymous with political parties. The model of party government that we have examined in the preceding chapters has undergone considerable change since it first entered academic discourse in the 1950s. That model emphasized the representation and accountability functions of political parties and placed parties at the heart of representative democracy. The model remained largely unquestioned until the 1970s, as mass parties remained organizationally strong and politically dominant within their respective countries.

The ongoing questioning of the role of political parties that began in the 1970s has led many scholars to revisit the key assumptions of the party government model. Kay Lawson stressed the linkage function of political parties within government, making parties the natural intermediary between the citizen and the state.[2] A series of studies in the 1980s re-evaluated the applicability of the party government model in the face of changing patterns of party competition and the organizational basis of many established parties.[3] Moreover, Scott Mainwaring and others showed that party institutionalization has been slower and less well developed in Third Wave democracies.[4] They attributed this to political elites having less incentive to build mass parties, and instead choosing to mobilize voters via the mass media and non-party organizations. But even in the new democracies, political parties remain central to the party government model.

Critics of the party government model often point to the evidence of party decline—for example, declining party memberships, and the increasing reliance of government on non-party actors for policy support—which we reviewed in Chapter 1. Other evidence that is often advanced for party decline is the low standing of political parties in the eyes of the public. Our response to this argument is to distinguish between the images that parties project and the functions that they carry out.

It is indisputable that the public image of political parties is poor. Across most countries, the popularity of parties and politicians among the public ranks along with real-estate agents and used-car salesmen.[5] Stories of expenses scandals, corruption and graft, and sexual and other infidelities involving politicians fill the mass media almost on a daily basis. Yet, like a battered and slightly slow bus that takes passengers to work each morning, parties still perform a vital function and accomplish it with reasonable efficiency. And like the bus, without a viable alternative to get people to work on time, parties maintain their monopoly on carrying out their linkage function.

The distinction between how citizens see the image of parties and their function is aptly demonstrated by the responses to two questions in the first module of the CSES project. The module asked people what they thought of parties. The survey first asked if they believed that parties cared what ordinary people thought.[6] Across the thirty-two countries in the survey, an average of just 10 percent believed that parties cared what people thought. This ranged from a low of 3 percent in Canada, to a high of 27 percent in Peru. By any standards, parties were held in low esteem across all of the thirty-two countries.

By contrast, when people were asked if they considered parties to be necessary to make the system work, 46 percent agreed with the statement.[7] Citizens in Thailand were most supportive of parties (70 percent), while those in the USA were least supportive of their role (25 percent). This is a clear illustration of how voters distinguish between image and function. Like the battered commuter bus whose passengers wish it was cleaner, faster, and more comfortable, voters realize that parties perform a vital function and that democracy in its current form would be impossible without them.

In this final chapter, we examine how and why parties have retained their predominant position within democracies in the face of so many predictions (and occasionally apparent evidence) of their imminent demise. We argue that while there is evidence for party decline, there is at least as much evidence of party adaptation. The first section reviews our broad findings, with particular reference to their implications for the party government model. The second section focuses on party adaptation and examines how, and in what ways, parties have adapted to the changing circumstances in which they find themselves. The third section outlines the mechanisms through which parties have maintained their dominance, from institutional design to organizational change. The fourth and final section covers the unanticipated threats that can emerge to damage parties that, by definition, they have difficulty adapting to.

Parties and Democratic Linkage

This book has marshaled the latest survey and other evidence to assess the role of contemporary political parties as agents of representation between citizens and the state. Our analysis is framed around five main forms of linkage between parties and citizens: campaign, participation, ideology, representation, and policy (see Chapter 1).

In the first instance, we see parties playing a continuing key role in the election campaign process (Chapter 2). Parties almost uniformly control the selection of candidates for election and dominate the political discourse of campaigns. Parties themselves also benefit through the provision of generous state subsidies, both financial and in-kind. Parties have also designed "light-touch" regulatory mechanisms that do little in practice to constrain them in any meaningful way. And not least, parties have introduced various controls over the electoral process that are designed to ensure the primacy of party. Party leaders in new democracies have quickly insitutionalized these party-benefiting rules they have learned from established democracies. Unlike Katz and Mair,[8] who argue that these steps are aimed at preserving a cartel of elite parties, we argue that the campaign linkage of parties serves to protect the genus of parties *tout court.*

Parties also play a key role in turning out the vote at elections (Chapter 3). Participatory linkage sees parties using traditional and modern means to mobilize their support base on polling day. Even in an age of declining voter turnout, most citizens still continue to vote in election after election, and our analysis provides irrefutable evidence that parties play an important role in this regard. We show that parties still have the ability to mobilize the vote at the local level. This appears to be particularly the case in the new democracies, where party members are increasing, in contrast to the established democracies, where membership has been in long-term decline.

Ideological linkage refers to how parties help voters determine who to vote for in an election. Our analysis in Chapters 4–6 shows that voters view their political preferences through the lens of the Left–Right policy continuum, even in a time when some differences between the major parties may be becoming less noticeable. Voters as a collective can also correctly identify the parties' locations on the same Left–Right continuum. And having done so, for the most part voters use this information to make informed choices between the parties. In short, the ideological or policy congruence between voters and parties continues to be an important determinant of voter choice.

Once elected, and (for those who "win") in government, attention next turns to the representative linkage between citizens and governments (Chapter 7). Parties promise certain policy objectives in an election campaign; we examined whether the electorate is well represented in the government resulting from intra-party government formation negotiations. Our examination of the dynamics of voter–party policy congruence provides good evidence of healthy representative linkage. Moreover, the levels of congruence improve between pre-election and post-election governments. And particularly important for the future of parties, these trends are at least as marked in the new democracies as in the old.

Finally, Chapter 8 finds substantial evidence that parties provide a meaningful policy linkage, supporting the perspective that it "matters" which party or coalition of parties are in office. Voters seek out parties for their policy goals and, for the most part, parties implement those goals when they gain office. While the measurement issues in following these linkages are considerable, we show that the linkages operate effectively across the broad range of countries in our analysis. In short, the policy outputs of governments are broadly consistent with the ideological profiles of the parties that form them.

This cumulative evidence thus suggests that voters choose parties in elections based on the broad political goals that they wish to see implemented. Voters sift through the information that is available to them, which, more often than not, is fragmentary and fleeting, and then make a choice. In turn, parties deliver on the wishes of their voters if they are elected to government. This is the essence of the party linkage model, with parties providing a crucial link between citizens and the state. As we have shown in this book, it largely works, regardless of whether the country is a new or old democracy, has a parliamentary or a presidential system, a two-party or a multiparty system, or differs on a host of other criteria.

Decline or Adaptation?

Why is the evidence for the continuing importance of party government so strong if much of the party literature emphasizes party decline? The answer to this question largely rests in the processes of adaptation that parties undergo. Once a party identifies a challenge to its continued existence, it should move to address it. Thus, through a continuous process of adaptation and change, parties can ensure their survival in a constantly changing environment. As Paul Webb has put it, in the context of a study of British parties, "it may be more appropriate to speak of the phenomenon of party adaptation rather than that of party decline."[9] Decline or new challenges are therefore the first part of the process; adaptation is the second part. If implemented successfully, adaptation can effectively arrest or even reverse the decline.

An example from British politics makes this point well. In the 1980s and early 1990s the British Labour Party was facing slow electoral death. The causes were fundamental socioeconomic changes within the electorate, the party's outdated class-based appeal, and the free-market policies of the Thatcher Conservative government that appealed especially to upwardly mobile working-class voters. The party was clearly out of step with current trends within the electorate; many observers thought that a fundamental party system realignment was under way, with Labour likely to be replaced by the Liberal Democratic Party as the main opposition to the Conservatives.

In response to this threat, a group of reformers led by Tony Blair and Peter Mandelson rebranded the Labour Party as "New Labour," the new title emphasizing both continuity and change.[10] The popular appeal of New Labour stressed equality of opportunity, thus skillfully retaining Labour's traditional working-class supporters while recruiting former Conservative voters. New Labour also committed itself to retaining some of the policy changes introduced by the Thatcher and Major Conservative governments that appealed to the public.[11] The effect was that Labour turned what many thought was a realignment in British politics into a decisive electoral win in 1997, which heralded the longest period of Labour government since the party's formation.

Other examples of party adaptation are more organizational. For instance, parties were forced to adapt to the advent of television in the 1960s, and the ability of the new medium to convey an appeal through visual images and personalities. They did that by ensuring that their leaders had, for the most part, the visual appeal and communication skills that suited the new medium. When a new party leader is chosen, it is taken for granted that one of the main selection criteria is how they present themselves on television. For example, when Koizumi wanted to signal a new style of Liberal Democratic Party (LDP) politics, he did it by appointing a very telegenic cabinet in 2003. Koizumi himself marked a sharp departure from the traditionalism of previous Japanese prime ministers, from his campaign style to his release of an Elvis CD in 2001 with his personal commentary on his favorite songs. His personal appeal pushed up his own approval ratings and the electoral success of the LDP.

Organizationally, political parties have also been forced to adapt to declining party memberships. A case in point is how the Irish political parties have adapted their district campaign strategies in the light of fast declining memberships. Ireland's highly localist political culture, combined with its candidate-centered single transferable vote electoral system, promotes a strong emphasis on traditional vote-chasing activities on the ground.

One prominent feature of this is known as the "lamppost wars," in which lampposts the length and breadth of the country are festooned with candidate posters (often two to three per lamppost). Traditionally, teams of volunteer party members with crotchety ladders spent long evenings hanging posters (and re-hanging them, for the other feature entails surreptitiously ripping down opponents' posters). The lamppost wars have continued in an age of membership decline: indeed, if anything they have intensified. Only now the teams hanging the posters are paid professionals.

Placed in a cross-national context, the evidence of party adaptation in response to change is impressive. In many of the Anglo-American democracies, the major parties pre-date the First World War; indeed, many are a century old or more, often retaining the same party labels. In the United States, for example, the oldest political party is the Democratic Party, while the Republican Party dates from 1854. In Britain and many of the British colonies, the expansion of the franchise created the mass political parties that still exist today; the Labour Party was founded in 1900 and the modern Conservative Party dates from 1912. In Australia, the Labor Party was formed in 1891 by the trade union movement, and in New Zealand the Labour Party dates from 1910, while its Irish counterpart was founded in 1912.[12]

The continuity of party labels in many Anglo-American democracies often belies the degree to which the parties have changed their appeals in order to adapt to changing circumstances. For example, the Australian Labor Party at the end of the nineteenth century was a party mainly supported by manual workers, trade unionists, and agricultural workers. In the 2000s, the party is unselfconsciously the advocate of the upwardly mobile middle class. Similarly, the modern Democratic Party in the USA is not the party of Lincoln, nor are the modern Republicans the party of Jefferson.

It might be argued that the stability of Anglo-American parties is atypical, in part because of the high electoral thresholds of non-proportional systems. For instance, Wren and McElwain find that about 40 percent of the parties existing in 1960 in the established democracies had disappeared by 2000. In France only the French Communist Party (PCF) has existed continuously since 1958. The *mani pulite* scandals in Italy in the 1990s resulted in a full-scale restructuring of their party system. The past few decades have witnessed spates of new parties—most prominently among them Green and populist parties—emerging across the world's established democracies, which is seen in statistics of growing party system fragmentation. Furthermore, long-term and established parties are remade (sometimes even renamed) to reflect new issues and new contexts.

All of this speaks to a successful process of party adaptation, involving a healthy mix of long-established parties that tack and change in order to survive, and the emergence of new parties to represent new issues that are not adequately covered by the existing parties, or to fill voids created by parties that fail to adapt. The characteristic that remains prominent throughout all of this is the genus of parties.

The experience of political parties is similar to the changes that take place in the private sector as part of economic development. Few major manufacturers or banks have survived the twentieth century unscathed, and those that retain their original name have often experienced numerous transformations, amalgamations, and takeovers. For example, although retaining its name, the Ford Motor Company, founded in 1903 by Henry Ford, is a radically different organization today compared with its origins, perhaps sharing only the goal of manufacturing and selling motor cars with Ford's 1906 logo as the trademark. Even more significantly, most of the car companies that were set up at the same time as Ford have long since disappeared—to be replaced by new companies that are better adapted to contemporary manufacturing and marketing standards.

How Parties Adapt

In keeping with the wide-ranging functions that they are expected to undertake, parties use many, often complex mechanisms to adapt to the ever-changing circumstances of modern democracy. A party sometimes makes these changes independent of other parties. For example, in the late 1990s the center-right Liberal Party in Australia was losing votes to the new One Nation Party, which was located farther on the right. In response, the Liberals sought to obviate the threat from One Nation by neutralizing anti-immigration sentiments among voters which One Nation was exploiting to its advantage.[13] The Liberals' policy shifts were successful and One Nation sank into electoral oblivion.

Often, the process of adaptation may involve some degree of collusion among the major parties, either implicitly or explicitly, in order to retain their dominant positions—one of the core features of Katz and Mair's "cartel party" model. As we reviewed in Chapter 2, this is most obvious in the allocation of state resources for political parties, either through the provision of state funding that disproportionately favors the more established parties, or regulations on TV access that in some instances effectively freeze out minor parties. An example of this was provided by the Irish 2007 election, when two separate party leaders' debates were held—most voters viewed the one involving the leaders of the two main parties, rather than the second TV debate that included the leaders of all the minor parties.

The major mechanisms that parties use to adapt to changing conditions can be grouped under four broad headings, covering institutional design, policies, organization, and government. We examine each of these in turn.

Institutional Design

Political institutions form the arena within which parties compete. The "rules of the political game" that govern how political institutions operate are therefore critical to party success. The most obvious institutional design feature that political parties seek to manipulate is the electoral system. Since electoral systems are rarely constitutionally embedded, they can be manipulated more easily than other fundamental design features of a polity, such as deciding between presidentialism or parliamentarism, for example.[14] This has led Sartori to view the electoral system as "the most specific manipulative instrument of politics."[15] Relatively small changes in electoral systems (such as, for example, the size of an electoral district or the level of a legal threshold) can result in major changes to a party's electoral fortunes or to the number of parties within parliamentary seats.[16]

The parties in new postcommunist systems have often used existing knowledge of electoral system effects to design a system that benefits the major parties and places barriers to new entrants. In Russia, the early debates about the electoral system were dominated by the adoption of a mixed member majoritarian system that would disadvantage the communists and favor the pro-reform parties led by Boris Yeltsin's party "Our Home is Russia."[17] Certainly this system resulted in some highly disproportional outcomes.[18] More generally, for the CSES nations examined in this book, disproportionality (the gap between party vote shares and seat shares) is greater in new democracies than in established democracies. This is probably a conscious goal of the major parties in new democracies.

Other countries, such as Italy, have moved in the opposite direction, undoing earlier majoritarian-leaning reforms and returning to a party list system with a threshold in 2005. New Zealand is currently debating whether to move away from the mixed member proportional (MMP) electoral system introduced in 1993. The issue is a complex one; large-scale electoral reform is rare and often it creates problems separate from those that it was designed to solve.

Parties have also been active in the institutional design of media access (see Chapter 2). In the 1960s, parties were forced to come to terms with the potential of television, and a wide range of measures were introduced to restrict advertising and provide free airtime for the major parties. In Britain, for example, free airtime during election campaigns has usually been allocated based on a complex formula combining votes and seats at the previous election. Thus, in the 1983 general election, when the new Social Democratic

Party-Alliance won 25.4 percent of the vote and Labour 27.6 percent, the Conservative and Labour parties were allocated 60 minutes of free airtime each, while the Alliance received just 20 minutes.[19]

The parties have also had to come to terms with leaders' debates, now an established part of election campaigns in almost all of the established democracies. Compared with a pre-television era, when leaders were seldom seen live and virtually never with their rival, this changes the dynamics of campaigns and stimulates the personalization of politics. In all the countries in which leaders' debates are held, the timing, format, and logistics are a matter of intense debate between party officials.[20]

In new democracies, the electronic media are essential sources of political information and electoral cues since voters typically lack partisan attachments and the social bases of the parties are weak. Consequently, the major parties have gone to great lengths to ensure favorable media attention. For instance, in the 1989 Brazilian presidential elections, the favorable coverage accorded to the conservative candidate, Fernando Collor de Mello, is generally viewed as having been decisive in his election.[21]

A final area in which the "rules of the political game" can be effectively manipulated to parties' advantage is the state funding of political parties. Like media access, the rules for state funding are often based on prior electoral performance. In practice, therefore, this denies funding to new entrants and forces them to rely on members or private benefactors to provide funds for organizational support. But once parties become established, this creates new resources that can substitute for declining party membership or even expand party information and mobilization efforts. For instance, German parties are entitled to receive state funding if they won at least 0.5 percent of the valid votes cast at the most recent European or Bundestag elections, or if they polled at least 1 percent of votes cast at one of the most recent Landtag elections. Parties receive €0.85 ($1.12) per valid vote in European, Bundestag, and Landtag elections up to a total of four million votes, and €0.70 ($0.92) for every additional vote. There are partial state matching provisions for individual donations to a party. In addition, the parties receive generous subsidies to support their party foundations and their educational/informational activities between elections. Such provisions create a distinct incentive structure for existing and new parties.[22]

Parties in the established democracies have had to adjust to changes in several of these institutional factors in recent decades. To survive, and perhaps prosper, this requires that a party adjust to the new incentive structures created by institutional reform. If they fail to adjust to these new structures, they risk the emergence of new parties that will take advantage of the new opportunities. This is a particular challenge for parties in new democracies. They must institutionalize themselves and, at the same time, they often have to learn to function and survive in an unfamiliar and changeable institutional environment. In the end, however, some parties will compete in the elections, vie for voter support, and represent their voters in the governing process. These are the parties that survive.

Policy Development

Parties appeal for support based on the policies that they would implement if elected to government. In theory, a party is not a serious contender for political office unless it possesses a comprehensive and coherent policy platform. Parties also depend on having a sufficiently large number of members with the skills to develop policy across a range of areas. It also assumes that a party will have the organizational resources and sophistication to have its policies adopted by the mass membership. Of course, by definition, single issue and protest parties do not require a comprehensive policy platform; their goal is to influence policy in their area of concern rather than to implement it by forming a government.

Largely as a result of the resources at their disposal, the major parties generally dominate policy development. Their proximity to political office brings them into regular contact with the public service. The periods of time that they spend in office, in addition to giving the parties access to administrative support to develop policy, also serve to socialize their members. Studies of elites consistently show that cabinet and shadow cabinet members have higher ethical standards and levels of tolerance than their backbench colleagues, net of a wide range of other factors.[23] This presumably reflects their greater mastery of policy detail, and their close contact with the senior public service. Even parties in opposition and minor parties, while not having control of the public service, still have frequent contact with, and briefings from, public servants.

Although the parties are constantly offering policy proposals, one of the main challenges they face is to respond to the changing policy demands emanating from society and the economy. Globalization, for instance, has forced parties to adapt their economic policies to new circumstances if they are to be electorally successful. Other issues—environmentalism, gender equality, immigration—create new bases of electoral debate. Perhaps this is clearest in international relations. International events are often exogenous shocks that require policy adaptation to new conditions. Thus the collapse of the Soviet empire required a major readjustment of foreign and defense policies in the West, and more recently the rise of jihadist terrorism has created a new need for adaptation.

Consequently, an important part of responding to changing policy demands is parties' ability to determine the political agenda. While their capacity for agenda-setting has undoubtedly declined, largely as a result of greater electronic media coverage of politics and the lobbying activities of political groups, the major parties still exercise an important role in directing the agenda toward issues that benefit them and away from those that will harm them. This agenda-setting capacity also means that the major parties can often adapt to new issues that may emerge by absorbing and then neutralizing them. For single issue and protest parties, this usually robs them of their electoral support.

Minor parties can also benefit from policy development, despite their relative distance from political power. Bonnie Meguid argues that what she calls "niche parties"—minor parties often promoting a single issue—can benefit electorally particularly where the larger parties fail to gain "ownership" of an issue. Meguid maintains that the Labour and Conservative parties in Britain failed to gain ownership of the devolution issue in the 1980s and 1990s at a time when the Scottish National Party's fortunes were rising. The net effect was that the Scottish nationalists were able to mobilize electoral support on the issues, without any serious opposition from the major parties.[24] The rise of Green parties in the 1980s and new right parties in the 1990s attests to the potential for new parties to capture public support when new issues enter the agenda and established parties fail to respond sufficiently.

Organizational Adaptation

In order to survive, political parties must be like sharks, they must keep moving to adapt to changing conditions. A key condition of successful adaptation comes from party elites who are committed to maintaining the organization, much like the successful firm depends on its CEO. Party leaders, typically, are committed to the party's heritage and ideology, and want to influence policy. But their livelihood is also often dependent on the party. Thus, when conditions change, party leaders have a strong motivation to adapt the party to the new conditions so that the party (and their status) continues. And alternative party leaders are looking for opportunities to improve the party's electoral showing and their personal status. Like most organizations, the entrepreneurial incentives are key to the degree and direction of organizational change.

One example of organizational adaptation involves party membership. The mass party model has its roots in the late nineteenth century, with the expansion of the franchise and the need for a large membership to provide subscriptions to fund a party's activities. In its early years, the mass party model was used most frequently by parties of the left, but by the 1950s it was common among parties of the right as well. This "contagion from the left," as Duverger coined it, led him and others to argue that the mass party model would become the norm within the established democracies.[25] The decline of party membership has proved this not to be the case. But it is perhaps instructive that the membership-based party has become popular in the new democracies of Central and Eastern Europe, with countries such as Croatia and Slovakia recording levels of party membership at over 5 percent of the population.[26] In these countries at least, the mass party model is thriving.

The decline of party membership has meant that the mass parties have sought other ways to fund their activities. We have already discussed how the state has replaced fee-paying members as a provider of funds (see Chapters 1 and 2). Parties have also adapted in other, more significant ways to offset the roles once performed by the mass membership. The Scandinavian parties have experimented with different classes of membership, with "trial" members and "cyber" members existing alongside traditional members. Susan Scarrow has called this "multi-speed parties," and it is arguably a major organizational change for parties as they seek to mitigate the dramatic declines in party memberships.[27] Another response has been to professionalize many activities formerly conducted by the mass membership. This can vary from the development of computerized mail systems and the reliance on mass media, to the growth of a professionalized party staff.

The internet has been a major driver of organizational change. Howard Dean's candidacy for the US Democratic Party's presidential nomination in 2004 was a milestone in the use of the internet for election campaigning. Dean reportedly raised one million dollars in donations in a single day, and his use of online discussion groups and the targeting of key bloggers presaged many of the techniques later used by Barack Obama even more successfully in his 2008 presidential election campaign. The Obama campaign raised nearly $750 million, and internet contributions were a sizeable share of this total.

The issue of whether online communication actually wins votes has been more contentious. Australian evidence points to a significant though modest vote advantage,[28] while other research suggests that internet use has reinforced rather than challenged the dominance of the existing actors.[29] Again the most dramatic example may be the 2008 Obama campaign; it coordinated activities through internet forums, created a social networking site for its supporters to interact with each other (MyBo), and used viral videos to spread the campaign's message. What is clear, however, is that parties are adapting to the potential of the internet.

Party in Government

In many respects, party actions to control government represent the peak function for parties. Much of party activity is organized around the goal of winning political power. Once a party has secured office, then its goal is to retain it for as long as possible, through the implementation of public policies that were supported by voters in an election. As we discussed in Chapter 1, modern government is usually referred to as *party* government, with the party in office being accountable for its actions through elections. The power-seeking function of political parties means that their effectiveness is usually measured by their strength while in government. When parties cease to fulfill their governmental functions—what V. O. Key referred to as the party as an organization of public officials—then parties should gradually weaken at election time.[30] Not surprisingly, then, much party effort is devoted to adapting to changes in government in order to preserve their dominant position.

Within legislatures, parties adapt constantly to a changing environment. One significant change is the growth of regional assemblies and supranational bodies. Examples include the Parliament of the European Union, Italy's creation of new regional governments in the 1970s, French decentralization to local and regional governments in 1982, and regional devolution in Britain and the gradual federalization of Belgian politics.[31] This decentralization trend has forced parties to adapt to the dispersion of national power.[32] In turn, the devolution of power and the potential fragmentation of party organizations make it more difficult for national party leaders to find collective solutions.

Similarly, the internationalization of politics has impacted on parties, and they now have to accommodate politics not just within their national boundaries, but often further afield as well. This is nowhere more prominently laid out than in the twenty-seven member countries of the European Union, whose parties have formed transnational alliances and who operate as increasingly cohesive parliamentary parties in the European Parliament.[33]

If parties are in decline within legislatures, one indicator would be weakening party cohesion. Yet the evidence collected by Shaun Bowler from a wide range of established democracies over an extended period of time suggests that this is not the case.[34] There is little evidence that elected representatives are any less disciplined in their party voting behavior, which perhaps points to the effectiveness of parties in maintaining their legislative recruitment procedures.

How do parties manage to maintain such a remarkably high level of discipline among their elected representatives? One approach is to ensure that potential defections are nipped in the bud, with suitable threats toward any member who is contemplating defection.[35] In the Irish case, the operation of its electoral system keeps potential recalcitrants in line, because defectors tend to be punished at the polls.[36] Another approach is to avoid issues on which members are divided, for example by making votes on contentious issues (especially moral issues such as abortion or gay marriage) a matter of conscience not of party discipline. A third approach is to enforce central control over the selection and recruitment of candidates, before they stand for election. On the demand side, history shows that parties that receive defectors do not accept them warmly. In Australia, for example, when the leader of the Australian Democrats, Cheryl Kernot, defected to Labor in 1997 she was allocated a marginal seat that she lost in the 2001 election, causing much bitterness.[37]

Corporatist policymaking outside of the legislative process presents a particular threat to the policy function of parties while in government since it may weaken the power of a party to promote the policies on which it was elected. This outcome may risk a party's ability to retain power at any subsequent election.[38] However, time-series analysis has cast doubt on this claim. Siaroff has suggested that there has been no change in the levels of corporatism that are apparent in twenty-four of the major democracies.[39] What seems to have occurred is that parties have adapted to interest groups. As policy has become more complex and interwoven through the political system, the parties in office have used input from these interest groups to develop policy—what has been recognized implicitly as "stakeholder democracy" which gained wide currency in the 1990s.

It is clear that parties have a range of mechanisms by which they can adapt to changing circumstances, ranging from institutional fixes to changes in how they make policy. These mechanisms can be used independently or, depending on the severity of the perceived threat, used as a portfolio of measures. All of this is, of course, given heightened relevance by the monopoly position that parties occupy within the political system. Parties can take measures to cope with the threats that they can anticipate. Different scenarios emerge when they must come to terms with unanticipated threats; this is examined in the next section.

Unanticipated Threats to Parties

So far, we have identified the extent to which parties may adapt to changing institutions and political circumstances. As we have seen, parties constantly survey the strategic environment and evaluate potential threats to their position, adapting themselves continuously as circumstances change. But what threats may emerge that parties find more difficult to anticipate and address effectively?

Antipartyism

A constant theme in public opinion is antipartyism, and it is manifested in many of the indicators that we have identified in this book—declining party memberships, partisan dealignment, and a rising vote for new parties. Antipartyism represents a particular threat because it is sometimes difficult to anticipate and may emerge with little or no warning. It may come about through disaffection with parties per se, or through parties risking becoming irrelevant due to changes in technology. When antipartyism is directed at the major parties, the outcome is likely to be the rise of "antiparty parties," such as the Reform Party in Canada or Berlusconi's Forza Italia. It can also result in electoral support for independents, such as Ross Perot in the 1992 US presidential election. If the antipartyism sentiments are directed at all parties then they are more likely to lead to abstention.[40]

Antipartyism usually has its roots in the general trends that drive partisan dealignment, such as generational change and parties creating unrealizable expectations. Parties can often anticipate and respond to these trends. But if antipartyism is caused by "random shocks," then it is more difficult to anticipate and neutralize. In Britain, the expenses scandal in 2009–10 was unique because it tarnished all three parties equally, and had the potential to generate substantial popular disaffection with the parties. In the event, however, the results of the 2010 general election suggested that the apocalyptic fears raised by the scandal failed to materialize.[41] Yet the anti-incumbent sentiments in the United States led to large electoral swings in 2008 and 2010—albeit in opposite directions. Indeed, public skepticism about political parties has generally been increasing in most established democracies, but still parties continue to structure the process of representative democracy. This has been one of the paradoxes of our findings. Parties are adapting or enduring even in this more critical environment.

Charismatic Leaders

The rise of a charismatic leader can cause conflict within a party. Bertie Ahern's thirteen-year dominance over Ireland's Fianna Fáil party ended in ignominy over issues relating to his personal finances in 2007. The dramatic economic collapse that followed directly after has resulted in political meltdown for the electorally most successful political party in Europe. Silvio Berlusconi's dominance of Forza Italia during the 1990s and early 2000s caused major tensions and eventually led to the creation of the People of Freedom Party, which was effectively a vehicle for Berlusconi himself.

Charismatic leaders are a particular danger to parties in new democracies since party attachments within the mass population are generally weak and parties often ephemeral. Vladimir Putin's period as Russian president between 2000 and 2008, and since 2008 as prime minister, is an example of how a leader has come to dominate the political system at the expense of a competitive system of political parties.[42] Similarly, Roh Moo-hyun ran in 2002 as the representative of a young, dynamic generation that had brought democracy to Korea. He ironically won the presidency as a candidate of the conservative Millennium Democratic Party. But within a year he left the party and took his followers to his new leftist Uriu Party, which won the 2004 elections after a failed attempt to impeach Roh in 2003. His personal appeal created a restructuring of Korean party alignments and election outcomes.

Direct Democracy

Direct democracy, which links citizens directly to government, is a particular threat to political parties since its implementation might undermine the fundamental rationale for political parties. Moreover, surveys show that the idea of direct democracy is uniformly popular with voters.[43] With the exception of Switzerland, the use of referendums to provide citizens with a greater role in decision-making is relatively rare, although countries such as Germany have significantly increased their use of referendums.[44] More common, parties and governments seek to redesign institutions in order to allow for more popular participation. Changes have resulted in greater popular involvement in the selection of public officials, local level referendums on particular community issues, and the use of "community cabinet" meetings in order to hear citizens' views on major policy issues.

The threat to parties of direct democracy lies not just in the popularity of the premise that underlines it, but also in the fact that the technology that could make it feasible is rapidly coming to fruition.[45] While the technology so far is restricted to the advanced societies, the feasibility of its use in the new democracies is only a matter of time; this will present particular problems for parties in countries where the party role is weak and/or contested. So far, parties in most countries are only vaguely aware of the threat, and have made little attempt to address it. However, in a potential triumph for party adaptation, Ian Budge maintains that parties may find ways to use direct democracy to strengthen their political position.[46]

In the parlance of Donald Rumsfeld, it is difficult to know the unknowns that are unknown. But it seems predictable that political parties will face further challenges from antiparty movements, charismatic leaders, direct democracy, and other sources which will force them to adapt to survive and prosper. This is the nature of party politics in representative democracy.

Conclusion

Parties are nothing if not survivors. They represent continuity in democratic politics and they are central to the successful operation of representative democracy. The ubiquity of parties in old and new democracies confirms their role as the main organizing principle of modern government. Yet much of the literature on parties focuses on party decline, vulnerability, and weakness rather than on resilience, adaptation, and survival. The survival of Christian Democratic parties in a secular era, or of agrarian parties in an age of urbanization, is an apt example of the capacity of parties to adapt even as support for their founding rationale has gradually ebbed.

One explanation for party survival is that they are part of the state, and perform functions that are integral to the operation of modern government; to remove parties from the equation would require modern government to be radically reorganized. A second explanation is that there is no obvious alternative to political parties, or any alternative means of organizing the competition for power and the allocation of resources by the modern state. So far, the potential of interest groups, corporatism, direct democracy, social movements, or a host of possible alternatives to parties has proved unequal to the job of replacing parties. Rather, these other political factors seem to complement party activities and often provide new vehicles for party action.

The third explanation for party survival, which we have focused on in this book, has been party adaptation. Parties are strategic actors, surveying the political landscape, evaluating threats, and responding in such a way as to resolve them. Parties are constantly using their control of the political system to redesign political institutions in ways that will benefit themselves and in order to deter non-party competitors. They constantly seek new ways to perpetuate their influence on voters and policy outcomes. They innovate to endure and succeed, even if it means changing their style or political goals, sometimes in fundamental ways.

The best prognosis for the future of political parties is what has happened in the past. As we have shown in this book, parties constantly evolve and adapt in order to survive or they emerge in new forms; they are here for the long haul.

Notes

1. See, for example, David Everson, The decline of political parties, *Proceedings of the Academy of Political Science* (1982) 34: 49–60; William Crotty and Gary Jacobson, *American Political Parties in Decline*. Boston: Little, Brown and Company, 1980; Martin Wattenberg, *The Decline of American Political Parties, 1952–1994*. Cambridge, MA: Harvard University Press, 1996; Peter Mair, Continuity, change and the vulnerability of party, *West European Politics* (1989) 12: 169–86; John Coleman, *Party Decline in America*. Princeton, NJ: Princeton University Press, 1996; Howard Reiter, Party decline in the West: A skeptic's view, *Journal of Theoretical Politics* (1989) 1: 325–48; Peter Mair, Party politics in contemporary Europe: A challenge to party, *West European Politics* (1984) 7: 170–83.

2. See Kay Lawson, ed., *Political Parties and Linkage*. New Haven, CT: Yale University Press, 1980; Andrea Römmele, Piero Ignazi, and David Farrell, eds, *Political Parties and Political Systems: The Concept of Linkage Revisited*. Westport, CT: Praeger, 2005.

3. For example, see the Future of Party Government series coordinated by Rudolf Wildenmann: Francis Castles and Rudolf Wildenmann, eds, *Visions and Realities of Party Government*. Berlin: de Gruyter, 1986; Richard Katz, ed., *The Future of Party Government: Party Governments—European & American Experiences*, vol. 2. Berlin: de Gruyter, 1987.

4. Scott Mainwaring and Edurne Zoco, Political sequences and the stabilization of interparty competition, *Party Politics* (2007) 13: 155–78; Scott Mainwaring and Mariano Torcal, Party system institutionalization and party system theory after the Third Wave of democratization. In Richard Katz and William Crotty, eds, *Handbook of Political Parties*. London: Sage Publications, 2006. See also Margit Tavits, The development of stable party support: Electoral dynamics in post-Communist Europe, *American Journal of Political Science* (2005) 49: 283–98; Ian McAllister and Stephen White, Democracy, parties and party formation in postcommunist Russia, *Party Politics* (1995) 1: 49–72.

5. Russell Dalton and Steve Weldon, Public images of political parties: A necessary evil? *West European Politics* (2005) 28: 931–51.

6. The question was: "Some people say that political parties in [country] care what ordinary people think. Others say that political parties in [country] don't care what ordinary people think. Using the scale on this card, (where ONE means that political parties care about what ordinary people think, and FIVE means that they don't care what ordinary people think), where would you place yourself?"

7. The question was: "Some people say that political parties are necessary to make our political system work in [country]. Others think that political parties are not needed in [country]. Using the scale on this card, (where ONE means that political parties are necessary to make our political system work, and FIVE means that political parties are not needed in [country]), where would you place yourself?"

8. Richard Katz and Peter Mair, Changing models of party organization and party democracy: the emergence of the cartel party. *Party Politics* (1995) 1: 1–28.

9. Paul Webb, Are British political parties in decline? *Party Politics* (1995) 1: 319.

10. The rebranding is well described in Peter Mandelson, *The Blair Revolution Revisited*. London: Politico's, 2002, and Tony Blair, *A Journey*. New York: Random House, 2010.

11. See Anthony Heath, Roger Jowell, and John Curtice, *The Rise of New Labour: Party Policies and Voter Choices*. Oxford: Oxford University Press, 2001.

12. Ross McMullin, *The Light on the Hill: The Australian Labor Party 1891–1991*. South Melbourne: Oxford University Press, 1991.

13. See Rachel Gibson, Ian McAllister, and Tami Swenson. The politics of race and immigration in Australia: One Nation voting in the 1998 election. *Ethnic and Racial Studies* (2002) 25: 823–44; Murray Goot and Ian Watson, One Nation's electoral support: Where does it come from, what makes it different and how does it fit? *Australian Journal of Politics and History* (2001) 47: 159–91.

14. Shaun Bowler, Elisabeth Carter, and David Farrell. Changing party access to elections. In Bruce Cain, Russell Dalton, and Susan Scarrow, eds, *Democracy*

Transformed? Expanding Political Opportunities in Advanced Industrial Democracies. Oxford: Oxford University Press, 2004.

15. Giovanni Sartori, Political development and political engineering, *Public Policy* (1968) 17: 273.

16. See David Farrell, *Electoral Systems: A Comparative Introduction*, 2nd edn. London and New York: Palgrave Macmillan, 2010.

17. Stephen White and Ian McAllister, Reforming the Russian electoral system, *Journal of Communist Studies and Transition Politics* (1999) 15: 17–40. See also Sarah Birch, Frances Millard, Marina Popescu, *Embodying Democracy: Electoral System Design in Postcommunist Europe*. London: Palgrave, 2002.

18. Farrell, *Electoral Systems*, pp. 113–16. Russia ultimately replaced its mixed member majoritarian system with proportional representation list.

19. Ian McAllister, Campaign activity and electoral outcomes in Britain, 1979 and 1983, *Public Opinion Quarterly* (1985) 49: 492.

20. Stephen Coleman, ed., *Televised Election Debates: International Perspectives*. New York: Palgrave Macmillan, 1999; Lawrence Le Duc, Party strategies and the use of televised campaign debates, *European Journal of Political Research* (1990) 18: 121–41.

21. See Thomas Skidmore, ed., *Television, Politics and the Transition to Democracy in Latin America*. Baltimore, MD: Johns Hopkins University Press, 1993.

22. For instance, the upstart Pirate Party won approximately 900,000 votes in the 2009 Bundestag election, which qualified it for about €750,000 in new state support. Public funding can thus be a real boon even for small, minor parties.

23. Ian McAllister, Keeping them honest: Public and elite perceptions of ethical conduct among Australian legislators, *Political Studies* (2000) 48: 22–37; John Sullivan et al., Why politicians are more tolerant: Selective recruitment and socialization among politicians in Israel, New Zealand and the United States, *British Journal of Political Science* (1993) 23: 51–76.

24. Bonnie M. Meguid, *Party Competition between Unequals: Strategies and Electoral Fortunes in Western Europe*. Cambridge: Cambridge University Press, 2008.

25. Maurice Duverger, *Political Parties*. New York: Wiley, 1954. p. xxvii. See also Leon Epstein, *Political Parties in Western Democracies*. New York: Praeger, 1967, pp. 126ff.

26. See Susan Scarrow, Party activism and party members. In Russell J. Dalton and Hans-Dieter Klingemann, eds, *The Oxford Handbook of Political Behavior*. Oxford: Oxford University Press, 2007, p. 638.

27. Susan Scarrow, *Multispeed Membership Parties*, manuscript in preparation.

28. Rachel Gibson and Ian McAllister, Do online election campaigns win votes? The 2007 Australian *YouTube* election, *Political Communications* (forthcoming); Rachel Gibson and Ian McAllister, Does cyber-campaigning win votes? Online communication in the 2004 Australian election, *Journal of Elections, Public Opinion and Parties* (2006) 16: 243–63.

29. See, for example, Bruce Bimber and Richard Davis, *Campaigning Online: The Internet and US Elections*. Oxford: Oxford University Press, 2003.

30. V. O. Key, *Politics, Parties, and Pressure Groups*. New York: Crowell, 1958. This is the argument made by Kaare Strom, Parties at the core of government. In Russell Dalton and Martin Wattenberg, eds, *Parties without Partisans: Political Change in*

Advanced Industrial Democracies. Oxford: Oxford University Press, 2000. See also Kaare Strom and Lars Svasand, eds, *Challenges to Political Parties: The Case of Norway.* Ann Arbor, MI: University of Michigan Press, 1997.

31. Christopher Ansell and Jane Gingrich, Trends in decentralization. In Bruce Cain, Russell Dalton, and Susan Scarrow, eds, *Democracy Transformed? Expanding Political Opportunities in Advanced Industrial Democracies.* Oxford: Oxford University Press, 2003.

32. See Jonathan Bradbury, British political parties and devolution: Adapting to multi-level politics in Scotland and Wales. In Dan Hough and Charlie Jeffrey, eds, *Devolution and Electoral Politics.* Manchester: Manchester University Press, 2006.

33. Simon Hix, Abdul Noury, and Gerard Roland, Dimensions of politics in the European Parliament, *American Journal of Political Science* (2006) 50: 494–520.

34. Shaun Bowler, Parties in legislatures. In Russell Dalton and Martin Wattenberg, eds, *Parties without Partisans: Political Change in Advanced Industrial Democracies.* Oxford: Oxford University Press, 2000. See also Shaun Bowler, David Farrell, and Richard Katz, eds, *Party Discipline and Parliamentary Government.* Columbus: Ohio State University Press, 1999.

35. In the British House of Commons, one of the most powerful officials is the party whip, whose job it is to enforce discipline. Traditionally, the party whip kept a "black book," containing the sexual and financial misdemeanours of members, which could be used against them to enforce discipline. See Tim Renton, *People, Power and Patronage in Westminster.* London: Politico's, 2006.

36. David Farrell, Séin Ó Muineacháin, and Matthew Wall, Individualized Representation and Intra-Party Cohesion in Ireland (mimeo).

37. Cheryl Kernot, *Speaking for Myself Again: Four Years of Labor and Beyond.* Sydney: HarperCollins, 2002.

38. Gerhard Lehmbruch and Philippe Schmitter, eds, *Patterns of Corporatist Policy-Making.* London: Sage, 1982.

39. Alan Siaroff, Corporatism in 24 industrial democracies: meaning and measurement, *European Journal of Political Research* (1999) 36: 175–205.

40. See Eric Belanger, Antipartyism and third party vote choice: A comparison of Canada, Britain and Australia, *Comparative Political Studies* (2004) 37: 1054–78; Dalton and Weldon, Public images of political parties.

41. David Denver, The results: How Britain voted, *Parliamentary Affairs* (2010) 63: 588–606.

42. See Stephen White and Ian McAllister, The Putin phenomenon, *Journal of Communist Studies and Transition Politics* (2008) 24: 604–28; Stephen White and Ian McAllister, It's the economy, comrade! Parties and voters in the 2007 Russian Duma election. In Richard Sakwa, ed., *Power and Policy in Putin's Russia.* London and New York: Routledge, 2009.

43. Todd Donovan and Jeffrey Karp, Popular support for direct democracy, *Party Politics* (2007) 12: 671–88.

44. Susan Scarrow, Direct democracy and institutional change, *Comparative Political Studies* (2001) 34: 651–65.

45. Bruce Bimber, *Information and American Democracy: Technology in the Evolution of Political Power.* Cambridge: Cambridge University Press, 2003.

46. Ian Budge, *The New Challenge of Direct Democracy.* Cambridge: Polity Press, 1996.

Index